Authenticity in Fusion Music

Authenticity in Fusion Music

A Case Study among Indigenous Churches in Brazil

Elsen Portugal

Foreword by Robin Harris

WIPF & STOCK · Eugene, Oregon

AUTHENTICITY IN FUSION MUSIC
A Case Study among Indigenous Churches in Brazil

Copyright © 2024 Elsen Portugal. All rights reserved. Except for brief quotations in critical publications or reviews, no part of this book may be reproduced in any manner without prior written permission from the publisher. Write: Permissions, Wipf and Stock Publishers, 199 W. 8th Ave., Suite 3, Eugene, OR 97401.

Wipf & Stock
An Imprint of Wipf and Stock Publishers
199 W. 8th Ave., Suite 3
Eugene, OR 97401

www.wipfandstock.com

PAPERBACK ISBN: 978-1-6667-6953-1
HARDCOVER ISBN: 978-1-6667-6954-8
EBOOK ISBN: 978-1-6667-6955-5

VERSION NUMBER 04/19/24

Scripture quotations marked (ESV) or English Standard Version are from The ESV® Bible (The Holy Bible, English Standard Version®), copyright © 2001 by Crossway, a publishing ministry of Good News Publishers. Used by permission. All rights reserved.

Scripture quotations marked (NKJV) or New King James Version are taken from the New King James Version®. Copyright © 1982 by Thomas Nelson. Used by permission. All rights reserved.

Scripture quotations marked *The Logos Bible* are from: Paul W. Esposito, *The Logos Bible*, (Stauros Ministries, 2010/14). MySword Bible.

Contents

Figures | ix
Foreword by Robin Harris | xi
Acknowledgements | xiii
Prelude | xv

1. Introduction | 1
    - 1.1 Research Context | 1
    - 1.2 Thesis Overview | 8
    - 1.3 Research Objectives | 23
    - 1.4 Literature Review | 25
    - 1.5 Theoretical Framework | 37
    - 1.6 Research Methodology | 40
    - 1.7 Chapter Summaries | 41

2. The Xerente and Christian Faith | 43
    - 2.1 Historical Background of Indigenous Missions | 43
    - 2.2 Xerente Cultural Heritage | 52
    - 2.3 Evangelical Missions among the Xerente | 56

3. The Xerente and Their Musics | 61
    - 3.1 Traditional Music | 61
    - 3.2 Brazilian Genres in Contact with Xerente Society | 67
    - 3.3 Music in the Xerente Church | 70
    - 3.4 The Xerente Fusion: Not an Exception | 89
    - 3.5 Chapter Summary | 90

4. Fusion Genres | 91

    4.1 Genre Development or Fusion | 91
    4.2 The Question of Absolute Genres | 94
    4.3 Actions Leading towards Fusion | 105
    4.4 Genres and the Xerente Christian Identity | 107
    4.5 Functions and Meanings in Musical Fusion | 108
    4.6 Chapter Summary | 109

5. Musical Meaning Development in Christian Genres | 111

    5.1 Musical Semiotics and Meaning Development | 111
    5.2 Perceived Meanings among Local Christians—
        An Ethnographic Report | 122
    5.3 Venues and Other Characteristics | 138
    5.4 Conclusion: Local Meanings and Functions | 141

6. Signposts of Authenticity | 143

    6.1 Introduction | 143
    6.2 Meaning as a Signpost of Authenticity | 145
    6.3 Function as Signpost of Authenticity | 151
    6.4 Competence among Musicians as Signpost of Authenticity | 157
    6.5 Agency as Signpost of Authenticity | 161

7. Considerations of Authenticity in Xerente Church Fusion Genres | 166

    7.1 The Meaning of Authenticity | 166
    7.2 Signpost of Meaning | 170
    7.3 Signpost of Function | 173
    7.4 Signpost of Competence | 175
    7.5 Signpost of Agency | 176
    7.6 The Significance of Authenticity for Spirituality | 178
    7.7 The Dichotomies Challenged | 179
    7.8 Chapter Summary | 181

8. Applications and Conclusion | 182

    8.1 Xerente Contextualization | 182
    8.2 Implications of This Study | 184
    8.3 Summary of Content | 206
    8.4 Conclusion | 211

Appendix A: Characteristics of Xerente Music | 213
Appendix B: Xerente Musical Instruments
  by Rinaldo de Mattos (in Portuguese) | 218
Appendix C: Xerente Music Recordings, Transcriptions, and Lyrics | 222
Appendix D: Musical Symbol and Meaning
  by Elsen Portugal: Abbreviated Article | 243
Appendix E: Xerente Mission Records | 250
Bibliography | 255

Figures

Figure 1: Traditional Xerente song displaying a typical two-part form | 63

Figure 2: Traditional Xerente musical genres | 67

Figure 3: First page of the song *Ĩpkẽ wadkâ wa waza Jesus dawa* | 75

Figure 4: Traditional melody with Christian lyrics—*Waptokwa Zawre Dawarze* | 77

Figure 5: Traditional song *Arê Arê* | 78

Figure 6: Transcription of the first two pages of the melody of the song *Kâ psêktabdi* | 80

Figure 7: *Waptokwa Zawre damã danõkrêze* | 82

Figure 8: *Waptokwa Zawre Dawarze* | 84

Figure 9: *Dazakru sĩm warewdêhu* | 85

Figure 10: *Aisi hawim hã nã* | 86

Figure 11: *Baiäo* by Luís Gonzaga | 102

Figure 12: Peirce Trichotomy 1—Semiosis | 115

Figure 13: Xerente Territory and Population (2 parts: T. I. Xerente and T. I. Funil) | 125

Figure 14: Picture taken during the 2017 workshop. Workshop leaders Héber Negrão and Elsen Portugal with singer Lázaro Rowakro | 134

Figure 15: Recording sessions during the workshop in Cabeceira Verde, July 2017 | 165

Figure 16: Model of Signposts of Authenticity | 170

Figure 17: Linear continuum of music categories | 189

Figure 18: Palette representing potential musical style options | 189

Foreword

In July 2016, I had the pleasure of accompanying Elsen Portugal and his wife Michelle to Brazil. There he co-facilitated an Arts for a Better Future (ABF) workshop with colleague Héber Negrão in Portuguese, their first language. My role for the event, along with Brian Schrag (who wrote the textbook for the course), was to certify Elsen and Héber as ABF Master Facilitators. I was deeply impressed with Elsen's engaging teaching style, his ability to connect with the participants, and his passion for the field of ethnodoxology. Previously, I have enjoyed Elsen as a student in World Arts courses at Dallas International University—courses he took to prepare for a doctoral program elsewhere. I knew of his native speaker fluency in languages like German and English, but this was the first time I had seen him in a workshop setting. He was *amazing*. Elsen worked effectively with participants ranging from talented indigenous artists to expat missionaries with advanced degrees.

In late 2018, Elsen was invited to join the board of the Global Ethnodoxology Network (GEN) and has since then served alongside me as a colleague and collaborator. When B. H. Carroll Theological Institute (now Seminary) invited me to serve as an outside reader for Elsen's PhD dissertation, I was grateful for the chance to participate in the outcome of this important dissertation—the first ever undertaken for a PhD in ethnodoxology. Elsen did not know the identity of his "mystery outside reader" and was stunned to see me when I showed up at the defense the next day, after I had hosted him at our home the night before without dropping any clues about my role.

The volume you hold in your hands is particularly significant because it is the product of several aspects of ethnodoxology in which Elsen excels: An ability to work respectfully and fruitfully with people across cultural boundaries, remarkable facility at an academic level in multiple languages, his deep connection to the Xerente people of his native Brazil, and his passion to see them thrive in their worship.

If you have ever wondered about the role of fusions in ethnodoxology or have doubted their usefulness for revitalizing and developing heart music for communities, this book is a must-read for you. Elsen points out that genre boundaries are always in a state of malleability—it is what gives them life. The appropriateness of authentic fusions in the Brazilian context is clear, and sheds light on processes occurring in more and more contexts.

Outlining several signposts that speak to the authenticity of contemporary indigenous musical developments, the book traces the streams of fusion material that come from both local and external sources. It notes the agency of the Xerente in creating these fusions, and how they leverage an amalgamation of musical materials to form uniquely powerful and culturally authentic expressions of contemporary faith.

Get ready for a fascinating journey into the world of Xerente music creation. You will come to admire their ingenuity, imagination, and determination to create their own voice, one that integrates present realities and older traditions in surprising ways.

Robin Harris, PhD (Ethnomusicology)
Dallas, TX
March 31, 2023

President, Global Ethnodoxology Network (GEN)
Associate Professor of World Arts
Chair, Center for Excellence in World Arts
Dallas International University
Worship and Mission for the Global Church: An Ethnodoxology Handbook
(William Carey Publishers)
Storytelling in Siberia: The Olonkho Epic in a Changing World
(University of Illinois Press)

Acknowledgements

To those prone to accept things to simply "be" as they are without wondering how they developed and why, the inclination towards philosophical examination may be puzzling. To some, however, research is fulfilling and purposeful. One could say that actions such as asking how and why, although often not immediately changing the status quo, have, in time, often fundamentally transformed the way life is conducted and developed alternative worldviews. This research, while focused on a local occurrence of a little-known people group in South America, has indeed been fulfilling to me and exists for the purpose of understanding the power of communicative artistic forms used by human beings all over the globe, as well as of developing a deeper knowledge of the integral part they play as expressions of worship and the mission of God.

To this end, multiple people have supported me in this work. My wife, Michelle, has once again demonstrated her love and support for her husband by permitting me to take up long hours of our lives to use for study and writing, as well as agreeing to the multiple times we had to be apart for the sake of ministry and research. I owe my introduction into the world of ethnoarts and the developing field of ethnodoxology to the influence of Dr. Robin Harris and Dr. Brian Schrag, both ethnomusicologists who, through their applied studies in arts and missions, helped me to broaden my comprehension of the mission of God to include, especially, God's artistic gifts. Under the direction of the B. H. Carroll Theological Seminary and the leadership of Dr. Stan Moore and Dr. Karen Bullock, multiple seminars have led to deep studies of a broad scope of knowledge and perception in the application and importance of ethnodoxology. They were also responsible for inviting Dr. Robin Harris into the committee, a privilege that grants this research even stronger support than I originally envisioned. To all my professors and guides, I am truly thankful.

The experience of being with the Xerente and learning from their culture has, likewise, been invaluable. I am indebted to the Brazilian Baptist National Mission Board (JMN) and its leaders involved in indigenous work for their indication of the Xerente as an option to assist in the area of music. Through this connection I had the privilege to meet and develop friendships with several dedicated missionaries—both husbands and wives—some of which have literally spent four-fifths of their lives seeking to bless the Xerente people through practical social helps as well as through the preaching of Christ. I am particularly thankful for the insights and support of Pr. Rinaldo de Mattos, a highly respected part of the Baptist mission among the Xerente, a musician, an anthropologist, a frequently cited source on the Xerente even in secular publications, and a committed servant of God. The Xerente Christian community and their musicians have been a delight to know. It is my hope that the help they offered towards this research, will turn in to a blessing for themselves and to other indigenous Brazilian communities.

I am especially thankful for my supervisor Dr. Todd Saurman, whose decades-long experience in this field, and often "out-of-the-box" thinking, helped hone my skills in research practices. His insights and suggestions, while never quenching any opposite opinions I might have had, had more sway in my choices than he may realize. I count him as a friend. Although we live on opposite sides of the globe, a kindred spirit developed between us during these the years of this research.

Most of all, however, I am mostly thankful to God for His grace throughout all of my life, and for the physical and mental health to accomplish the works appointed for me to do. To God be the glory.

Elsen Portugal, PhD
Hot Springs, Arkansas
March 21, 2023

Prelude

INDIGENOUS EVANGELICAL CHURCHES IN Brazil display a wide variety of musical preferences and practices ranging from genres essentially identical to local traditional cultural forms to patterns of musical worship practices in non-indigenous Brazilian congregations. Focusing on the current fused musical styles used by Christians among the Xerente (pronounced "Sheh-ʹren-teh"), a people with several decades of interaction with evangelical Christian missions, this research seeks to evaluate the authenticity of contemporary indigenous musical practices on the basis of relevant signposts. The "fusion" musical genres presently used by these churches bring together elements from within and without the local cultural tradition. This project responds to tensions concerning the use of local and external musical genres for church services within Christian missions and envisions the possibility that the styles' meaningfulness and functionality, as well as the internal competency and control of such amalgamation of musical characteristics extant in Xerente churches may serve as a token of cultural authenticity within their contemporary society. Attention is given to the processes of genre development, particularly in Brazil, in an attempt to assess the value of the progressive stages of the fused musical practice in contemporary Xerente Christian churches.

The doctoral dissertation from which this book derives[1] argues that the authenticity of a genre is not primarily entirely dependent on the timespan of a tradition, its origin, or on similar tangible markers, but likewise on intangible characteristics such as emotional, contextual,

---

1. Portugal, "Fusion Music Genres in Indigenous Brazilian Churches: An Evaluation of Authenticity in Xerente Christian Contexts," (Irving, TX: B. H. Carroll Theological Institute, 2019) PhD Dissertation, https://www.tren.com/e-docs/search.cfm?p150-006.

practical, and even theological connections of the people to the genre at a given time. It conceives of authenticity, in its relationship to ethnicity (or ethnic identity), not as a slave of a society's past but as a fluid or dynamic feature. Authenticity of musical and artistic genres, as proposed in this book,, may, therefore, be identified through signposts indicating the presence of communal and individual meanings, integrated functions within the community, local competence of creation and reproduction in the genre, as well as local agency in the administration of such musics.

1

Introduction

1.1 RESEARCH CONTEXT

1.1.1 Historical Introduction to Research Context

FOLLOWING A MONTH-LONG VOYAGE in the waters of the Atlantic Ocean, Captain Pedro Álvares Cabral's secretary Pero Vaz de Caminha wrote a letter to the King of Portugal describing the first encounters in the land which they called *Terra de Vera Cruz* (Land of the True Cross).[1] On the twenty-second day of April of 1500, members of the crews of the Portuguese fleet came on land and, for the first time, met the naked indigenous inhabitants of the land which was later to be called "Brazil." During the first few days they attempted to communicate with them through simple gestures and obtained a mixture of positive and negative responses that laid a foundation for long-term perceptions of Brazilian Indians.[2] A little more than a week after their arrival, on May 1, Caminha stated his impressions of the indigenous population in his letter to the king of Portugal: "They seem to me to be people of such innocence that, if one were to understand them and they us, they would soon become Christians, since they, as it appears, neither have nor understand any belief [system]."[3] He

---

 1. Fundação Biblioteca Nacional, "Carta de Pero Vaz," 1.

 2. Descendants of the original people groups that lived in South America at the time of the European landing in Brazil in 1500. They are still called "Indians" (índios) in Brazil.

 3. Fundação Biblioteca Nacional, "Carta de Pero Vaz," 12. Translation mine.

urged the King to "care [provide] for their salvation. And it will please God that, with little work, it should be so."[4]

Apart from alleged visits to the northern regions of Brazil between 1498 and early 1500, including one by Captain Duarte Pacheco Pereira in 1498[5]—still contested theories—Cabral's fleet's interaction with the Brazilian Indians above was the earliest contact between the Portuguese and the inhabitants of South America on record. The magnitude of change that would occur on that continent during the following five centuries was beyond the grasp of those early visitors. The perceived state of 'innocence' attributed to the Indians by Caminha would give way to descriptions like that of the sixteenth Jesuit priest José de Anchieta, who suggested that some of them had a "nature resembling that of beasts rather than that of men."[6] The interactions between Europeans and Indians (later involving also African slaves) gave rise to the development of a Brazilian national society (including multiple regional variations), laid the groundwork for multiple processes of ethnogenesis in the continent, moved—or provoked the move of—countless tribal communities to areas in Brazil where they did not reside when colonization began, and brought about the demise of large numbers of Indians through war and disease.[7] Yet, through purposeful displacement, group protective retraction, or an original geographical distance from the colonizing forces, hundreds of indigenous ethnic groups remained distinct—on the whole—from the dominant culture. According to "Povos Indígenas no Brasil" ("Indigenous Peoples in Brazil"), a site dedicated to the advancement of Brazilian Indians in various ways, 266 indigenous groups still maintain their ethnic distinction in modern Brazil.[8]

1.1.2 The Reality of Blended Cultural Forms

Along with the painful memories of exploitation, slavery, and destruction, however, a comparatively more benign development occurred

---

4. Fundação Biblioteca Nacional, "Carta de Pero Vaz," 12. Translation mine.

5. UOL Educação, "Invasão do Brasil."

6. See "Carta de Piratininga (1554)," in Anchieta, *Cartas, Informações, Fragmentos Históricos*, 46. Translation mine.

7. Many of these developments and tragedies took place as early as the sixteenth century and are described throughout the correspondence of the Jesuit priest Joseph de Anchieta, in *Cartas, Informações, Fragmentos Históricos*.

8. Povos Indígenas do Brasil, "List of Indigenous Peoples."

through the blending of cultures and ethnicities along the course of the last 500 years of Brazilian history. Countless mixtures and fusions led to the creation of multiple artistic genres that are now emblematic of Brazilian identity. The tensions, longings, loves, and passions of the peoples that were brought together, often by forces greater than their own, served as wombs for the creation of new musical genres such as *samba, forró, chorinho,* and *bossa nova,* to mention just a few. Most of these genres, while intentionally developed by creative musicians, arose through contact with other cultures and situations.

Although one could assume that a cultural power with the strongest political status in a developing nation consistently predicates which musical genres become dominant in the process of lending and borrowing features, a careful observation of the development of Brazil demonstrates that the strongest influences have often come from the opposite direction. This view of the capricious factors involved in the struggle for cultural supremacy and the rise of new cultural practices or customs is portrayed by the Brazilian poet Oswaldo de Andrade in his poem entitled "Erro de Português"[9] with ambiguity and humor:

> Quando o português chegou
> Debaixo de uma bruta chuva
> Vestiu o índio
> Que pena!
> Fosse uma manhã de sol
> O índio tinha despido
> O português[10]

---

9. The title of this short poem is a play on words. The immediate impression on the fluent Portuguese language speaker is that Andrade is making a reference to a linguistic mistake in the Portuguese language. However, the poem is actually suggesting that the Portuguese (a generic term for the conquering people that colonized Brazil) made a mistake in not adapting to the native custom.

10. Andrade, "Erro de Português," 146–47.

Translation:

*When the Portuguese arrived
Under a brutal rainfall
He dressed the Indian
What a pity!
If it had been a sunny morning
The Indian would have undressed
The Portuguese*

In this poem, Andrade suggests that the Portuguese colonizers affected the predominant character of cultural norms in the newly discovered land. While this is true in multiple aspects of Brazilian society, artistic developments throughout Brazilian history, however, demonstrate a much more complex blend and have often leaned away from the politically dominant culture in the developing nation. Not unlike the general Brazilian society, indigenous communities that have maintained their cultural and ethnic distinction into this century, despite their lower status of power, have participated in—and even determined—the choices of cultural elements which they wished to preserve, alter, or substitute for their people along the course of Brazilian colonization.[11]

1.1.3 The Xerente Context

In this study, we will consider the current Christian music situation within the communities of one specific indigenous Brazilian people group in central Brazil: the Xerente (pronounced "Sheh-´ren-teh"). Although they have reportedly been in contact with European colonists and their descendants for about 250 years,[12] the Xerente have been able to maintain a distinct identity until the present.[13] They call themselves *Akwẽ*, a term

---

11. Machado, "Trajetória da Destruição," 17–20. In her thesis, Machado refers to the late Brazilian anthropologist John Monteiro, who, among others, recognizes that indigenous people, contrary to traditional histories, pursued interests with force comparable to that of the Portuguese, albeit weaker in terms of political, technological, and military power.

12. Povos Indígenas do Brasil, "Xerente," esp. "History of Contact." This length of time probably refers to the beginning of regular interaction. The same page, under "History of Contact," indicates that "the first contacts between the *Akwẽ* and non-indigenous segments of society occurred in the seventeenth century, with the arrival of Jesuit missions and colonizers (frontier expeditions and raids) to the Brazilian central West" (para. 6).

13. Wewering, *Povo Akwẽ Xerente*, 7. This publication, while copyrighted under

that also serves as designation for their language. *Akwẽ*, however, also refers to up to four groups generally known as Xavante, Xerente, Acroá, and Xacriabá.[14] The Xerente language belongs to the *Jê* family, one of three major indigenous linguistic branches in Brazil.

Although oral history indicates that they may have come from coastal areas,[15] documents show that the Xerente have inhabited the area of the Brazilian States of Goiás and Tocantins since at least the eighteenth century. After a forced *aldeamento* (a colonial strategy of civilization and integration) under Jesuit control between 1725 and 1775, which the Indian community remembers essentially as slavery, the different *Akwẽ* groups moved to separate regions. After more than a century and a half of difficult survival and frequent conflict with "white colonists," the Brazilian government's SPI (*Serviço de Proteção aos Índios*—Indigenous Protection Service) arrived in 1940 to offer some assistance. Notwithstanding, living conditions continued to be extremely precarious for several decades. After the extinction of the SPI, the new governmental agency responsible for indigenous matters—FUNAI (*Fundação Nacional do Índio*—National Foundation for the Indian)—instituted yet further governmental rules on the Xerente. "After many struggles and great conflicts, the 'Xerente Land' was finally delineated on the 14th of September of 1972,"[16] effectively creating a protected area of land in which primary control rests on Xerente leadership.

1.1.4 Mission and Music in the Xerente Church

Brazilian Baptists began missionary work among the Xerente in 1959/1960. Their efforts, which included church planting, social work, and Bible translation, have demonstrated continuous growth through the years.[17]

As in other indigenous evangelical churches in Brazil a wide variety of musical preferences and practices exist among Xerente Christians. The

---

Wewering's name, presents the history and customs of the Xerente from their own perspective and in their own way of expression, albeit in Portuguese. Its introduction explains that the book resulted from a joint community effort, and it (the book) speaks as the voice of the Xerente people.

14. Povos Indígenas do Brasil, "Xerente," para. 7.
15. Povos Indígenas do Brasil, "Xerente," para. 6.
16. Wewering, *Povo Akwẽ Xerente*, 7.
17. Portugal, "Musical Choices."

spectrum of Brazilian indigenous Christian music ranges from genres essentially identical to the traditional cultural forms to those that follow patterns of musical worship practices in non-indigenous Brazilian congregations.[18] Current musical styles among the Xerente have developed from a fusion of musical elements derived both from sources within and without the cultural tradition. In this aspect, the Xerente community resembles the ongoing processes of hybridization, blending, or fusion of elements that have taken place along the last five centuries on Brazilian soil.

At the inception of the evangelical message among the Xerente, churches utilized Western hymnody as had been the trend around the world for centuries. This stance, however, did not stem from intentional ethnocentric and prohibitive attitudes emanating from the missionaries. I discuss this developmental process in greater depth in the article "Musical Choices in the Early Baptist Missions among the Xerente."[19] Notwithstanding, the early and subsequent musical components of Xerente life appear to have fused into a genre (or genres) displaying both their time-honored origins and a distinct local character. Presumably, musicians and other church members have made their own personal or corporate choices to adopt these styles for their songs of encouragement, praise, and worship. As the long-term missionaries related to me in personal conversations, after an initial introduction of extra-Xerente Christian music elements, an "awakening" toward traditional cultural features took place about twenty years later after the beginning of the Baptist mission. By the end of the twentieth century, several Xerente had learned to play Western musical instruments and become significantly competent both to play and compose in the most popular genres. The consequent interplays of musical styles and performance practices, most of which derived from the northeastern part of Brazil, gave rise to the genres that the Xerente church uses today.[20]

18. Although I am not aware of the existence of any comprehensive written record of the multiplicity of styles being used in Brazilian indigenous churches, this variety can be observed, apart from multiple visits to distinct ethnic societies, at CONPLEI conferences. CONPLEI (pronounced "Con-Play") is a nationwide network of Brazilian indigenous evangelical pastors and leaders that has become intensely involved in indigenous evangelism and discipleship among numerous ethnic groups in Brazil. This network hosts nation-wide conferences at two- or four-year intervals, as well as multiple yearly regional and youth meetings. Furthermore, the organization has been very intentional in the validation of local expressions of worship, including all modalities of art. See: http://www.conplei.org.br/.

19. Portugal, "Musical Choices."

20. The Xerente openly acknowledge the incorporation of musical features, styles,

1.1.5 The Dichotomy of Traditional and Western Forms

The long history of interaction between peoples around the world reveals a lamentable pattern of subjugation of politically, economically, or militarily weak or weakened peoples. This conquest, among many important aspects, often involves the control of cultural artistic expressions by the dominant society. While a worldwide simultaneous conquering era began with the explorers in the late 1400s, manifesting a general inclination to impose European values as the highest and most desirable, the cultural suppression that took place did not eradicate all native aspects of the conquered. In many instances, local elements were incorporated into the general ethos. Some of the multiple reasons for this phenomenon are briefly discussed in this book.[21]

As a result of this polarizing set of influences around the world, it is common to default to a dichotomy of "local traditional" versus "Western," "global," or "modern" musics when discussing musical and artistic genres. According to Bruno Nettl, writing in the late twentieth century, even the field of ethnomusicology, while attempting to "separate itself from practical society and politics," had surprisingly maintained "nineteenth-century ideas of musical and cultural purity."[22] Indeed, in spite of the broader contemporary vision of evangelical missions efforts in the twenty-first century characterized by the incorporation of arts into cross-cultural approaches, this dichotomy continues to affect (presumably unintentionally) the understanding and the application of arts in multiple settings in practical ways.

Christian arts advocates affirm with conviction the importance of allowing the community to choose artistic paths that will bring good effects for their communities.[23] Roberta King, in her dissertation on the Christian music of the Senufo people in the Ivory Coast, voiced this perspective in tune with a chorus of ethnodoxologists declaring that

---

and instruments from the northeastern part of Brazil, and this fact can be clearly observed by the outsider who is familiar with the surrounding popular styles.

21. This is discussed, for instance, in Walls, *Missionary Movement in Christian History*, as well as in records of colonists and priests in sixteenth-century Brazil, such as Anchieta, *Cartas, Informações, Fragmentos Históricos*.

22. Nettl, *Study of Ethnomusicology*, 405.

23. This is one of the emphases of the course "Arts for a Better Future" elaborated and taught by members of the Global Ethnodoxology Network (formerly the International Council of Ethnodoxologists). See Global Ethnodoxology Network, "Arts for a Better Future."

"culturally appropriate"[24] music can best communicate to and involve local communities in worship and evangelism. Despite the currently strong character of this affirmation resounding from cross-cultural works and ethnodoxologists, calls for a re-evaluation of what "culturally appropriate" music actually represents have increased through lectures and ethnographies addressing musical blends, diaspora musical practices, and other musical phenomena found in cultural "borders."[25] Arts advocates have been challenged to strongly consider that "culturally appropriate music" may not simply refer to that which is rooted exclusively in the cultural heritage of the community before an intense contact with Western culture began, *but that it may incorporate all that is meaningful or authentically applicable in a given local community.*

1.2 THESIS OVERVIEW

1.2.1 Thesis Statement

This research responds to requests to evaluate the present-day musical communication taking place in the Xerente church. It evaluates the authenticity of contemporary indigenous church musical practices in answer to tensions concerning the use of local and external musical genres within Christian missions. It is grounded on the point-of-view of the contemporary Xerente society and focuses particularly on genres involving fusion of traditional and recently adopted elements. It contends that the local meanings and functionality of these genres, the competence to either develop a genre, compose with its elements, or simply perform it, as well as the presence of local agency (or administration) of these musical practices serve as signposts of their cultural authenticity.

If an authentic character of Xerente Christian music genres can be recognized, it could be a summons to affirm fused musical styles and a call to those who interact with them to identify and encourage musical genres that can have spiritual significance for the church while remaining culturally appropriate to communicate with the unchurched Xerente. It is my hope that, as a result of a study like this, the local community will

---

24. King, *Pathways in Christian Music Communication*, 10.

25. For instance: the 2018 Missiology Lectures at Fuller Theological Seminary in November of 2018 in which nearly half of the lectures addressed examples involving blended genres. See https://www.fuller.edu/missiology/save-the-date/.

maintain ownership of its on-going musical development, and that such local practices would be encouraged among other people groups.

At its core, this research investigates whether the contemporary Xerente music genres could legitimately be called authentic or "genuinely" Xerente, or if they remain indeed "foreign" and disruptive. On one hand, local Xerente musicians have relearned the value of their cultural music genres and some have become motivated to incorporate their elements in their new compositions or new renditions.[26] On the other hand, contemporary Xerente individuals (musicians included) have already grown up with a blend of musical styles. Within this context, the signposts suggested in this dissertation propose that the authenticity of musical and artistic genres are not dependent on the timespan of a tradition or its documented origin, but on connections involving emotional, contextual, practical, and spiritual meanings perceived by present-day participants. It conceives of authenticity, in its relationship to ethnic identity, not as a slave of a society's past but as fluid or dynamic, attaining local—and at times indispensable—functions within the community. Furthermore, this study proposes that choices made by the people and the observable competence of Xerente musicians to create blends, as well as the ability to compose, perform, and administer the regular practice of the fused styles, give evidence of their genuine Xerente character.

1.2.2 Ethnodoxology and Other Foundational Research Fields

The focus of research on musical genres used for the expression of Christian worship and its message is at the heart of the interdisciplinary field of ethnodoxology. The term *ethnodoxology*, adopted in the early part of the twenty-first century particularly through the influence of Dave Hall[27] and Roberta King,[28] describes "the interdisciplinary study of how Christians in every culture engage with God and the world through their own artistic expressions."[29] Ethnodoxology incorporates multiple research

---

26. This motivation was shared with me by all the Baptist missionaries whom I interviewed and who work among the Xerente at the present. I personally observed this intentional practice during visits and workshops with Xerente musicians between 2017 and 2019.

27. Hall, "Centrality of Worship."

28. Evangelical Dictionary of World Missions, "Ethnomusicology," 327.

29. Global Ethnodoxology Network, "Ethnodoxology," esp. "What is ethnodoxology?"

practices from the fields of ethnomusicology, anthropology, missiology, and the social sciences.[30] Its applications involve primarily Christian worship practices in multiple cultural settings and the fulfillment of Christian missional goals through the exercise of the arts. Its relevance, however, as will be elaborated in the conclusion of this volume, can also be demonstrated through the broader perspective it brings to the fields that contributed to the discussion.

Despite the apparent young character of ethnodoxology as a field, its development began long ago in various parts of the world, particularly as cross-cultural workers with artistic training, or at least a keen eye for the variety of musical expressions in their particular fields, perceived the richness and the potential for the use of local music as an integral part of communicative strategies. By the end of the twentieth century some missions organizations, faith-based non-governmental as well as other para-church organizations, had already begun to incorporate this innovative approach into their formal structure.[31]

Throughout the centuries, isolated voices have called for the contextualized communication of the Christian faith wherever it might be introduced. More recently, in the early twentieth century, some theologians and missionaries began to look for possible applications of local "traditional" music and artistic genres in worship settings. Daniel Fleming, professor at Union Seminary in the early part of the twentieth century,[32] for instance, stressed the importance of contextualization in missions and the use of local forms long before this practice had become a trend. John F. Butler suggested similar undertakings in his book *Christian Art in India*.[33] The very first edition of the *Evangelical Missions Quarterly* in October of 1964[34] contained an article by Raymond Buker (a former missionary) referring to the value of local music for proper communication

---

30. The Global Ethnodoxology Network's core values provide the following representative list of disciplines "that provide holistic views and positions" for the field of ethnodoxology: performance studies, creativity studies, musicology, orality, missiology, worship studies, and various anthropologies of the arts. See Global Ethnodoxology Network, "Core Values." Linguistics, ethnomusicology, sociology, communication theory, semiotics, history, and theology are also important contributors to the field.

31. For instance, Dye, *Bible Translation Strategy*, 110–13. Also see Chenoweth, *Melodic Perception and Analysis*.

32. This is a relevant topic addressed in Daniel Fleming's books such as *Whither Bound in Missions* (1925) and others listed in the bibliography.

33. Butler, *Christian Art in India*.

34. Buker, "Missionary Encounter with Culture."

based on an experience in the Ivory Coast.[35] These seemingly lonely calls finally began to be heeded in the 1970s and a conversation about the value of arts in worship and their importance in the practice of Christian mission finally ensued.[36] Ethnodoxology today has a growing corpus of literature and practitioners all over the world.

Although some of the scattered voices calling for contextualized art for Christian worship addressed not only the local musics, but also the potential of local architecture, painting, and other artistic modalities,[37] the precursors of ethnodoxology were mostly linked to ethnomusicological principles during the last decades of the twentieth century. Through the years, practitioners have matured from a relatively closed dichotomous view of Western versus traditional musics,[38] developing ideas on cultural and individual "heart music(s)" (later also "heart musics and arts"), to the acknowledgment of the interaction of the multiple artistic modes through the development of the current term "ethnoarts." In fact, today, the field prefers to apply the term "genre" to a broad concept that encompasses multiple artistic modalities within the same event.[39] In his most recent definition of "local arts," Brian Schrag describes the wide spectrum of artistic potential of community with as those forms which it "can create, perform, teach and understand from within, including its forms, meanings, language, and social context."[40] In spite of the range of application to the arts for which the definitions of ethnodoxology gives space, each practitioner may unadvisedly apply his/her own closed categories to the interpretation of authenticity in local artistic expressions. This book aims at providing greater clarity to aspects of genres and their developments as well as to what may indeed be the elements that constitute authentic expressions.

The creation of the Global Ethnodoxology Network—GEN (formerly known as the International Council of Ethnodoxology—ICE) in 2003 provided increased opportunities for ethnodoxologists to exchange

---

35. The case briefly addressed by Buker in the above-mentioned article could be the same case of the Senufo in Roberta King's dissertation written over two decades later.

36. The present-day broader validation of the importance of the arts in Christian worship probably received impulse from a variety of global evangelical conferences such as the one held in Lausanne, Switzerland in July of 1974. See: Lausanne Movement at https://www.lausanne.org/our-legacy.

37. Fleming and Butler, for instance.

38. Chenoweth, "Spare Them Western Music," locs. 3894–4008.

39. See the discussion on the term "genre" in the next section.

40. Schrag, *Make Arts*, 296.

and develop new ideas.⁴¹ The network has grown to hundreds of members who are engaged in arts in Christian worship from all around the world. Beyond simply facilitating the exchange of information and the creation of connections, GEN actively advocates for local- and broad-based artistic creativity through articles, academic and practical courses in ethnodoxology and arts advocacy, and through many other venues. In line with the proposals of this book, GEN acknowledges the dynamic reality of cultures and values the results of their artistic expressions.

Through diasporas and multiple types of cultural exchanges, "the kinds of arts" developed and enjoyed by communities are impacted, giving birth to events demonstrating fusion or hybridity as well as to new self-perpetuating genres.⁴² In this century, ethnodoxology has broadened its perspectives to recognize and value the countless potential blends of musical languages and genres present and under development currently around the world.⁴³ It is a field that uses a phenomenological approach to study what people are doing in the present and encourages "forward-focused"⁴⁴ actions "for a better future."⁴⁵ In this spirit, Proskuneo Ministries cofounder Joy Kim, for instance, celebrates the creativity and authenticity of the "diaspora musicians"⁴⁶ in the multicultural context of Clarkston, Georgia. Her research demonstrates how "musicians from diverse ethnic backgrounds create new music together"⁴⁷ and develop an "innovative fusion"⁴⁸ that is able to ultimately impact the new identity of the community. As an active collaborator in the field of ethnodoxology, Joy Kim expresses the need for more case studies of "multicultural, multilingual, urban context(s)" echoing Megan Meyers,⁴⁹ who states that "ethnodoxologists need to be better equipped to understand the increasingly globalized reality of worship in today's urban churches."⁵⁰ Although

41. Harris, "Dealing Effectively with Opponents," loc. 9318.

42. Global Ethnodoxology Network, "Ethnodoxology Values."

43. For a more comprehensive outline of ethnodoxology during the last few decades see Kim, "Diaspora Musicians."

44. Kim, "Diaspora Musicians."

45. "Arts for a Better Future" is GEN's community arts development week-long workshop. Global Ethnodoxology Network, "Arts for a Better Future."

46. Kim, "Diaspora Musicians," 74.

47. Collinge, "Moving from Monocultural," loc. 11021.

48. Collinge, "Moving from Monocultural," loc. 11012.

49. Megan Meyers is an ethnodoxologist working in Lusophone Africa.

50. Kim, "Diaspora Musicians," 154. Citation from Meyers, "Developing Disciples," 138.

not addressing a multicultural urban context, study on the Xerente fusion music genres is meant to contribute to the equipping of local or expatriate ethnodoxologists who cooperate with communities that use (or wish to use) fusion expressive arts, as called upon by both Kim and Meyers. It is my conviction that the concepts developed and advocated in this work can be applied to both multicultural urban and (relatively) monocultural rural communities.

1.2.3 Definition of Key Terms

Fusion and Hybridity

This book employs the term "fusion" to describe the contemporary genres among the Xerente churches. Some authors describe a blend of genres by the term "hybrid." Gerard Behague uses terms such as "amalgamation" and "mestizo" for the genres that developed in Brazil, whether among Indians or not. None of these terms, however, exist primarily as a description of music.[51] Two pertinent reasons have contributed to my preference for the term "fusion." Firstly, the term has already been applied to musical blends of the twentieth century with a measure of acceptance. One of the definitions for "fusion" listed in the *Oxford Learner's Dictionaries* describes it as a term for "music that is a mixture of different styles, especially jazz and rock."[52] Secondly, in certain contexts "hybrid" may lead to a Western connotation of a creation (or product) demonstrating "less than pure" characteristics, and, therefore, less valuable. Although, in fact, agricultural hybrids are intentionally created to gain some presumed advantage, the colloquial connotation derives meaning from classifications or categorizations of established models which have been elevated to ideal symbols. This study offers some historical examples of genre development that took place through the blending of diverse (often from different cultures) styles, giving special attention to this process within the South American continent. It is likely that a thorough research of the musics of all the ages in recorded history would lead to a conclusion that the large majority of all musics originated from a blend of elements. Because at distinct times specific genres have become established to such a degree that they are viewed as "ideals," "intermediary" forms of music

---

51. Behague, "Brazil," 3:224.
52. Oxford Learner's Dictionaries, "Fusion."

receive unfair treatment and are regarded as strictly "a step" in a supposed musical evolutionary process. "Fusion," on the other hand, besides its earlier use in the context of music, may connote a less negative product. Fusion of earlier genres, within this view, does not represent a degradation of an ideal model, but rather an expression of positive developments towards a new genre containing characteristics of more than one earlier genre. The likelihood of such scenarios developing in Christian music is highlighted by Schrag with a reference to Christian Kiswahili rap, which has "multiple origins wrapped up in unique ways."[53] He warns, "don't hold your definitions too tightly."[54]

The problem of hybridity or fusion of elements containing cultural, or specifically artistic, features recently adopted from outside an indigenous community exists because of a perceived dichotomy that still attracts followers even among advocates of indigenous cultural heritages. In "Body Paint, Feathers, and VCRs," Beth Conklin explains that there is a "Western commonsense notion of tradition that 'presumes that an unchanging core of ideas and customs is always handed down to us from the past.'"[55] Within this view, "authenticity implies integration and wholeness-continuity between past and present, and between societal values and individual agency, and between sign and meaning." This, she says, "leaves little room for intercultural exchange or creative innovation, and locates "authentic" indigenous actors outside global cultural trends and changing ideas and technologies."[56] These "distancing dichotomies"[57] involving "views that equate authenticity with purity from foreign influences"[58] are not atypical in Western-indigenous relations. They are directly challenged by "the appropriation of complex Western technologies by indigenous peoples"[59] as is the case of the Xerente and the subsequent development of fusion genres.

According to Martin Stokes, resistance to hybridity and fusion also exists among some ethnomusicologists. He states that this stance stems from the assumption that these mixtures take place due to "hierarchical

---

53. Schrag, *Creating Local Arts Together*, 61.

54. Schrag, *Creating Local Arts Together*, 61.

55. Conklin, "Body Paint, Feathers, and VCRs," 715. Citation from Handler and Linnekin, "Tradition, Genuine or Spurious," 273.

56. Conklin, "Body Paint, Feathers, and VCRs," 715.

57. Conklin, "Body Paint, Feathers, and VCRs," 726.

58. Conklin, "Body Paint, Feathers, and VCRs," 715.

59. Conklin, "Body Paint, Feathers, and VCRs," 715.

and exploitative relationships that (continue to) pertain between centers and peripheries, dominant and subaltern groups."[60] Those who strongly oppose the resulting mixtures "tend to lean toward an 'anti-hybrid nationalist' point of view that sees hybridity as *opposed* to authenticity."[61]

As this book seeks to demonstrate, however, the Xerente musical fusion, although not completely inoculated against power relationships, displays evidence of freedom of choice within the Xerente Christian community, and does not necessarily fit in the pattern suggested by Stokes. I concur with Conklin's indications that opposition to hybridity and fusion relies on "stereotypes of cultural purity":[62]

> Most indigenous people and anthropologists would agree that native political claims should not be judged by conformity to stereotypes of cultural purity. Yet pro-Indian rhetoric that invokes the content of "traditional culture" as an argument for native rights *relies on similar distancing dichotomies and oppositional representations of Indian and non-Indian cultures.*[63]

Genre

The Western concept of "genre" generally describes a subset of an artistic domain (music, literature, visual art, dance, etc.) that displays a collection of defining characteristics. The Merriam-Webster Dictionary describes it at as "a category of artistic, musical, or literary composition characterized by a particular style, form, or content."[64] Nevertheless, specific genres have porous outlines and can be variously defined depending on local, academic, or commercial interests. The "Music Genre List" site, for instance, while affirming the term "genre" as a subset of artistic domains, suggests that the term is appropriate for different forms of categorization. Genres could be defined by their time period, musical instrumentation, geographic or ethnic origin of the composer, associated culture, artistic or musical form, intended audience, practical functions, means of dissemination, as well as other pertinent criteria. The site, while attempting

---

60. Stokes, "Music and the Global Order," 59–60.
61. Kim, "Diaspora Musicians," 26. Citation from Stokes, "Music and the Global Order," 60. Emphasis added.
62. Conklin, "Body Paint, Feathers, and VCRs," 726.
63. Conklin, "Body Paint, Feathers, and VCRs," 726. Emphasis added.
64. Merriam-Webster Dictionary, "Genre."

to create a comprehensive collection of musical genres, admits that "there is no agreement or a single comprehensive system to talk about music genres at the present time."[65]

Franco Fabbri, in his 1981 article "A Theory of Musical Genres: Two Approaches," comments on the lack of clarity in the use of the term "genre," stating that "a record buying adolescent of today has clearer ideas on musical genres than the majority of musicologists who have made such a fuss about them."[66] As part of the response to this gap, Fabbri suggests the following definition: "a set of musical events (real or possible) whose course is governed by a definite set of socially accepted rules."[67] These rules involve not only form and technical rules, but also semiotics, behavior, social, ideological, economical, and juridical ones.[68] These factors guide the treatment of Xerente musical genres in this study in that it attempts to follow the lead of locally determined rules for the identification of traditional and fusion musical genres.

As I alluded to, earlier in this chapter, the desire to attain a holistic perception of artistic performance within its own cultural context and from a local perspective has led ethnodoxologists to utilize the term "genre" in a broader sense.[69] In this application, "genre" does not represent a subset of a Western artistic domain, but rather identifies "a community's category of communication characterized by a unique set of formal characteristics, performance practices, and social meanings."[70] The parts (including Western categories of artistic domains) of such artistic instantiations or events are often perceived by the community as integral to its category. Although Xerente events could potentially also be classified in these terms, this text uses the term "genre" primarily in its more colloquial and typical sense, that is, as a subset of the music category. Yet, within the Xerente context, there are indications that the enactment of musical performance of fusion music genres do indeed incorporate constant nonmusical features that could be viewed as integral.

65. Music Genres List, "What Is a Music Genre?," para. 1.

66. Fabbri, "Theory of Musical Genres," 3. Page numbers refer to the PDF cited for this source.

67. Fabbri, "Theory of Musical Genres," 1.

68. Fabbri, "Theory of Musical Genres," 3–6.

69. This use of the term "genre" is not unique to ethnodoxology. Folklore studies apply the term in similar ways as ethnodoxologists, particularly those within the GEN Network. For a perspective of "genre" in the discipline of folklore see Harris, "Genre."

70. Schrag, *Creating Local Arts Together*, 268.

Authenticity

Authenticity has been variously defined in the literature using this term. This is likely a result of the difference in field perspectives, in contexts of application, of point-of-view, and of the object of evaluation. Furthermore, the preceding viewpoints are not mutually exclusive but can combine in multiple ways and shade the definition and the focus of application. Studies in the last twenty years addressing perceptions and projections of authenticity have documented the difficulty of establishing a single characterization for this concept.[71] Therefore, to avoid unwarranted comparisons and misunderstandings, it is imperative that the framework for the application of the term be established.

Dictionaries provide us with multiple applications for the terms "authentic" or "authenticity." The Merriam-Webster Dictionary, for instance, offers two entries referring primarily to the truthful (or even identical) character of the reproductions of material or cultural items. The third of its definitions states, "true to one's own personality, spirit, or character."[72] The online Oxford Dictionary *Lexico* provides a description of the use of the term "authentic" that comes somewhat closer to its application in this book. In reference to its use in existential philosophy, *authentic* refers to that which relates to or denotes "an emotionally appropriate, significant, purposive, and responsible *mode* of human life."[73] Although these definitions may have some application to the subject at hand, they are still insufficient to determine the range of contexts to which this term refers. The primary value of these definitions for this study is their focus on the relationship between the "thing" being evaluated for authenticity and its relationship to an individual or community. With this perspective in view, cultural authenticity in Xerente Christian musical fusion genres can be demonstrated when the evidence indicates their genuine or true connection to Xerente individuals and/or society, and the local community deems them to be emotionally appropriate and significant, participating in the purposes (functions) of the community as directed by its leaders.

A number of research or academic fields make use of the term "authenticity" to describe situations from their particular perspective. Social theory, for instance, applies the term for the discussion of individual

---

71. Hodgson, "Perceptions of Authenticity." (An AU thesis corresponds to a US dissertation.)

72. Merriam-Webster Dictionary, "Authentic."

73. Merriam-Webster Dictionary, "Authentic." Emphasis added.

authenticity (also called "autonomy").[74] Anthropological and ethnomusicological analyses of authenticity meander between the social theory application of the term and the issue of a certain practice's cultural origin. Stańczyk's study of Polish music appropriations in the 1970s and 1980s is an instance of this challenging variety of usage and perception.[75] His study claims that, in order to be *authentic* (to themselves, their character, their anti-establishment views), a segment of the Polish musical scene constructed a social authenticity consisting of "alternative lifestyles" that were "connected to one's perceived otherness from the social majority and at times 'invented' *otherness* against both the dominant culture and the suppressive political power."[76] This *otherness* was expressed through the inclusion of "Oriental and exotic motifs,"[77] that is, through musical elements that would *not* be regarded as authentically Polish. Although in this instance Stańczyk uses the term from this social perspective, his study exists in fact because the cultural perception of what would be authentically Polish contradicts the musical situation he describes.

In *Singing the Congregation*, Monique M. Ingalls also applies the term as in the social sciences. In her study of the current contemporary Christian music scene, Ingalls seeks to describe to what extent those who participate in this type of worship expression perceive it as authentic. This aspect of authenticity is connected to ideas of sincerity and reality of the experience. Ingalls identifies the idea of value as key to evaluating the "worship experience itself."[78] She states that "evangelical conversations about authenticity in worship music parallel closely the authenticity discourses of other musical forms."[79] Citing Sarah Thornton, she states that "music is perceived as authentic when it *rings true* or *feels real,* when it has *credibility* and comes across as *genuine*."[80] The evaluation of the authentic nature of these worship experiences also leans on Jesus's words

---

74. Oshana, "Autonomy and the Question."
75. Stańczyk, "Authenticity and Orientalism."
76. Stańczyk, "Authenticity and Orientalism." See the abstract at https://link.springer.com/chapter/10.1007/978-3-030-17034-9_4.
77. Stańczyk, "Authenticity and Orientalism." See the abstract at https://link.springer.com/chapter/10.1007/978-3-030-17034-9_4.
78. Ingalls, *Singing the Congregation*, 47.
79. Ingalls, *Singing the Congregation*, 47.
80. Ingalls, *Singing the Congregation*, 47.

quoted in the Gospel of John through which he identifies as true worship that which exercised in spirit and in truth.[81]

The uses of the term cited above are indeed legitimate and of great importance. However, they do not represent the core meaning of the term in this book. In this work, the predominant focus is on the cultural authenticity of the artistic/musical practices of the Xerente, or else, whether the fusion genres do indeed possess the character of the contemporary Xerente culture. The authenticity (sincerity, true devotion) of Xerente Christians is not being brought into question, nor does this work cast doubt on the truthfulness of the expression of Xerente Christian experience found in their musical practices. Nothing in this research has indicated that the Xerente Christian community or the missionaries believe them to be inauthentic from this perspective. Indeed, even when the Xerente only sang the translated Western hymns in their congregations, no evidence indicates that they were not being (authentic) true to their newfound faith.

The context of application also frames much of the discussion of authenticity as seen in the literature I researched. Several resources serve to illustrate this dilemma. Renata Hodgson's dissertation on aboriginal artistic tourism in Australia, for instance, and Beth Conklin's article addressing the efforts of indigenous ethnicities in the Amazon region of Brazil to offer an impression of authenticity as a political tool. Joy Kim's thesis addresses a multicultural urban situation where the consideration of power issues is clearly relevant. But regardless of the factors leading communities to develop fused artistic expressions, a common thread does seem to exist: the fact that the emic perception, or else the internal view, provides the most faithful interpretation of authenticity. Along the same line of thought, "authenticity" as discussed in this study gives greater weight to local perception than to Western categorization methods and seeks to allow the voice of the Xerente people to be heard. In sum, I presume and accept that the attitudes and expressions about the musical genres of the Xerente people themselves can best describe their authenticity.

From the context of architectural and landscape preservation, several definitions are offered that reflect the importance of considering change through time as well as intangible characteristics of cultural expressions for the assessment of authenticity. Schrag also offers great insight into the reality of cultural dynamism in his *Creating Local Arts*

---

81. John 4:21–24.

Together.[82] These ideas are relevant to the proposals of this book and will be discussed in chapter 7.[83]

Signposts

The term "signpost" is the most flexible of the key terms in this research. It is used figuratively as a marker akin to such as one would encounter on roads indicating the name of a place, the likely presence of certain animals, directional signs, memorials celebrating events that occurred on particular location, and so forth. However, the significance of the signposts is not primarily the indication of the *presence* of meaning, function, competence, or agency. The demonstration of the presence of such characteristics is primarily the task of the evidence made relevant through this research. Rather, "meaning," for instance, if determined to be present in the community being studied, serves as an indicator of the likelihood of the quality of "authenticity" in the genres. In essence, signposts serve to indicate the potential quality of "authenticity," not simply the presence of either meaning, function, competence, or agency.

1.2.4 Xerente Musical Genres Currently in Use

Xerente cultural songs (from now on referred to as "traditional") have specific functions within the community's life and display enough variety to be locally identified as distinct genres. In the course of missionary (Pastor) Rinaldo de Mattos's[84] tenure among the Xerente, he was able to identify various types (or genres) of songs that are appropriate to specific life or cultural events. The genres, although to a certain degree distinguishable from one another in their structure, do share common melodic and verse patterns characteristic of the *Akwẽ*.[85] They are used to this day in their festivals (Pt.: *festas*), although these are not held as frequently as

---

82. Schrag, *Creating Local Arts Together*, 166.

83. The following article provides various definitions and criteria for the evaluation of authenticity especially in material culture. The content will be discussed in chapter 7. Nezhad et al., "Definition of Authenticity Concept."

84. Rinaldo de Mattos and his wife, along with Gunther Krieger and his wife, were some of the earliest Baptist missionaries among the Xerente.

85. See Appendix A.

in the past.[86] Chapter 3 of this book considers the musical and practical aspects of traditional music that are pertinent to this research.

Churches in the various Xerente villages use a combination of musical genres for their services. In contrast to a great number of Brazilian evangelical churches in the twenty-first century, church services still include many musical numbers that are presented by soloists, duets, or a group of people.[87] Current evangelical church practices in Brazil frequently resemble the contemporary binary styles of North America and other English-speaking nations, including music from the contemporary Praise & Worship genre followed by preaching.[88] Congregational songs or specials make use of traditional Western hymns translated into *Akwẽ*, a few contemporary Praise & Worship songs, northeastern genres like *forró*, or a blend of styles, the character of which will also receive special attention in chapter 3.

1.2.5 Authenticity in Blended Styles

The thesis of this work is predicated on a view of musical and artistic categories not bound to static stylistic frameworks. The question of authenticity rests upon the assumption that characteristics of fluidity and malleability in the creation of musical genres are the best representatives of the essential character of musical creativity. Furthermore, this work proposes that sufficient evidence exists from historical genre developments worldwide and particularly in Brazil that warrant a re-evaluation of prerequisites associated with formally acknowledged genres as determinants of a music style's authenticity.

According to authors Chris McGowan and Ricardo Pessanha, "Brazil has been a real melting pot for centuries, not a mixed salad like the United States."[89] Evidence of this development occurs not only in terms of racial combination (European, Indian, and African, primarily), but in

---

86. Personal conversation with Xerente Christian composer Lázaro Rowakro during Music Workshop in the village of Cabeceira Verde between July 18 and 28, 2017.

87. I obtained this information through participant observation in Xerente services in January and July 2017, and in June 2019. This was also confirmed by the missionaries who lead or attend the services on a regular basis.

88. I served as music director and president of the Minas Gerais Association of Baptist Musicians from 2014 to 2017 and had firsthand information as well as acquaintance with countless musicians from many Brazilian states who confirmed this practice.

89. McGowan and Pessanha, *Brazilian Sound*, loc. 215.

religious, cultural, and artistic blends. Many Brazilian musical genres are well known and loved by musicians worldwide and they present a sound that identifies the culture of Brazil in many circles. Yet, in the early 1500s (for most genres, even as recently as in 1900) no such Brazilian society or musical identity existed. *It developed—partly consciously but without foreknowledge of the outcomes—through cultural mixes.*

In *The Brazilian Sound*, McGowan and Pessanha constantly affirm the multiplicity of sources and genres that converged on Brazilian soil, and that, through a series of circumstances and social issues, they fused many times over to create new genres. These genres, after a period of public affirmation, developed stylistic boundaries in the perception of both experts and general audience. In time, as seems common in known cultures, the following generations (sometimes even the same generation) began to 'forget' that the genres were the result of (intentional or unintentional) blends and they became judges of the very processes that have brought their own preferred musics to life. In the same manner, while the apparent combination of stylistic musical practices present in Christian Xerente musical styles may be characterized by some as incongruent and inauthentic, Xerente ingenuity and imagination has probably followed the same process of genre development that has characterized most musical creativity on Brazilian soil and potentially around the world.

1.2.6 Meaning Development

Music, as other symbolic patterns of communication, has been shown to attain meaning based on cultural and individual interpretation. "Meaning is not 'transmitted' to us—*we actively interpret texts and the world according to a complex interplay of frames of reference.*"[90] The process of meaning development, or *semiosis*, represents a key element of the field of Musical Semiotics, and as such, accompanies the framework of this study. The pioneering concepts of semioticians Ferdinand de Saussure and Charles Peirce have served as foundation for multiple writers who have studied the process of meaning development.[91]

In consonance with the academic community of ethnomusicologists, this research affirms that "(m)usic is no more a universal 'language'

---

90. Chandler, *Semiotics*, loc. 480. Emphasis added.

91. The bibliography at the end of this book provides references to a few works by these authors.

than (verbal) language itself."[92] As part of the evaluation of authenticity, Peirce's concept of the type of sign identified as *symbol*[93] and its attainment of local or personal meaning can present a structured way to explain the development of singular meanings among the Xerente that are connected to the fusion genres currently in vogue.

1.3 RESEARCH OBJECTIVES

1.3.1 Research Questions

The initial impetus to partner with the Xerente church and missionaries to assist in developing their church music ministry came through a personal visit to their region in January of 2016. In multiple conversations with both indigenous and non-indigenous Christians, a number of differing opinions were expressed as to which stylistic direction(s) Xerente Christian music should take. A music workshop held in the village of Cabeceira Verde in July of 2017 was my first week-long interaction with Xerente musicians aiming at addressing this question and supporting local musical creativity. The responses from the musicians indicated that they felt deeply connected with Xerente society and that their traditional music had important meaning in their lives. At the same time, it became evident that many adopted musical practices that were not originally Xerente had gained a solid footing in church musical practices.

In view of the musical reality of contemporary Xerente churches, this work attempts to evaluate the evidence from musical creativity that does not simply reflect characteristics of traditional Xerente music. Furthermore, it considers the possibility that the conjunction of 'internal' and 'external' musical components mirrors an internal perception of true Xerente Christian identity. The questions and observations contained in this book seek to unveil the relevance of the contemporary music genres' functions and meanings for Xerente Christians to better determine their authentic nature. Could the choices for these genres and the musicians' capacity to create in them indicate such authenticity? Questions such as this one are not intended to determine the existence of the genres, nor to classify them, but to help confirm the internal prerogative of a people to determine the authentic nature of its artistic expressions.

---

92. Tagg, *Music's Meanings*, 38.
93. Tagg, *Music's Meanings*, 109.

1.3.2 Implications for Indigenous Peoples

This research values the desires and designs of Xerente Christians to continue to communicate their faith through the musical dialects with which they have come to identify themselves as a people. In essence, the implications of an affirmation of authenticity to these and other locally produced and sustained genres are indeed *practical*. If indigenous communities like the Xerente can be encouraged to describe themselves and their identity (in many cases refuting external closed systems that have been used for the identification of an authentic character by anthropologists, missionaries, governmental agents, et al.), then outsiders who look into their culture will be challenged to acknowledge as legitimate the dynamic processes of culture building that take place among them.[94] Such concession could result in a growth in mutual respect between cultures and affirm the legitimacy of choices made by indigenous communities, music being the aspect addressed as relevant in this work.

1.3.3 Implications for the Academic Community

As previously indicated, the study of ethnodoxology draws on concepts from various other existing academic fields. The evaluation of authenticity in locally developed fusion genres has important implications for the contributing fields of ethnomusicology, cultural anthropology, musical semiotics, and sociology. Systematic academic studies tend to fix and use categories which, while helpful for the understanding of an unfamiliar cultural milieu, can also distort the complex reality in view. While studies on authenticity struggle to determine a global definition, because of the concept's close connection to group and individual identities, the concept may be best understood as a local matter. After all, as Norwegian social anthropologist Frederik Barth explains, ethnic identity is "a matter of self-ascription and ascription by others in interaction, not the analyst's construct on the basis of his or her construction of a group's 'culture.'"[95]

---

94. The complex character of "authenticity" is addressed in the essays of ethnohistorian João Pacheco de Oliveira. Oliveira, *Nascimento do Brasil e Outros Ensaios*, 220. (All translations from this source are mine.)

95. Barth, *Ethnic Groups and Boundaries*, 6.

1.3.4 Implications for the Church and Its Outreach

Music, although not universal in its meaning, has served as a medium of communication in all known cultures of the world. The Christian faith, as a completion of the hopes of Hebrew writings, has incorporated the use of music through the centuries in a multiplicity of ways. It has followed both the Old Testament command to "sing unto the Lord"[96] and Paul's instructions to the churches in Ephesus and Colossae to speak to one another in psalms, hymns, and spiritual songs, making melody to the Lord.[97] Understandably, those who brought the Christian message to peoples such as the Xerente, were moved by a spirit of obedience to these Scriptures and communicated the desire to sing to those who became Christians.

The affirming signals of authenticity offered in this research rely on the testimonies of Xerente Christians and non-indigenous people who have ministered to them. On the basis of the evidence to which I had access, I felt compelled to pursue this study, confident that music and arts that genuinely represent a people's communicative forms are highly likely to connect with them on a spiritual level and to enhance their perception and response to the message of the song. Such interlinking of the spirit with the understanding (or the mind) is foundational for a holistic and fulfilled Christian life in Pauline thought. This is indicated in his first epistle to the Corinthians: "I will pray with the spirit, and I will also pray with the understanding. I will sing with the spirit, and I will also sing with the understanding" (1 Cor 14:15 NKJV). The spiritual value of genuine expressions of faith through music can be found in the potential strengthening of the churches, as well as in the development of relational forms of communication of the Christian faith to those outside the church.

1.4 LITERATURE REVIEW

1.4.1 Ethnodoxology, Ethnomusicology, and Semiotics

The implementation of "culturally appropriate" music and arts for Christian worship has gained continued interest and increased momentum since the last decade of the twentieth century among cross-cultural workers engaging minority language groups.[98] Multiple experiences

---

96. For instance: Pss 30, 95, 96, and 98, to cite a few.
97. Col 3:16 and Eph 5:19.
98. Christian ethnomusicologists have presumably begun to apply their research

worldwide have given evidence of the countless creative ways a culture can express itself in daily activities including Christian worship. Three ethnomusicology works have assisted in the formation of the conceptual framework of this research. The foundational contribution of these three and of other authors are outlined in the next pages.

Roberta King's 1989 dissertation *Pathways in Christian Communication*[99] provided valuable observations about the Senufo response to their local music style and informed the conceptual framework of this work. *Pathways* discusses Christian music commonly used among the Senufo people of the Ivory Coast and analyzes its communicative strength and its subsequent theological and formative significance. Its focus, however, differs from the concentration of this research addressing present-day Xerente Christian music in several aspects:

a. *Pathways in Christian Communication* studies an African people that has experienced a *distinct historical interaction with the West*[100] (or the middle East and Islam in the case of the Senufo) containing multiple variables that may have affected their response to non-traditional music.

b. Although the Senufo people have had evangelical churches about as long as the Xerente, after a short-lived use of Western hymns the Senufo themselves began to compose music in their traditional style and maintained these songs to this day. The Xerente, on the other

---

to develop (or encourage local peoples to develop) music for Christian functions (worship, community building, etc.) around the middle of the twentieth century. One traceable and important precursor of the recent ethnodoxology movement was Vida Chenoweth, a celebrated marimbaist who also served among the Usarufa in Papua New Guinea beginning in the early sixties (Goldsborough, "Vida Chenoweth"). Following this example, a few others applied her methods of generative song composition (or similar) methodologies to missionary interactions with peoples across the globe. *The Ethnodoxology Journal* (2002–5) provides a rich array of stories and resources that give evidence of the broader range of methods, as well as the increased interest, application, and various resources that have been developed. (A list of contents of the *Journal* is available at http://ethnodoxology.org/contents.htm. The actual articles can be accessed through the accompanying DVD of the *Handbook* cited in this work). In the twenty-first century, the focus on music began to broaden to include all artistic modalities (ethnoarts). Multiple new resources have now become available for education, training, and application in any ethnic contexts (https://www.worldofworship.org/).

99. King, *Pathways in Christian Music Communication*.

100. The italics in this outline of contrasts between Roberta King's and my dissertation (here in book form), apart for the title of her book based on the dissertation, serve to highlight the main thought of each point.

hand, were more readily accepting of Western hymnody and still use it to this day. They began to incorporate traditional elements much later and *have not adopted—as of this day—what one could term a "thoroughly traditional" style of music for their churches.*

c. *Pathways* focuses on the lyrics of these Senufo-composed songs and seeks to demonstrate both the weight given by the Senufo to certain topics and the theological depth of their churches. *In contrast, the study of musical authenticity of fusion genres in the Xerente church, while not ignoring the importance of textual content, addresses primarily musical forms, styles, and instrumentation.*

d. *Pathways* used a mixed research methodology but gave considerable weight to a quantitative analysis. Instead, *this research is qualitative in nature, and uses a phenomenological methodology.*

In contrast to the Senufo, the Maninka of Guinea responded to Western Christian hymnody with a full embrace. Dr. Katherine Morehouse's case study "'They're Playing Our Song'"[101] describes a context in which the people chose to adopt and continue to sing Western hymns, even after a fruitful music workshop during which Christian musicians composed many songs in a local genre. Dr. Morehouse also addresses the functions of these hymns for the development of an "Ethnic Christian Identity" (ECI)[102] among the Maninka. Her observation on the functions of the church music adopted in this case provides a comparative basis for the evaluation of authenticity by observing the functionality of musical genres among the Xerente.

Todd Saurman's article and dissertation on Tampuan (an ethnic group in Cambodia) traditional music revitalization affirms positive outcomes of "hybrid" songs.[103] "Singing for Survival" does not address Christian music, but rather the presence of music revitalization efforts within an Asian community that has undergone long-term pressure to adopt national Khmer customs. Unlike the case of Xerente Christian music, newly composed Tampuan musical hybrids have maintained the traditional musical system and modified primarily the context of its participation in community life.[104] Saurman explains that the culture-

---

101. Morehouse, "'They're Playing Our Song.'"
102. Morehouse, "'They're Playing Our Song,'" 2.
103. Saurman, "Singing for Survival," 5.
104. Saurman, "Singing for Survival," 7.

making capacity of music emerges from these texts once again as they attest to the changing character of cultural forms and their meanings in the course of time.

As ethnomusicologists have long acknowledged that music is "not a universal language,"[105] this assessment invites members of all cultures to acknowledge the fact that "there is no single artistic language that communicates completely across lines of time, place and culture."[106] Since meaning develops primarily within the receptor's environment or mind on the basis of a multiplicity of factors, local testimony of cultural perceptions of songs and whole genres demonstrates the most accurate interpretation of their meanings and functions. Leaning on pioneering concepts of semioticians Ferdinand de Saussure and Charles Peirce, music and art semioticians during the latter part of the twentieth century such as Umberto Eco, Eero Tarasti, Thomas Turino, Oscar Salgar, José Luis Martinez, Philip Tagg, Jean-Jacques Nattiez, and many others,[107] provide validation for the reality of meaning creation in human experience. Although not focused on indigenous Christian music, these authors provide relevant understanding as to how local (or individual) perception of meaning may indicate authenticity in the creation of new genres in the Xerente church.

In the 1970s, the Italian author Umberto Eco "was responsible, in part, . . . for turning the theory of semiotics toward a reappraisal of the American philosopher Charles Peirce, making Peirce's key ideas the cornerstone of his own semiotic theories."[108] His literary work incorporated the concept of an "open work." According to Eco, a work of art contains meanings "instigated by the artist," but invites the audience to collaborate to create meaning with their "subjective perspectives."[109] The American ethnomusicologist Thomas Turino published an article in 1999 which sketched "a theory of music, emotion, and identity"[110] on the basis of Peirce's principles of meaning using his categories related to the concept of "'sign." Turino proposes that "authenticity," as it is used in this text, "relates directly to how signs are interpreted within given social contexts."[111] More recently, British-born musician Philip Tagg brought

---

105. Meyer, *Emotion and Meaning in Music*, locs. 179–80.
106. SIL International, "Arts and Ethnomusicology," para. 7.
107. Works by these authors are listed in the bibliographical section of the book.
108. Bondanella. *Umberto Eco and the Open Text*, locs. 55–56.
109. Elmo Raj, "Text and Meaning," 331.
110. Turino, "Signs of Imagination," 222.
111. Turino, "Signs of Imagination," 247.

together semiotic concepts developed during the last decades by multiple semioticians and philosophers in his large volume entitled *Music's Meaning*.[112] The initial five chapters serve as an introductory course in music semiotics in the author's website. Tagg's conceptual approach to music semiotics invites the reader to seek to find ways to respect one another's perceptions of specific musical pieces or genres. Through the works of the above-mentioned authors and others of a similar vein, semiotics can provide a structural outline for a better understanding of the meaningful connection between Xerente Christians and their music.

1.4.2 Historical and Cultural Development of Brazilian Indians

The Xerente, as is the case of multiple indigenous peoples of Brazil, have participated to some degree in the creation of the broad Brazilian national identity. They belong to a historical line of interaction with European peoples initiated approximately 500 years ago. Numerous historians, therefore, have provided insight into the multifaceted experience of nation building during the initial years of discovery, centuries of colonization, decades as an independent empire, and lastly as a republic.

Modern scholarship has profited from reports and books written by the early explorers about their early experiences in Brazil. They open a window into an age of distinct expectations (religious, economic, cultural) and allow the modern reader to better understand how the early interactions could have served as catalysts for later practices. One of these books is *History of a Voyage to the Land of Brazil*, written by Jean de Léry, a French Huguenot who had participated in the failed attempt to establish a French colony along the Bay of Guanabara where the city of Rio de Janeiro was later founded. First published in 1580, it serves as one of the earliest documents of indigenous music, particularly of the *Tupí*[113] who were spread along the coast of Brazil.[114] From his observations, he arrived at the conclusion that their music had no "composers," and noted that "the function of music in the indigenous environment is

---

112. Tagg, *Music's Meanings*.

113. *Tupí* (pronounced "Too-'pea") is often used very broadly for numerous people groups and their language(s) first encountered along the coasts of Brazil.

114. Camêu, "Música Indígena." A short survey of the short history of the French colonial establishment in present-day Rio de Janeiro (called *France Antartique*) is available online: Vidal, "Présence Française."

connected directly to community life, and [is] not perceived as an individual manifestation."[115]

The well-known Portuguese Jesuit priest José de Anchieta described sixteenth-century conflicts, events, social issues, and religious advances in the new colony in his letters to his superiors. These writings have been collected and published as *Letters, Information, Historical Fragments, and Sermons of Father José de Anchieta: (1554–1594)*.[116] Anchieta provided catechism among Indians through various means and stated a willingness to embrace "some customs of these gentile(s)[117] that are not against [the] catholic faith," including music that was not "dedicated to idols."[118] First published two centuries after its writing,[119] Gabriel Soares de Souza's *A Descriptive Treatise of Brazil* also provides "a true repository of indispensable information" about the "geography of the coast of Brazil, as well as [its] topography, colonization, agriculture, flora, fauna, ethnography, etc. of [the modern State of] Bahia."[120] These primary sources relate early European impressions of an exotic and unexplored world they had just "uncovered" and, hence, are invaluable for the comprehension of this historical period.

Since the centuries of colonization until the present republic, the countless and complex experiences involving Europeans, their (often mixed) descendants, Indians, and Africans have shaped both the national identity and the image of the Brazilian Indian in the national conscience. According to Brazilian ethnohistorian John Monteiro (1956–2013), traditional historiography has granted insufficient recognition to the role played by indigenous peoples in the creation of a Brazilian national identity.[121] His 2001 dissertation "Tupís, Tapuias, and Historians: Studies in Indigenous History and Indigenismo"[122] testifies to Monteiro's

---

115. Camêu, "Música Indígena," 30.

116. Anchieta, *Cartas, Informações, Fragmentos Históricos*.

117. The Roman Catholic Church at that time applied the term *gentile* to those who were not considered Christians, or, in other words, *pagans*. It was not used in the traditional biblical sense as a term referencing *all* nations other than Israel. The theological modification displays an absolute identification of the "Church" as the real "Israel" since Christ. Oliveira and Costa Freire, *Presença Indígena*, 25.

118. Monteiro, "Tupis, Tapuias e Historiadores," 40.

119. Biblioteca Brasiliana Culta José Mindlin, "Souza, Gabriel Soares de."

120. Carone. "Tratado Descritivo do Brasil." Translation mine.

121. Monteiro, "Tupis, Tapuias e Historiadores."

122. Monteiro, "Tupis, Tapuias e Historiadores." The term "indigenismo," according to the Portuguese Aurélio Dictionary, refers in this case to "a set of ideas proposed by

"decisive and striking influence" towards a significant renewal in the comprehension of the place of indigenous cultures in the development of Brazil.[123] Monteiro notes that "the powerful image of the Indians as eternal prisoners of isolated and primitive forms has made difficult the understanding of the multiple processes of *ethnic transformation* that would help explain a considerable portion of the social and cultural history of the country."[124] Historical research since the beginning of the twenty-first century has further reinforced this broader perspective. João Oliveira and Carlos Freire's official publication *The Indigenous Presence in the Formation of Brazil*,[125] for instance, was organized around the idea that the Indian "has always been an essential part of this process of territorial and political formation."[126] Likewise, Marina Monteiro Machado's "The Trajectory of Destruction" insists that "we should not believe that [indigenous peoples] were simply manipulated by the colonists ... even though their choices may have contributed to their own destruction."[127]

Friedrich Câmera Siering's thesis "Conquest and Domination of Indigenous Peoples" identifies the importance of indigenous resistance along the coastal lands of the State of Bahia in the seventeenth century for the creation of ethnic identities. He states that, beyond the (tragic) decimation of populations and destruction of indigenous societies, through a number of interethnic alliances "these sets of [cultural/ethnic] clashes also produced new societies and new types of society."[128] Furthermore, his study "seeks to dismantle the radical opposition between "original purity/post-contact contamination," a dichotomy which persists in its resistance, and it [the study] underscores the continuous process of cultural innovation."[129] The above-mentioned and other corroborating works demonstrate the development of a greater consciousness of indigenous participation of Brazilian nation-building and of their own distinct

---

organizations or individuals connected to the State, relative to the situation of Brazilian indigenous populations and to the problems that arise in reference to their incorporation into the 'nation-state.'" Schiavini, "Indigenismo e Politica Indigenista," para. 11. Translation mine.

123. Almeida, "John Manuel Monteiro (1956–2013)." Translation mine.
124. Monteiro, "Tupis, Tapuias e Historiadores," 5. Emphasis added.
125. Oliveira and Costa Freire, *Presença Indígena*.
126. Oliveira and Costa Freire, *Presença Indígena*, 18.
127. Machado, "Trajetória da Destruição," 26. Translation mine.
128. Siering, "Conquista e Dominação," 14.
129. Siering, "Conquista e Dominação," 14.

societies. They contributed to this research by supporting evidence of a continuous process of cultural change in Brazil, by challenging the dichotomy between traditional and Western culture, and by strengthening the importance of local choices that have ultimately affected the shape of indigenous communities.

The Xerente experience has been studied by many researchers with various interests, including anthropologists, linguists, sociologists, and missionaries. The Brazilian Digital Library of Dissertations and Theses displays eight dissertations and around twenty-five theses addressing primarily anthropological, linguistic, and sociological topics involving the Xerente.[130] While they provided some cultural information for the content of this text, none of them addresses in depth the traditional musical aspects of the society nor the current church musical genres. Nevertheless, these, along with books, informational sites, as well as unpublished notes from Baptist missionaries who have lived among them for almost sixty years have all contributed to a broad understanding of the present Xerente musical scene. Particularly relevant among these, the communally produced book *Povo Akwẽ Xerente: Vida, Cultura, Identidade* (*The Akwẽ Xerente People: Life, Culture, Identity*) presents an indispensable internal view of the community. In this publication, with the assistance of the editor Silvia Thêkla Wewering, the Xerente express their desire for, and effort towards, the affirmation and preservation of their culture.[131]

1.4.3 Hybridity and Fusion

The industrial and scientific age could be regarded as one of the greatest catalysts of cultural change in known history. Compared to previous ages, the accelerated developments of the twentieth century have quickly juxtaposed tradition and modernity, creating innumerable social blends in the process. Nestor Garcia Canclini addresses the ramifications of these combinations, particularly in Latin America, in the book *Hybrid Cultures*. His analysis of hybridization leads him to conclude "that today all cultures are border cultures."[132] Through the multidirectional transfer of goods and artistic products, "cultures lose the exclusive relation with

---

130. http://bdtd.ibict.br/vufind/Search/Results?lookfor=Xerente&type=AllFields.
131. Wewering. *Povo Akwẽ Xerente*.
132. Canclini, *Hybrid Cultures*, 261.

their territory, but they gain in communication and knowledge."[133] Canclini substantiates the growing perception that the *opposing concepts of "pure versus contaminated"* arts and crafts would serve culture best *by being abandoned.*[134]

Although Canclini focuses on visual arts and crafts, similar blending processes can be identified in the development of musical genres across South America. As mentioned earlier in this chapter, Brazilian musical genres have developed through the interaction and integration of elements from various ethnicities. *The Brazilian Sound*,[135] a recently written history of the principal genres of modern Brazil, attests clearly to the process of genre creation that has taken place repeatedly, particularly since the late nineteenth century. In the same vein, Gerard Behague, in his article on Brazilian music for the *New Grove Dictionary of Music and Musicians*, affirms as "genuine" what he terms 'mestizo' musical traditions of Brazil.[136] Carolina Bertolini's 2016 thesis "Musical Performance and Recognition" also gives evidence in modern times of the potential of multi-ethnic blends which she observed among the Sateré-Mawé and Tikuna peoples in Manaus. Her research demonstrates the necessity of shifting away from "the common classical perception which establishes a direct correspondence between one [specific] ethnic group, [or] a people group, and one [style of] music."[137]

1.4.4 Ethnogenesis, Identity, and Ethnicity,

The development of cultural and artistic blends relates also to a lesser-known field of study termed "ethnogenesis." Jonathan Hill applies the concept of ethnogenesis as "a theoretical approach to hybridity and syncretism"[138] to the rise and reformulations of ethnic identity in the Americas in his publication *History, Power, and Identity: Ethnogenesis in the Americas, 1492–1992*. The approach is grounded on the distinguished work of his forerunner Frederik Barth *Ethnic Groups and Boundaries: The Social Organization of Culture Difference*, which affirms that

133. Canclini, *Hybrid Cultures*, 261.
134. Canclini, *Hybrid Cultures*, 175. Emphases mine.
135. McGowan and Pessanha, *Brazilian Sound*.
136. Behague, "Brazil," 224.
137. Bertolini, "Performance Musical e Reconhecimento," 167.
138. Hill, *Power, and Identity*, 27.

"ethnic identity is a matter of self-ascription and ascription by others in interaction,"[139] focusing on "the on-going negotiations of boundaries between groups of people."[140] Citing James Clifford, Hill argues that, through ethnogenesis, cultures undergo "a process of 'authentically remaking' new social identities through creatively rediscovering and refashioning components of 'tradition', such as oral narratives, written texts, and material artefacts."[141] A formal survey of theories of ethnicity and ethnogenesis has been organized in the first section of *The Hurons—Ethnicity and Ethnogenesis* by Josef Sprotte, former professor of ethnology at the Free University of Berlin. Section two of Sprotte's work focuses on the Hurons, offering valuable perceptions and assessments of the dynamic changes that occurred among them.[142]

1.4.5 Authenticity

While it is unlikely that an overarching *definition* of "authenticity" would be applicable to every context, authors addressing the topic in various applications of the term—for instance: tourism, music production, politics, architecture—seem to prefer identifying *demonstrative signs* of "authenticity" for each case. Beth Conklin's 1997 article "Body Paint, Feathers, and VCRs: Aesthetics and Authenticity in Amazonian Activism"[143] addresses the question from a geopolitical perspective among Amazonian Indians and suggests that their activism may have led them to act "inauthentically."[144] Within the article she identifies an emphasis by anthropologists on local *competency* and *control* since the 1990s. With the modification of the term *control* to *agency*, these demonstrative signs have been integrated into the thesis of this dissertation as two of the four "signposts" of authenticity.

In an evaluation of authentic cultural experiences in Australian tourism, Renata Hodgson states that "prominent philosophers who reflected upon the notion of authenticity include existentialist writers such as Camus (1975), Hegel (1977), Heidegger (1996), Kierkegaard (1985), Nehemas

---

139. Barth, *Ethnic Groups and Boundaries*, 15.
140. Boston University Anthropology, "Emeritus Professors: Frederik Barth," para. 3.
141. Hill, *Power, and Identity*, 28.
142. Sprotte, *Hurons*.
143. Conklin, "Body Paint, Feathers, and VCRs."
144. Conklin, "Body Paint, Feathers, and VCRs," 729.

(1999) and Sartre (1992)."[145] Responding to the lack of a clear definition of authenticity, her emphasis, embodied in the title of her 2007 doctoral thesis, turns to "Perceptions of Authenticity,"[146] based on four meanings suggested by E. M. Bruner.[147] Restating J. P. Taylor's question, Hodgson asks "who should hold the power to define the authenticity of a cultural experience?" indicating the need to identify who has 'authority' to declare a given cultural object (performance, tangible objects) truly authentic.

In the 2014 article "Music, Culture, Politics: Communicating Identity, Authenticity and Quality in the 21st Century" Ulkik Volgsten states that "music is not just an interchangeable stimulus, but an important aspect of many persons' and groups' identity processes."[148] Volgsten's discussion on the functions of music and his proposition that "a hermeneutic concept of culture, identity, authenticity and quality are rather about intersubjective production of meaning,"[149] provide support to the signposts of *function* and *meaning* that frame the discussion of authenticity in this book.

Lastly, in an article focused on the authenticity of cultural landscapes, particularly that of historic architectural objects, Somayeh Fadaei Nezhad (University of Tehran) and colleagues, discuss a series of definitions and tests of authenticity suggested along the course of the last six decades.[150] The article highlights two key commonalities found in the works written since the 1980s that offer support to the choice of signposts applied in the evaluation of authenticity in this work: 1. questions of authenticity need to consider the dynamic character of the culture; and 2. a truthful assessment of authenticity should consider both "tangible" and "intangible" aspects. Both of these ideas provide foundational support for the signposts chosen to evaluate the authentic character of Xerente music fusion genres and will be discussed accordingly.[151]

---

145. Hodgson, "Perceptions of Authenticity," 57.
146. Hodgson, "Perceptions of Authenticity."
147. Bruner, "Abraham Lincoln as Authentic Reproduction."
148. Volgsten, "Music, Culture, Politics," 116.
149. Volgsten, "Music, Culture, Politics," 117.
150. Nezhad et al., "Definition of Authenticity Concept."
151. Nezhad et al., "Definition of Authenticity Concept," 97.

1.4.6 Missiological Perspectives

Missiological perspectives of historical church policies and practices are of equal importance for the consideration of authentic and appropriate Christian music genres. Although a number of authors could be introduced as key sources—and many were indeed studied or consulted—a few resources are particularly pertinent to this topic because of their stress on aspects which most authors seldom mention or subjugate to negligible ranks. Andrew Walls' *Missionary Movement in Christian History: Studies in the Transmission of Faith* presents the argument in favor of "contextualization" (although Walls finds this jargon "appalling"), or the adaptation of the essential elements of faith to the linguistic and cultural forms of local culture. Walls states that "the process is clearly visible within the New Testament itself,"[152] and explores the evidence of its practice along the centuries of church history.

Daniel Fleming, a theologian/missiologist of the early twentieth century represents one of the early academic voices in modern history in favor of contextualization of the Christian message. His 1925 publication *Whither Bound in Missions*[153] voices his conviction that every "nation" (ethnic group) should have the privilege of expressing their worship and Christian principles through forms that communicate appropriately with its society.

Missionary Raymond Buker addressed the applicability and advantage of local musical tunes in cross-cultural settings in an article of the *Evangelical Missions Quarterly* in 1964. The example he cites from Donald McGavran related to church musical practices in the Ivory Coast in 1962 leads him to conclude that "this example of adopting the local cultural situation to the need in Christian development of a given group is indicative of what may well be done in any culture."[154] This particular article has the distinction of being featured in the very first edition of the *Evangelical Missions Quarterly*.

Although many Brazilian sources are relevant to this research, one author/missionary and his wife stand out in the field of missiology. Ronaldo Lidório and his wife have served in missions with a minority people group in Africa and with indigenous groups in Brazil for many

---

152. Walls, *Missionary Movement in Christian History*, loc. 192.

153. Fleming, *Whither Bound in Missions*. Fleming produced also other valuable works that accord with the same vision as this *Whither Bound*.

154. Buker, "Missionary Encounter with Culture."

years. Ronaldo Lidório is a respected anthropologist and speaks with authority on indigenous missiology. Among his many publications, *Communication, Transculturality, and Ethics*, written by the Lidórios about their communications model termed MEDICI,[155] and *Communication and Culture*[156] relate to intercultural conversations and support certain important aspects of this dissertation.

1.5 THEORETICAL FRAMEWORK

1.5.1 Foundational and Collaborative Fields of Ethnodoxology

Ethnodoxology proposes to study the practice of Christian worship within the context of any given culture.[157] It encompasses two major branches of the humanities which merge together to form the interdisciplinary field of ethnodoxology: Christian theology, with a particular emphasis on worship and mission, and the arts, a term not restricted to the "fine arts" but incorporating also crafts and skills applied for the creation of tangible or intangible objects. Ethnodoxologists consider the creative ability in human beings to be a reflection of the image of God and that human creative acts can honor God.[158] The field has roots in the principles of ethnomusicology and anthropology which continue as conversation partners in contemporary academic discussions. In addition to the foundational fields, as the literature review indicates, musical semiotics, music and Brazilian history, missiological theory of contextualized communication, as well as sociological subfields involving ethnic identity, cultural hybridity, and authenticity represent essential collaborative fields for the positive outcome of this research.

1.5.2 Elaboration of Theoretical Framework

The contemporary Xerente Christian context and its music served as the springboard for raising the question of musical authenticity. The dichotomy of traditional versus Western or modern, as previously introduced,

---

155. Lidório and Lidório, *Comunicação, Interculturalidade e Ética*.

156. Lidório, *Comunicação e Cultura*.

157. For further details and examples of this field of applied arts access, see Global Ethnodoxology Network, "Ethnodoxology," esp. "What is ethnodoxology?"

158. Schaeffer, *Art and the Bible*.

dictates a widespread perception of fixed genre categories. It has important ramifications and is demonstrated through the application of labels of "inauthentic"—or devoid of value or genuineness—to music styles or genres that appear incongruent with accepted music categorizations.

By way of affirming ethnodoxology's emphasis on the importance of meaningful and culturally appropriate worship[159] expressed through a community's "own heart languages, heart musics, and other arts,"[160] this book challenges models of evaluation of local worship arts that are rooted in the dichotomy of fixed genre categories (internal or external) and that lend themselves to mere external assessments of authenticity, and similarly demonstrate reluctance to accept the non-static character of living cultures. In this work, I attempt to demonstrate that, throughout recorded history, musical genres have generally been adaptable and versatile, often as a result of human creativity in an environment of cultural exchange. Based on this framework, an evaluation of what may be deemed authentic and "culturally appropriate" music genres for worship and other Christian messages is most reliable if it rests primarily on internal indicators, here designated as *signposts* (not that a local community is dependent on external approval). Four such signposts can serve as strong markers of authenticity for musical genres, and potentially any artistic expression:

1. *Meaning*—a genre's significance for individuals and the community, including the potential to help form identities.

2. *Function*—the presence of roles for a music genre integrated into the life of the community (or church) in indispensable ways (or so perceived by the community).

3. *Competence*—the ability of local musicians to envision a combination of features that fuse as a genre, as well as the competence to compose and perform music of such genre.

4. *Agency (Control or Administration)*—the local community's decision-making practices concerning the local genre's performance within Christian meeting venues and in the Christian's private life; the presence of local administration of a genre.

Presumably, local musical genres maintain certain features from long-standing, traditional genres of the culture. They may play a role in

---

159. Bailey, "Cultivating and Contextualizing Arts," locs. 7197–205.
160. Harris, "Great Misconception," loc. 3065.

developing a genre's meanings and functions, as well as in facilitating competent creativity and control of its integration in the life of the community. Through an analysis of the original songs recorded in the Xerente village of Cabeceira Verde, characteristics typically associated with local and non-Xerente traditions have been found to be fused together into a new whole.

1.5.3 Spiritual Applicability of Framework

Although even the most accurate perception of cultural realities and social implications cannot guarantee that humans will behave appropriately towards one another, a framework such as this one seeks to provide reasonable evidence of a hermeneutical position that supports a spiritual attitude of respect and understanding. Human tendencies to impose one's own views on others can be so clearly identified in historical records and daily news that presumably even a child of ten years of age would have experienced such pressures in his or her own lifetime. Christian virtue, however, calls upon the individual to exercise respect and exhibit love to other members of the Christian community, as well as to those outside it. The apostle Paul addresses similar issues in his New Testament letter to the Romans. Considering that Christians hold to differing opinions and practices determined by various backgrounds and sensitivities, he admonishes them by asking: "who are you to judge another's servant? To his own master he stands or falls. Indeed, he will be made to stand, for God is able to make him stand."[161]

In matters related to cultural differences, Christians are often still drawn to evaluations supported primarily—or solely—by the principles of their own nationality or social rank. This paradigm affects not only a Christian's relationship with other people(s) but it may also indicate a potential weakness in one's relationship to God. Charles Kraft's *Christianity and Culture* challenges several assumed paradigms including the presumed superior stance of Western culture above others.[162] Although for a spiritual transformation leading an individual to move away from unwarranted perceptions of superiority to take place, a personal spiritual encounter with God is needed, the framework offered in this book is

---

161. Rom 14:4 NKJV.
162. Kraft, *Christianity in Culture*, 18.

designed to encourage a re-evaluation of one's own perception of cultural realities unlike one's own.

1.6 RESEARCH METHODOLOGY

The discussion of potential local authenticity of Xerente Christian music genres relies on contributions from the various fields mentioned in in previous sections of this chapter, on recordings, as well as on personal interviews with local stakeholders—the Xerente Christians. This study intends to unveil the functions and meanings of Xerente Christian music genres through the various voices of members of the community regarding their genuine local character. The research also investigates the competence of and administration by Xerente Christian musicians in the compositional and performance practices of their fusion music genres.

This qualitative research involves a phenomenological approach that used eight strategies applied along the course of three years (2016–19). These strategies guided and permeated my three personal visits to Xerente villages (January 2016; July 2017; June 2019) as well as all opportunities of interaction with missionaries actively involved with the Xerente and other indigenous peoples of Brazil. They are as follows:

1. Analysis of literature discussing cultural blends and hybridity. This strategy involved a review of literature relating to and discussing the historical interaction and power struggles between cultures around the world and, in particular, between Europeans and indigenous peoples beginning with the first centuries of Brazilian colonization. Issues of cultural authenticity, identity, and religious views discussed in the texts were of particular interest for this study.

2. Analysis of literature related to evangelical missions around the world and in Brazil, with a specific focus on indigenous missions.

3. Review and analysis of a corpus of recorded indigenous music. This review provided a broad view of Brazilian indigenous Christian music genres from approximately two dozen ethnic groups. The recordings were studied for readily observable stylistic elements but not transcribed or further analyzed for this study.

4. Interviews with Xerente Christians (pastors, musicians, and other church members) from several villages.

Introduction

5. Discussions with certain CONPLEI[163] leaders about their perception of the topics of local worship arts and of authenticity.

6. Participant observation at a) church services in Xerente villages and inquiries about other venues such as all-night vigils; b) some representative "traditional" activities such as group dances and body painting.

7. Musical transcription of contemporary Xerente Christian songs and analysis of their musical elements. The sources used for this analysis include professional recordings of Xerente singers and new songs recorded during the music workshop which this author offered in the Xerente village "Cabeceira Verde" in 2017 in collaboration with colleague and ethnodoxologist Heber Negrão. An evaluation of potential connections between the songs and the attested meanings obtained during interviews follows the transcriptions and their analysis.

8. Final conclusions drawn from the resources.

Even multiple interviews could not exhaust the potential new avenues of examination which the open-ended questions raised. However, the interviews highlighted evidence of the general perception of *meanings* and *functions* in the consciousness of the people, as well as the Xerente musicians' *competence* to create and perform within this musical framework and the manifestation of control (or *agency*) exercised in its practice. On this basis, the degree of authenticity in the Xerente church genres was evaluated. Although interviews were done in Portuguese, the responses of the indigenous contributors were checked for accurate meaning by missionaries who speak both Portuguese and *Akwẽ* to make the possibility of misunderstanding to be negligible.

1.7 CHAPTER SUMMARIES

This opening chapter presented the foundational concepts that led to the topic and its core questions. It introduced the thesis of this research and its primary objectives, discussed the key literary works contributing to the understanding of the topic, and outlined the framework and methodology of the research.

Chapter 2 provides a historical background for situating the Xerente as actors of a developing pluricultural society. It surveys relevant

---

163. See footnote 18 in this chapter for a brief explanation of the CONPLEI network.

information concerning events or trends of interaction between the broader Brazilian society and indigenous communities.

Chapter 3 looks at the musical world of the Xerente including their cultural (traditional) music genres, as well as the influences they received from the majority (and neighboring) culture and from the contemporary musical practices of Brazilian evangelical churches. This chapter also describes the characteristics of Xerente Christian music fusion genres by means of transcriptions and musical analysis.

Chapter 4 discusses the process of genre creation by means of musical fusion. It demonstrates the dynamic character of musical contexts from multiple areas of the world, focusing in particular on the creation of new musical genres in Brazil during the last 150 years. It argues for a potentially normative fluidity of development that resists absolute definition through confinement to closed genre systems. Attention is given to how the non-static character of genre formation may indicate authenticity and value of Xerente fusion genres through local meanings, functions, musical competence, and local agency.

Chapters 5 and 6 relate personal interviews with members of the Xerente community and give gathered evidence demonstrating the presence of the 4 proposed signposts of authenticity.

Chapter 7 argues for the validity of the signposts as demonstrative of genuineness and/or authenticity of these and other fusion genres or blends which seem to be manifesting in increasing numbers across the world. It is a formal challenge to the dichotomous paradigm of traditional and Western (or modern) absolute genres.

Lastly, chapter 8 ponders the implications of this study for the principal related fields of ethnomusicology, ethnodoxology, cultural anthropology, social studies, and missiology, considering in particular the spiritual significance of the discoveries. It concludes with a call to respond to this information through transformative action and invites a continuation of research into potential applications of this evaluation.

2

The Xerente and Christian Faith

2.1 HISTORICAL BACKGROUND OF INDIGENOUS MISSIONS

2.1.1 "Discovery" and Brazilian Colonization

EUROPEANS BEGAN INTENSE PROGRAMS of exploration in distant lands during the fifteenth century. The literature suggests that motivations for this enterprise included legitimate curiosity, economic prosperity, political power, and religious advancement. Roger Crowley assigns the launch of this worldwide expansion to the Portuguese conquest of the Muslim port city of Ceuta in Morocco in 1415.[1] The comparatively poor nation of Portugal became attracted to the riches of the middle and far East during the remainder of the century and became the first European nation of that era to navigate under Africa and gain direct access to India in 1498.[2]

With the financial backing of bankers from Genoa and Florence, "the eyes of Europe were turning toward Lisbon"[3] and Pedro Álvares Cabral's armada consisting of 1,200 crewmen and thirteen ships headed for the seas on March 9, 1500, intent on reaching India. Crowley identifies this historical moment as "the shift from reconnaissance to commerce

---

1. Crowley, *Conquerors*, xxii.
2. Crowley, *Conquerors*, xxiii.
3. Crowley, *Conquerors*, 85.

and then conquest."[4] After a series of maneuvers which led the fleet much farther west than planned, they landed in what is now Brazil and met the indigenous population. That early encounter, described in the introduction of this book, ended on May 2 when Cabral's fleet set sail again for India leaving only two convicts in the new land.[5] Numerous expeditions returned to the newly discovered land during the subsequent decades, primarily focused on the exploration of Brazil wood (in Portuguese: *pau-brasil*). Concerted colonization efforts, however, began officially with the arrival of Martim Afonso de Souza's expedition in 1531.[6]

According to the ethnologist Curt Nimuendaju there were "approximately 1400 indigenous peoples in the territory that corresponded to Brazil at [the time of its] discovery." "They were peoples belonging to great linguistic families—tupí-guaraní, jê, karib, aruák, xirianá, Tucano, etc—diverse in geographic location and social organization." Estimates of the total population range from 1.5 to 5 million individuals.[7] The limited knowledge the Portuguese had of the indigenous population and their resistance to subjugation led to the development of a dichotomous categorization of "Tupís and Tapuias"—the former being Indians open to subjugation and the latter hostile ones.[8] The contemporary understanding of linguistic families, ethnic identities, and social processes was achieved only gradually along centuries of difficult interaction, but also of copious blending with the local populations.

4. Crowley, *Conquerors*.
5. Crowley, *Conquerors*, 88.
6. História do Brasil, "Brasil Pré-Colonial," paras. 11–12.
7. Oliveira and Costa Freire, *Presença Indígena*, 22. Translation mine.
8. Oliveira and Costa Freire, *Presença Indígena*, 24. Note: Under "Information" in *Carta*, Anchieta makes a variant description of who the Tupís and the Tapuias were. He explains that the Tupís themselves related that the Tapuias originally inhabited the coasts but started to move inland. The Indians affirm their earlier presence along the coasts, he says, because of the names of places given to them by the Tapuias (see Anchieta, *Cartas*, 298–300). In the nineteenth century, however, the term "Tapuia" obtained a different connotation in the Amazon region, having become a term for Indians who were already "christians," distinct from yet another segment of "indios bravos" (mean Indians) (see Oliveira and Costa Freire, *Presença Indígena*, 92).

2.1.2 Missionary Efforts until the Early Twentieth Century

Missionary initiatives among Brazilian Indians began with the Jesuits in the sixteenth century.[9] Since the beginning of Jesuit catechism, their "reports about the new world identified the indigenous [peoples] as 'gentiles' (pagans), 'brasis', 'negros da terra' [land negros] (enslaved Indians), and 'Indians' (Indians [who lived] in [colonist-created] villages) (Cunha, 1993)."[10]

One of the most celebrated Jesuit priests who had come from Portugal to Brazil was Father Anchieta (*Padre Anchieta*). He learned *Tupí*, the primary indigenous language along the coast of Brazil at the time and penned the first grammar of the newly discovered language.[11] Besides religious instruction, catechism in this environment also involved battles, conquests, the domination of "unbelieving barbarians (Neves, 1978),"[12] as well as "mechanisms of compensation for the Indians, such as the conquest of *sesmarias*,[13] payment of salaries, etc."[14]

Anchieta's letters to his superiors reveal the mindset of the age which was set on "evangelizing" by means of "civilizing."[15] On the whole, it assumed that most native customs were either inferior in content or importance, or irrevocably linked to idolatry.[16] Nonetheless, allowance was made for particular local speech modalities which could accommodate the content of the Jesuits' message and demonstrate their love for the people.[17] By means of dramatization and other artistic devices Anchieta sought to communicate Bible stories and to catechize the Brazilian Indians (in Portuguese, *Índios do Brasil*) by using both Tupí and Portuguese. The forms they chose to utilize, however, appear to have been frequently foreign to the indigenous population. This approach represents a distinctive feature of catechism (in contrast to evangelism),

---

9. Anchieta, *Cartas, Informações, Fragmentos Históricos*.
10. Oliveira and Costa Freire, *Presença Indígena*, 25. Translation mine.
11. Leite and Franchetto, "500 Anos," 22.
12. Oliveira and Costa Freire, *Presença Indígena*, 49. Translation mine.
13. Uncultivated or abandoned piece of land. Priberam Portuguese Dictionary, "Sesmarias."
14. Oliveira and Costa Freire, *Presença Indígena*, 49. Translation mine.
15. Oliveira and Costa Freire, *Presença Indígena*, 47.
16. Monteiro, "Tupis, Tapuias e Historiadores," 40.
17. Monteiro, "Tupis, Tapuias e Historiadores," 40. The author cites Father Manoel da Nobrega, Anchieta's Jesuit colleague, who suggests that adaptation to the local people's mode of speech (discourse methods, not only the language) *would demonstrate love to them*.

according to anthropologist Ronaldo Lidório, which maintains a form of communication based "on the symbols and the structure of the church which conducts it."[18] In spite of these debatable practices and the overall negative assessment of indigenous peoples made by the European incoming population, Anchieta's reports indicate that he sincerely cared for the local population.

The subsequent centuries of colonization brought about countless encounters, both positive and negative, with new ethnic groups in the vast territory of Brazil. Since colonial times until the recent past, a variety of policies were instituted, most of which (until approximately the middle of the twentieth century) were intent on administering the potential integration of indigenous individuals and whole communities with the general Brazilian society.[19] Along the course of history, multiple indigenous groups resisted colonization,[20] while most were assimilated, and their communities fragmented.[21] While a complete history of this situation lies outside of the scope of this report, the frequent and constant cultural incursions produced by colonial, imperial, governmental, or local policies toward Indians may have had (at a minimum) significant consequences on present-day musical developments among indigenous societies.

2.1.3 Evangelical Missions to Indigenous Peoples

Known records demonstrate very little action by protestant or evangelical churches among the Indians except for pastors on the border of Brazil with the English Guyana around the 1880s. Due to that activity, a portion of that border region was eventually turned over to the English Guyana.[22]

Ongoing evangelical missions among indigenous populations had its beginning among the *Terena* people in Mato Grosso do Sul in 1912. Scottish missionaries John Hay and Henry Whittington had originally visited Paraguay in view of establishing a work among its indigenous population. During their first visit to the *Terena* in southwestern Brazil, however, they were invited by the indigenous leadership to establish schools in their villages. After a period of furlough in Scotland, the

18. Lidório, *Comunicação, Interculturalidade E Ética*, locs. 549–55. Translation mine.
19. Oliveira and Costa Freire, *Presença Indígena*.
20. Oliveira and Costa Freire, *Presença Indígena*, 51–60, 84–94.
21. Oliveira and Costa Freire, *Presença Indígena*, 61–92.
22. Oliveira and Costa Freire, *Presença Indígena*, 138.

missionaries returned to Brazil and settled among the Terena in 1913.[23] During the following decades of the twentieth century many other missions organizations initiated works of Bible translation, social work, or church planting in numerous other indigenous ethnic groups.[24] Today, according to a 2010 report of the Research Coordination of the Department of Indigenous Affairs[25] of the Brazilian Association of Transcultural Missions,[26] "182 ethnic groups have an evangelical missionary presence." Moreover, indigenous Christian leadership is now also strongly represented within the context of twenty-first-century indigenous missionary activity in Brazil.[27]

2.1.4 Governmental Agencies and Interventions

Along the centuries, Portuguese and Brazilian governments sought to establish policies to regulate the interaction with the original peoples of Brazil. During the centuries as a colony (early 1500s until Brazil's independence in 1822), the concept of "just war" reigned supreme in times of conflict with the Indians involving the Portuguese Crown and the colonists. According to the Law of April 28, 1688, a war was considered "just" if enacted "against the enemies of the Catholic faith and against the Indians who did not acknowledge royal dominions [lands], thus threating the Portuguese State."[28] In 1724 and 1726, for instance, troops were organized to war against the Manao Indians by the Negro River,[29] who were thus identified as "criminals."[30]

In 1755, during the term of the Portuguese Minister for Brazil Marquês de Pombal, a document named *O Diretório dos Índios*[31] was formulated to "express important aspects of indigenous policy." The text declares

---

23. Instituto Antropos, "Terena," para. 5.

24. For instance, New Tribes Mission (interdenominational): Missão Novas Tirbos do Brasil. "História da Missão"; Junta de Missões Nacionais (Baptist): Missões Nacionais, "Who We Are"; ALEM (interdenominational partner of the Wycliffe Global Alliance): Associação Linguística Evangélica Missionária. "História."

25. In Portuguese: DAI—*Departamento de Assuntos Indígenas*.

26. In Portuguese: AMTB—*Associação de Missões Transculturais Brasileiras*.

27. Grupo Povos e Línguas, "História da Missão."

28. Oliveira and Costa Freire, *Presença Indígena*, 58.

29. In Portuguese: *Rio Negro*, a tributary of the Amazon River.

30. Oliveira and Costa Freire, *Presença Indígena*, 58.

31. Almeida, *Diretório dos Índios*.

"the intention of the government of the Kingdom of Portugal, at that time, of avoiding the enslavement of the Indians, their segregation, and their isolation, as well as of suppressing the treatment of indigenous persons as second-class people among the colonists and white missionaries." The 95 articles that comprise the *Diretório*[32] prohibit the use of the term "negro" in reference to indigenous individuals (article 10), "encourages the marriage of white colonists with Indians (88–91)," establish "the substitution of the General Language (Portuguese: *língua geral*)[33] by the Portuguese language (6)," and "punishment against discrimination (84, 86)."[34]

The *Diretório* makes its goal clear in article 3, stating the will of the Crown "to Christianize and civilize these heretofore unfortunate [unhappy] and miserable peoples, so that, by leaving ignorance and the rustic character to which they are reduced, they may be useful to themselves, to the residents, and to the State."[35] Despite the advances in the promotion of equality for the indigenous peoples manifested through this policy statement, its guidelines were not consistently applied to all Brazilian Indians during the period of the *Diretório's* validity (until 1798). Policy reversals took place during the nineteenth century through Crown edicts and numerous conflicts related to land ownership.

After Brazil's independence from Portugal in 1822, the Brazilian statesman José Bonifácio de Andrada e Silva "proposed that the rights of the Indians over the lands that remained to them should be acknowledged."[36] On this premise, various pieces of legislation were formulated through the remainder of the century, although not always proving to be advantageous to indigenous persons, particularly if they had been "assimilated."[37]

In 1910, the formation of the SPI (Indigenous Protection Service),[38] a governmental agency specifically created for the protection of the

---

32. The word *diretório* describes a certain set of guidelines for a board of directors. It should not be confused with the English word "directory."

33. *Língua Geral* (General Language) refers to the particular dialect of the indigenous *Tupí* language which had become colloquial throughout Brazilian territory up to that time.

34. Nacaodomestica.org, "Diretório que se Deve Observar." All citations in this paragraph stem from this internet page.

35. Nacaodomestica.org, "Diretório que se Deve Observar," para. 3.

36. Oliveira and Costa Freire, *Presença Indígena*, 76.

37. Oliveira and Costa Freire, *Presença Indígena*, 74–75.

38. Portuguese: *Serviço de Proteção aos Índios*.

Indians, set the stage for newer developments in indigenous affairs.[39] Under the leadership and influence of Cândido Rondon, who had served as chief of the Telegraphic Lines Building Commission of the State of Mato Grosso since 1900,[40] the SPI was created with the following goals:

> a) establish a peaceful coexistence with the Indians; b) act to guarantee the physical survival of the indigenous peoples; c) instill in the Indians the gradual adoption of "civilized" customs; d) influence indigenous life in a "friendly" manner; e) fixate the Indian to the land; f) contribute to the settlement of the interior of Brazil; g) have the power to access or produce economic assets; h) use the indigenous work force to increase agricultural productivity; i) strengthen the indigenous perception of belonging to a nation.[41]

The above-mentioned goals would be pursued by a variety of strategies promoting the maintenance of local family organization and intertribal peace, yet consciously allowing the introduction of cultural innovations, including agricultural and cattle raising techniques, and the enlistment of workers for the Telegraph Commission.[42] At the heart of the plan laid "the idea that the condition of 'Indian' would always be transitory . . . and thus, that the indigenous policy would be aimed at transforming the Indian into a national worker."[43] This new policy period is typically identified as "Indigenous Tutelage," under which indigenous persons would be viewed having a special right under the tutelage of the Brazilian State and, whether intentionally or not, practically establishing a unified, generic perception of Indian identity.[44]

The "tutelage" regime, as Pacheco de Oliveira identifies, was naturally ambiguous and cannot be understood only as having a "humanitarian dimension (pointing to the ethical or legal obligations), nor simply as a tool for domination." The effects of this tension, he suggests, have lasted into the twenty-first century notwithstanding the changes that indigenous legal policies underwent through the remainder of the twentieth century.[45]

---

39. Oliveira and Costa Freire, *Presença Indígena*, 69.
40. Oliveira and Costa Freire, *Presença Indígena*, 107.
41. Oliveira and Costa Freire, *Presença Indígena*, 113.
42. Oliveira and Costa Freire, *Presença Indígena*.
43. Oliveira and Costa Freire, *Presença Indígena*.
44. Oliveira and Costa Freire, *Presença Indígena*, 114.
45. Oliveira and Costa Freire, *Presença Indígena*, 115.

The application of SPI strategic actions, like previous approaches, was also fraught with conflict and inconsistency that brought into question its efficacy. In 1939, under the dictatorship of then President Getúlio Vargas, a new agency in the form of a Commission (CNPI)[46] was organized to study the issues and propose suggestions through the SPI.[47] This Commission inherited the call to sustain earlier goals, but had to face "the transition from the positivist, protectionist plan to the paradigms defended by the Interamerican Indigenous Institute and the anthropology of the post-war era."[48] In this atmosphere, the plans were made to create yet a new agency: FUNAI, the one which remains active to the present. The National Foundation for the Indian (FUNAI)[49] was established by law on the 5th of December of 1967 with the purpose of maintaining the same paradoxical strategies of the SPI: "'respect for the indigenous person as well as tribal institutions and communities' coupled with 'spontaneous acculturation of the Indian' and the advancement of 'basic education appropriate for the Indian in view of his/her progressive integration into the national society.'"[50] On the legal front, it was the Brazilian Constitution of 1988 that finally "broke with the tutelage inheritance" established in the early twentieth century and allowed indigenous persons, "individually or through their organizations [to] enter into judicial dispute to defend their rights and interests,"[51] a right that aided the subsequent greater affirmation of local indigenous cultures.

The historical overview of indigenous policies and agencies above is by no means a complete record of relevant occurrences that have affected the national Brazilian society, indigenous peoples, and their level of interaction. The historical markers and policy statements included here, however, are primarily focused on the evidence of the philosophical mindset of the agencies coupled with the inconsistent practices which have been partially responsible for the fusion of cultural elements in certain places, while not in others. They also display an admission of a long-term goal—or at least expectation—of the eventual integration of the indigenous society into the overall Brazilian society. This line of thought represents

---

46. *Conselho Nacional de Proteção aos Índios* (National Council for the Protection of the Indians).
47. Oliveira and Costa Freire, *Presença Indígena*, 128.
48. Oliveira and Costa Freire, *Presença Indígena*, 130.
49. FUNAI—*Fundação Nacional do Índio* (National Foundation for the Indian).
50. Oliveira and Costa Freire, *Presença Indígena*, 131.
51. Oliveira and Costa Freire, *Presença Indígena*, 133.

an uncomfortable blemish which contemporary FUNAI agents seek to ignore when attempting to construct a case against missions' activities among indigenous peoples for presumed cultural damage.

2.1.5 Contemporary Indigenous Missions

Brazilian missiologists today identify "Three Waves" of missionary activity on South American territory which have made an impact on indigenous communities. The first "wave" denotes the *foreign* missionary activities throughout the last five centuries, more specifically the evangelical missions established in Brazil in the nineteenth century followed by the early-twentieth-century outreach among indigenous peoples. The second one identifies the beginning of *national* Baptist missions among the Krahó people in the years 1925 and 1926, along with some initial work with Xerente communities. This "wave" resulted from a set of "interactive factors: such as the beginning of courses specific for the indigenous field,[52] offered by New Tribes [Mission] (1956) and SIL (1959) . . . and the inclusion of Brazilians in the membership of foreign missions [organizations]."[53] The third "wave" recognizes the increased inclusion of *indigenous Christian workers* in missionary efforts to their own peoples and to other indigenous ethnic groups, as well as the intentional development of Bible training organizations for indigenous Christians:

> Isaac Costa, in his research, reports that the first institution [that was established] primarily for the preparation of indigenous evangelical leaders was constituted through the adaptation of the Bible Institute Cades Barnéia [English: Kadesh-Barnea] in 1980, under the direction of the South American Indian Mission (SAIM), which now is directed by Terena Indians.[54]

More than thirty missions agencies, denominational as well as nondenominational, are listed on the site of the group *Povos e Línguas do*

---

52. The SIL courses taught at that stage of indigenous missions in Brazil were primarily in the field of linguistics as aids for language acquisition, literacy, and eventual Bible translation.

53. Povos e Línguas do Brasil, "História de Missão," paras. 4, 7. Translation mine. All the information found in this paragraph can be accessed at this site. It references at least four sources for this systematic view of Brazilian indigenous missions, including works by the Brazilian anthropologist and missionary Ronaldo Lidório cited elsewhere in this dissertation.

54. Povos e Línguas do Brasil, "História de Missão," para. 8.

Brasil (Peoples and Languages of Brazil) as supportive of a joint effort of all "Three Waves" as partners to bring the Christian message to all the indigenous population of Brazil.[55] Current missiological theory promotes a spirit of collaboration and encouragement for further intercultural partnership. Christian anthropologist Ronaldo Lidório affirms this overall positioning by stating that "Brazilian evangelicals are motivated by affirming the *worth of all peoples*, as made in the image of God, the divine provision of natural resources and land, for each people to live their lives and to seek after the Creator, and that the destiny of all peoples is through the knowledge of peace with God through Jesus Christ."[56]

2.2 XERENTE CULTURAL HERITAGE

2.2.1 Xerente Society in the Late 1950s

While the Xerente managed to maintain their ethnic identity through the centuries, interaction with the Brazilian national society since the eighteenth century has taken its toll on their society. Amidst struggles for land rights, forced resettlements (*aldeamentos*) under governmental and religious orders, natural droughts, and all the consequences of these changes,[57] a population numbered at 2,200 in 1851 had been reduced to 1,364 in 1924. David Maybury-Lewis, one of the principal sources of Xerente life in the 1950s, reported in 1963 that there remained only 330 individuals.[58] Maybury-Lewis and his wife lived among the Xerente environment for a period of eight months during 1955–56, as he relates in his 1965 book *The Savage and the Innocent*.[59] He describes his initial reception by the people as he unloaded his cargo from the boat as passive. It was only after he mentioned having come from Rio de Janeiro and that he had government ties that the Xerente demonstrated an increased reaction. The first few weeks, and indeed the entire stay, proved to be challenging to the couple as they struggled to comprehend their unique responses and wants through the language barrier.[60]

---

55. Povos e Línguas do Brasil, "Conheça os Nossos Parceiros."
56. Lidório, "Indigenous Peoples of Brazil," para. 4.
57. Wewering, *Povo Akwẽ Xerente*, 13–14.
58. Povos Indígenas do Brasil, "Xerente," para. 5.
59. Maybury-Lewis, *Savage and the Innocent*, preface.
60. Maybury-Lewis, *Savage and the Innocent*, 37–69.

Maybury-Lewis' descriptions reveal a people weary of their fight for physical survival. Pr. Guenther, one of the pioneers of the Baptist mission among the Xerente, recalls that, "when he arrived in the region, the Xerente people did not amount to 450 people." The older generation would express their painful acknowledgment, saying: "Once we were many, but now we are few; all that's left is for us all to be finished."[61] Without outside intervention, such an outcome would have been likely since "the Xerente nation was being decimated by infirmities arising from the contact with the white man for which they had neither antibodies nor medicine."[62]

2.2.2 Traditional Xerente Worldview, Customs, and Religion

The origin and explanation of things, people, and situations within the traditional Xerente context are explained through a number of mythological legends that compose the people's overall worldview. These stories portray events related to an earlier "mythological era in which all was good,"[63] and when *Bdâ* (god or sun) and *Wairê* (moon), the two principal heroes, were both present.[64] "The entire set of ideas, philosophy of life, cosmogony, etc that composes the Xerente worldview, even its temperament, stem from these legends."[65] Although no practical worship rituals are directed to either of the above cultural heroes, *Bdâ* is understood as being wise and the author of good, while *Wairê* is a reckless and impetuous character which some have syncretized with the apostle Peter[66] since the Xerente encounter with Christianity through Roman Catholicism.

The Xerente worldview can be further characterized as an *existential messianism*. It differs from *historical messianism* primarily due to its two-era division of the world: one of paradise-like characteristics, and the "era of Reality, present, in which the People lives with pain and suffering."[67] Unlike *historical messianism* that holds a third (future) era of restored bliss in

---

61. Graciana, "Pastor Guenther Carlos Krieger," para. 5. Translation mine. The phrase cited in Portuguese is *"Um dia fomos muitos, agora nóis é pouco, só falta nóis acabá tudo."*

62. Graciana, "Pastor Guenther Carlos Krieger," para. 5.

63. Mattos, "Messianismo Existencial Xerente," 28. Translation mine.

64. Mattos, in Wewering, *Povo Akwẽ Xerente*, 93.

65. Mattos, "Messianismo Existencial Xerente," 28.

66. Mattos, "Messianismo Existencial Xerente," 30.

67. Mattos, in Wewering, *Povo Akwẽ Xerente*, 93.

view, this worldview does not contain any such expectation.[68] It displays, rather, a latent nostalgia and an existential attitude about the here-and-now in multiple aspects of Xerente life including the people's expectancy of economic success. In spite of its fatalistic character, certain responses to the legends demonstrate enough hope (through disappointment) that have led some to categorize the Xerente worldview as *messianic*. Three traditional legends describing decisions made by the Indian or by *Wairê* characterize this longing hope: the Legend of Death, the Legend of the Trips to Heaven (Sky), and the Legend of Economic Prosperity. Invariably, at the point when the storyteller describes the crucial decision that brought about suffering and disappointment (either disobedience to a command of *Bdâ* or rejection of a gift), one individual or even several begin(s) to speak out laments such as, "Ah, if he had not thrown the stone, we would not be crying today over the death of our relatives," or "if he hadn't looked back, we would still be going up and down to visit our Father until today," or even "if they had not rejected . . . [Bdâ's gifts]."[69] Through these storytelling practices, as well as through other personal interactions with the people, Pr. Rinaldo de Mattos has identified that "the Xerente has, in the essence of its belief [system], a deep desire of conquering death and live forever, . . . of climbing to heights and reaching the transcendent, . . . [and] of being completely happy, prosperous, and fulfilled."[70]

2.2.3 Social Organization and Other Identity Markers

Three key twentieth-century anthropologists depict Xerente society from perspectives of different time periods: Curt Nimuendaju, David Maybury-Lewis, and Agenor Farias. The accounts of their research, respectively relating their experiences in the 1930/40s, 1950/60s, and 1980s, display group descriptions and terminologies which demonstrate that certain changes may have taken place along the course of the last eight decades.[71] These may have resulted from multiple factors including demographic and political shifts along the course of those decades. The variances, however, give evidence of an inherent ethnic capacity for holding traditions in high esteem, while creatively adapting to new sets of circumstances.

68. Mattos, in Wewering, *Povo Akwẽ Xerente*, 93.
69. Mattos, "Messianismo Existencial Xerente," 34–36.
70. Mattos, "Messianismo Existencial Xerente," 36.
71. Schroeder, "Política e Parentesco nos Xerente," 55–65.

Xerente society today displays a social structure containing two exogamous moieties: *Isake* and *Dohi*. Each moiety[72] is further subdivided into three clans: the *Isake* containing the *wahire*, *krozake*, and *krãiprehi*, and the *Dohi* the *kuzâ*, *kbazi* and *krito*.[73] The moieties and clans are visually marked by body painting, primarily used for special occasions, serving as "ID cards that place them in their social context."[74] According to Nimuendaju's research in the first half of the twentieth century, villages (*aldeias*) ideally demonstrated this social division in their area organization, but Maybury-Lewis failed to identify an inherent meaning in their physical layout during the time of his investigation.[75]

Xerente clans do not incorporate primarily all the members of an extended family. On the contrary, within the same family unit people belong to different clans. The concept of respect (*waze* and other related terms) among clans, which institutes rights and duties towards their counterparts, permeate and inform everyday life, rituals, and political conflicts, defining both when respect has been maintained and when it was absent.[76] Other important social structures are the associations (*dakrsu*) consisting of four age-related male associations and a single one among the women. These associations are involved, for instance, in *naming ceremonies* and festival events such as the "[tree] trunk race."[77]

The great Xerente feast (*Dasĩpsê*) usually takes place during the dry season (after April).[78] The *Dasĩpsê* combines a series of events—naming ceremonies, races, dances, and meals—which serve as a unifying force of Xerente identity, and affirm "a distinct way of life," reminding them of "how things were in order not to forget how they ought to be." The feast also shows traditional ways to the younger generation and visitors.[79]

Ivo Schroeder identifies the institutions in Xerente society as being "very active, acknowledging an ideal extracted from ancient traditions

---

72. "The moiety system is a more unusual form of unilineal descent and involves the occurrence of descent groups in linked pairs which assume complementary positions and functions. Each moiety (or half) of a pair will almost always be exogamous and take its husbands and wives exclusively from the matched group." University of Manitoba, "Moieties," para. 1.

73. Schroeder, "Política e Parentesco nos Xerente," 66.

74. Wewering, *Povo Akwẽ Xerente*, 41. In Portuguese, *"carteira de identidade."*

75. Wewering, *Povo Akwẽ Xerente*, 59.

76. Schroeder, "Política e Parentesco," 84.

77. Portuguese, *"corrida da tora."*

78. Wewering, *Povo Akwẽ Xerente*, 63.

79. Schroeder, "Política e Parentesco," 66.

that can always be recaptured and reinvented."[80] Relating this characteristic to musical and artistic practices, such adaptability may have been key to the people's capacity to incorporate features from the surrounding national society while maintaining a strong ethnic identity. Access, for better or for worse, challenges a community to make decisions regarding the positive and negative results of integrating outside features. In the face of this challenge, the Xerente appear to have adopted the stance cited in their collaborative work *Povo Akwẽ Xerente*:

> "Considering that the indigenous peoples of today wish to have access to the multiple material and technological resources of the modern world as a legitimate right, it is hereby confirmed the irreversibility of the contact with the white world . . . with its inevitable consequences, which requires from the Indians to rethink the conditions of existence and ethnic continuity, not in order to disavow them, but to update them according to their own wishes and desire. . . . The challenge is [how] to make it possible that the Indians themselves define the limit and the dynamics of the alleged integration."[81]

2.3 EVANGELICAL MISSIONS AMONG THE XERENTE

2.3.1 The Early Missionaries

Anna Muller was the first missionary, sent by the New Tribes Mission, to settle among the Xerente in the 1950s.[82] She would be followed by Pr. Guenther Krieger and Pr. Rinaldo de Mattos, who began to settle in the region between 1959 and 1960. These two men and their spouses helped give an impulse to evangelical missions' activities among the Xerente that lasts to this day.[83] Their long-standing relationship with the people has allowed them to attain a crucial firsthand knowledge of the people's culture, language, and social issues. Christian and secular institutions, as

---

80. Schroeder, "Política e Parentesco," 62.

81. Wewering, *Povo Akwẽ Xerente*, 38. This citation is a statement made by Luciano in *Índio Brasileiro*, chapter 6, "Economia Indígena." Translation mine.

82. Anais do XVI Encontro Regional de História da Anpuh-Rio, "Evangelho Não Destrói Culturas," 1.

83. Portugal, "Musical Choices," 82.

well as private researchers have consulted their observations throughout the years to prepare reports, websites, theses, and dissertations.[84]

In my first conversation with Rinaldo de Mattos[85] for this research, he explained the early history of their work as well as the process of music introduction in churches during a few distinguishable periods. Both he and Pr. Guenther had participated in the first, yet unofficial, course in linguistics offered by SIL in Brazil in 1958. It consisted of a three-month intensive course, still without official publications in Portuguese to guide them, led by a guest teacher from the United States who later moved on to work with another indigenous group. He described the study of anthropology during those days as still being "in diapers" in Brazil. Very few books were available on the topic, and, unless one had access to English or German literature on the subject, missionaries had little encouragement to discover cultural aspects of an indigenous population, let alone to contextualize the communication of the gospel. Beyond the course in linguistics, no further training in cross-cultural communication was provided for these missionaries at the time.

2.3.2 Brief History of Church Development

Responding to the felt needs of the Xerente at the time, the early evangelical missionaries began their work by seeking "to improve the precarious health conditions of the Xerente," introducing literacy, helping them to continue their education, and guiding them "into the knowledge of the Christian gospel."[86] However, it was only after the confrontation with the realities of the Xerente culture in day-to-day interaction that these missionaries comprehended the need for a deeper understanding of their worldview and cultural expressions. Since the Xerente had been in intermittent contact with Brazilian society throughout the years, many of them understood basic Portuguese. Hence, serious consideration of a New Testament translation into *Akwẽ* was delayed for about a decade.

---

84. For instance, Povos Indígenas do Brasil, "Xerente."

85. The core source of information contained in section 2.3 and other portions related to the development of Baptist missionary work among the Xerente and the transformation of their music are my personal conversations with Prs. Rinaldo and Guenther, as well as with other missionaries involved in the work. The first of these took place on October 24, 2016, with Pr. Rinaldo, following previous exchange of e-mails. Other sources are duly noted as references in this text.

86. Portugal, "Musical Choices," 82.

After further preparation in linguistics, Pr. Guenther became the principal actor of the translation project since he spoke both English and German and had, therefore, greater access to academic translation tools.

In the 1970s, as Pr. Rinaldo describes it, there was a "great awakening" among the missionaries in the understanding of culture. At that time, they came to a deeper realization that in order to accomplish Christian mission in a more effective manner, they would have to devote greater attention to the cultural anthropology of the Xerente. Don Richardson's books, such as *Peace Child,* were greatly influential in this process. Pr. Rinaldo first learned of this book through a short book review in a Reader's Digest (Pt. *Seleções*) publication. Although he was not yet fluent in English, he ordered the book from the United States and struggled to read it all. These newly attained perspectives of cross-cultural missions deeply affected the two pioneer missionaries' expectations and emphases in their work. The Xerente churches established in various villages in their territory certainly demonstrate the impact of this new vision.

2.3.3 Present-Day Xerente Churches and Workers

A 2018 report on evangelical churches in Xerente villages[87] demonstrates that local leadership of congregations has now become pervasive throughout the territory. The missionaries, while continuing to attend to various necessities related to leadership training, Bible translation, and finances, have reportedly led in such a way throughout the decades that Xerente Christians followed the invitation to grow into positions of leadership. Among the churches planted by the Baptist missionaries, six of them[88] are well established, three of which are led by ordained Xerente pastors. Eleven other churches are in a process of formation, but also have local leadership. Furthermore, twenty other small communities (small farms or villages with small populations) have a local Christian leader who occasionally holds meetings in view of establishing new congregations. The report also lists five other villages that have an evangelical presence of other denominations. The evangelical Christian population among the Xerente today revolves around 1,000, a full 25 percent of the total population.[89]

---

87. See Appendix E.

88. It is understood that one village has only one church. Thus, the number of churches is identical to the number of villages that have evangelical churches.

89. See Appendix E.

Although the process of developing local leadership (pastors, deacons, teachers, and other people engaged in church ministries) has been long, and sometimes frustrating, the local agency identified through this research among Xerente Christians demonstrate a strong sense of "ownership." Indeed, this cultural character has been decisive for the musical choices addressed in this study.

While the numerical growth of churches and their leadership are gratifying to both missionaries and local Christians, different political alliances related to local, regional, and national interests have negatively affected some of the congregations in the recent past.[90] As the overview of Xerente social structure demonstrates, the opposing clan identifications within the Xerente worldview establish responsibilities of reciprocal duty rather than partisanship. Nevertheless, a parallel tendency towards the development of factions has been identified by studies of *Jê* people groups of central Brazil. In the case of the Xerente such schisms do not coincide with clan divisions and occasionally "subordinate other social institutions and obscure their ritual activities."[91] Certain churches have suffered under this predisposition, raising serious concerns among church leaders. Notwithstanding the negative tone of this complicated cultural engagement, the power of such individual choices can help explain the variety of music identified in the churches.

2.3.4 Conclusion

This chapter reviewed the historical development of the Brazilian national society since the 1500s. By focusing on the interaction of European peoples, religious movements, and changing governments with the original inhabitants of South America, I have attempted to show that various policies and attitudes contributed to the development of an understanding of the character and place of indigenous individuals in the national society as well as within each indigenous people group on Brazilian soil. Along the course of history, indigenous peoples made choices of their own in response to the incoming influences and power they were obliged to face. These choices contributed to the state of cultural characteristics of the indigenous populations today.

---

90. Information obtained through personal conversation with two of the Baptist missionaries in 2019.

91. Schroeder, "Política e Parentesco," 238.

Reflecting the above character of South American colonization, Xerente society in the present displays characteristics that resulted from this historical intermingling of cultures—both through force and by mutual consent. The Xerente communities which the Baptist missionaries encountered in the 1960s stem from centuries of struggle to survive the pressures as well as diseases brought through the contact with the colonizing forces. In spite of the difficulties, the Xerente continued to hold to many traditional practices while appropriating external customs and acquiring new tastes, including musical ones. Missionary efforts, conscious of the need of local leadership, appear to have helped affirm Xerente choices along the decades, creating an environment that allows for internally directed growth for the churches.

This brief survey of indigenous (and particularly Xerente) history of interaction and responses demonstrates the potential within the people to shape the present and future character of their culture. Through features displaying either positive or negative immediate outcomes, the Xerente demonstrate a desire and capacity to administer their own institutions as well as to maintain substantial liberty for individual choices.

3

The Xerente and Their Musics

3.1 TRADITIONAL MUSIC

3.1.1 Musical Characteristics

ALTHOUGH TRADITIONAL XERENTE MUSIC is an inherent component of *Dasĩpsê* as well as of many other civic and religious rites, no ethnomusicological thesis or dissertation has been dedicated fully to the analysis of their cultural songs and traditional instruments. This chapter and the subsequent evaluation of the role of traditional Xerente music plays in the constitution of their contemporary genres rely primarily on two source groups: Pr. Rinaldo de Mattos's unpublished personal research and observations along the course of his sixty years of interaction with the people, and personal interviews undertaken with the missionaries and Xerente musicians from 2017 to 2019.

According to Pr. Rinaldo, the Xerente worldview does not acknowledge any human composer for traditional songs. "They were all 'left' by *Bdâ*, the cultural hero, just as the other aspects of their culture."[1] Songs are not intended for casual or daily "humming" but serve ritualistic functions exclusively. They are not "public property" but rightly belong to the *pajé* (shaman) or to the various associations, each of which has a

---

1. See Appendix A. Since the original notes by R. de Mattos are unpublished, references to them are specified with a number in parentheses in the dissertation or in this book. The number is the observation number as organized by Mattos.

particular repertoire.² The people are led by a *puxador*—the song leader—who initiates the collective practice by singing the first words or the first phrase.

Xerente traditional songs are monophonic using a pitch inventory usually stretching no wider than an octave and a half. Mattos noted that preference is given for major intervals and that melodies favor the use of the first, third, and fifth degrees of a Western major scale. The second degree is seldom found except as an octave above the low tonic, in other words, the ninth scale degree. Furthermore, the minor second between the third and fourth degrees and between the seventh and eighth are also rare. When used at all, only one of the two half-step intervals are found in a given melody.³ The rhythmic pattern of Xerente songs is binary and usually marked by the stomping of the feet or even a club on the ground (for example, in girls' naming songs) on the first beat. With the exception of lament songs, movement always accompanies the singing, whether the singer stands alone, in a circle, or as a participant in line dances.⁴

Traditional songs exhibit a short binary form commonly made up of only one stanza.⁵ The verses are "divided into two musical phrases. The first phrase serves as a question, and the second one, with the music and lyrics somewhat modified, as the answer."⁶ Each of the phrases is typically sung twice, and the people sing it repetitively until the *puxador* somehow indicates that they will stop. Mattos did not detect any specific musical marker that indicates that the singers have reached the end of the song, except some communal sense of completion.⁷

---

2. See Appendix A, points 5, 6.
3. See Appendix A, point 1.
4. See Appendix A, points 2, 4.
5. Mattos cites one exception, the *Wakedi* songs, that contain several stanzas.
6. See Appendix A, point 8. Translation mine.
7. See Appendix A, point 8.

Arê Arê

1—Traditional Xerente song displaying a typical two-part form.[8]

Mattos considers the identification of the addressee of Xerente traditional songs to be one of the most difficult aspects to determine. Presumably, by using a second-person singular pronoun, most songs are addressed to "mythological entities" or "spirits that inhabit the rivers and bushes . . . or to certain animals." The exception to this norm is the *Wakedi* set of songs, which are performed by the men to the women or vice-versa.[9]

Rinaldo de Mattos's research lists eight traditional musical instruments,[10] including both aerophones and idiophones:[11]

- *Kupawã*: an aerophone made out of *taboca* (bamboo)[12] resembling a cornet 35 to 45 cm in length and 4 to 5 cm in diameter.

- *Kupawãhârpo*: an idiophone made of two naturally resonant materials: an oblong gourd (30 to 40 cm in length, and 15 cm in diameter) and a bamboo tube (25 to 35 cm in length, and 3 to 4 cm in diameter). It was decorated with feathers and sketches in beige and

---

8. Music transcriptions of all Xerente songs presented in this book and the original dissertation were made by me.

9. See Appendix A, point 9.

10. The instrumental descriptions in this section are based on Mattos's research. The general descriptions stem from the original Portuguese document in Appendix B but the text is not a direct Translation, unless identified through quotation marks.

11. This classification is based on the Hornbostel-Sachs instrumental categories used for ethnomusicological studies. Musical Instrument Museums Online, "Revision of the Hornbostel-Sachs Classification."

12. Dicionário Online de Portugues (Dicio), "Taboca."

black. "It was traditionally used to announce the arrival of a Xerente group for a friendly visit."

- *Sdupuzâ*: an aerophone made of two shoots of *taboca* of different lengths and diameters (15 to 20 cm in length, and 1 to 1½ cm in diameter). The *Sdupuzâ* was valuable to allow for "continual communication among warriors without being noticed since their signals were confused with [the sounds] of singing birds."

- *Zâ*: a rattle-type idiophone consisting of a gourd (*cabaça*) approximately 15 cm wide, filled with fragments from snail shells and stones and managed by a wooden stick/handle. This instrument has traditionally been used exclusively by the shamans (in Akwẽ: *sekwa*; in Portuguese: *pajés*), who "besides using it in their shamanic sessions, also used it in the *warri nõkrêze*, the plaza songs, where the *pajés* serve as Masters of Ceremony."

- *Kupkrnãihirê*: an aerophone like a fife or flute made of a single bamboo shoot with seven holes. Used in pairs, these instruments were used for non-traditional festivities at night, and it was "probably inserted into the *Akwẽ* culture through contact with the white man festivities such as the Feast of the Divine.[13] According to the reports it is known that one of the flutes, with a lower pitch, played the 'bass', and the other, with a higher pitch, played the melody of the music."

- *Wanẽkumkrê*: an idiophone like a tabret made of a hollow wood trunk covered with *sucurijú*[14] skin. It was played with a small drumstick (*wanẽkumkrêtkaze*) or with the hands. It was used "to accompany the flutes used in the festivities of non-indigenous origins." Both the *Kupkrnãihirê* and the *Wanẽkumkrê* were considered secular [instruments], not being used by the shamans.

- *Wapsãwanẽ*: an aerophone in the form of a small, thin cornet made of a single bamboo shoot (15 to 25 cm in length, 3 cm in diameter) with a mouthpiece. It sounded like a dog bark and was played by the *sipsa*[15] to warn of upcoming danger or played to announce the coming of the dawn.

---

13. In Portuguese, "*Festa do Divino*" [Espírito Santo]. A Catholic festivity brought to Brazil by the Portuguese in the sixteenth century. Conferência Nacional dos Bispos do Brasil, "Festas do Divino."

14. Also known as *sucurí*, a type of giant snake. Dicionário Online de Portugues (Dicio), "Sucurijú."

15. *Sipsa*—a chaste young man.

- *Kukrãinmõrturê*: an aerophone made from a gourd, using the hole made at the gourd's stem for a mouthpiece and another hole on the side; it produced only two pitches; the *sipsa* played it when staying in the *warã*, and also visitors when approaching a village.[16]

According to local reports, with the exception of the *zâ* (the rattle called *maracá* in Portuguese), most of these instruments are now rarely used. The *zâ*, as indicated in the list above, has been used exclusively by the shamans. Because of this association with traditional Xerente religious beliefs, its use for Christian worship has been generally discouraged, although some of the churches have begun to review their position concerning the *zâ*. This move will be discussed later in this book.

3.1.2 Traditional Genres and Their Functions within Xerente Communities

Fabbri's theory of musical genres identified several categories of rules that determine the boundaries of a genre. The Xerente musical genre classification is primarily governed by their function (purpose), their meaning (semiotics), and by the enactor of the genre. The lyrical content and the point of application, therefore, define traditional genres.

During the music workshop in Cabeceira Verde, Héber Negrão and I joined in conversation with a group of Xerente musicians and discussed the classifications of traditional song and their potential for use in the church. The participants, and in particular Lázaro Rowakro, one of the elders and composers who attended it, identified three main "classes" (or "moments") of traditional musical genres. The first "belongs" traditionally to the *Sekwa* (the shaman). These song genres comprise a category termed *Dâsipê do pajé*.[17] Secondly, a group of six or seven songs identified as belonging to *Wairi (Dâsipê do Inksuinã)* encompasses music for social gatherings, naming ceremonies, as well as those used for the traditional feast. These are not property of the shaman and can be led by any elder. The third one involves the naming ceremony for the boys. During the course of the interviews the musicians mentioned two other specific song types: the elder's announcement song and lament songs. Further research

---

16. Appendix B.

17. This term combines Portuguese with *Akwẽ*. Despite the linguistic mixture, it was the informant Lázaro Rowakro (Xerente) who used it.

could possibly identify these as distinct group categories. However, this possibility was not pursued as it lay outside the scope of the discussion.[18]

The categories identified by the Xerente as "classes" or "moments"[19] may be the best candidates to qualify as "genres" in Western terms. The distinguishing features of each category relate little to musical structure but are deeply connected to the contexts and the "ownership" of the songs. The songs classified as *Wakedi* and *Kbuhukwa* demonstrate some melodic contours with certain accentuation that could mark their distinctive character, but this may only be confirmed by research focused specifically on these categories. They resemble cultural music used by the Xavante, the close relatives of the Xerente. Figure 4 below provides a general overview of the "genres" locally acknowledged as distinct in its first column. The second column contain sample songs[20] that belong to the "genre." Columns 3 to 5 describe details related to the contexts of their usage.

The Xerente have important emotional and functional connections with this song tradition. Lázaro expressed the emotional weight he senses when leading the songs as an elder. He explained that they remind him of elders who have passed away.[21] The songs address themes of nature, at times describing animals, at other times personal feelings. To collaborate with ideas during the workshop, the *cacique* (village chief) of Cabeceira Verde, also a Christian believer, sang a song that he believed would be appropriate to adapt to Christian practice. It initiates a period of festivities (*Wairi*) expressing hope that things will go well for them in the future.[22]

---

18. The categorization offered in this portion of the chapter is based on interviews and discussions that occurred during the Cabeceira Verde music workshop in July of 2017.

19. *Momentos* or *classes* were the terms used by the Xerente when they identified these categories in Portuguese.

20. A confusing misapplication of the Portuguese word *ritmo* (rhythm) came to be identified with the Western concept of "song" in multiple indigenous ethnic groups in Brazil. The *ritmos* (songs or melodies) are not necessarily distinct in rhythmic character. The historical reason or circumstance in which this term was introduced with a meaning deviating from the Portuguese language is unknown.

21. Music Workshop—Session 6 at 22 minutes. The recordings of this workshop teaching sessions and group discussions are not openly published. They are kept in Héber Negrão's and my personal digital archives. They can be reviewed by other researchers upon request.

22. Music Workshop—Session 6 at 40 minutes.

Main "moments" (Categories) GENRES	(Songs) "Ritmos"	Descriptions	Event	Participants
Dãsipê do pajé (Shaman's Dãsipê) (Akwẽ: Sekwa)	Sucurí Dance (Wanêku); Fish Dance (Tbê); Star Dance;	Songs using the Zã (rattle or maracá); typically used for circle dances.	Festival - Dãsipê	Led by the shaman; all are invited to participate
Dãsipê do Wairi	Girls' naming song: ex. Canto da Siriema	Played with a stick (Borduna; Akwẽ: Kuiró); Interpreting the siriema.	Girls' naming ceremony ('batismo')	Men and women. (Pattern yet unresearched)
	Wakedi (6 or 7 song cycle)	Expresses "saudade" (longing) or other sentiments; uses the Zã.	Not exclusive to any event	Men sing to women and women sing to men.
Waiñ nõkrẽze	- Song for when the Trunk (tora) is picked up: Kuiwde nitró - Song for when the Trunk arrives;	The old men sing when they arrive back at the feast location.	Cultural festivals	Older men
Kbuhukwa	Boys' naming songs (around 7)	Sung in the woods ('no mato'); themes of nature, expression of peace	Boys' naming ceremony	Only the men sing it; women and children are not allowed participate; when the men return to the 'patio', then the women join them.
Elder's Announcement Song	(Not yet researched)	Announcement, admonishment, invitation; It precedes the announcement.	Any opportunity when something needs to be announced to the community, at times in the middle of the night.	Community Elder
Lament	(Not yet fully researched)	Mostly improvised. (Not yet fully researched)	Mourning when visiting a deceased person's body and family	(Not yet researched); possibly only women
Dãsipê Kibazinprãinri	(Not yet researched)	Certain names are given to both boys and girls in this celebration (Tikwa, Prordó)		Men

2—Traditional Xerente Musical Genres

3.2 BRAZILIAN GENRES IN CONTACT WITH XERENTE SOCIETY

3.2.1 The Mode of Development of Brazilian National Genres

Colonial practices in Brazil generally dampened, but did not stamp out non-European musical practices. As long as indigenous peoples remained isolated from the developing national society, they continued to carry on their traditions. On the other hand, these were seldom integrated into the urban centers as acceptable forms of expression. For the greater part, the

Indians who became incorporated into the national society during colonial times adopted styles originated from Portuguese folk practices and baroque sacred forms.

Since the latter part of the eighteenth century, a wealth of liturgical works by Brazilian-born composers remains as a testimony of the tradition in the booming era of gold and diamond exploration in the southeastern State of Minas Gerais.[23] The move of the Portuguese royal family to Rio de Janeiro in 1808 gave a new impulse to musical life in the colony including the development of a tradition of concerts and operas. Although popular musical styles ran parallel to classical traditions in similar fashion to European counterparts, a nationalist movement began to develop in the 1860s through compositions that included urban popular music and its rhythms. Compositions by Alberto Nepomuceno in the last decade of the nineteenth century and later Hector Villa-Lobos during the early decades of the twentieth century, for instance, illustrate the characteristic nationalistic styles that have become iconic of Brazilian "classical" music.[24]

Few transcriptions are available, however, of folk and popular music from colonial times. The early development of their genres, therefore, is difficult to determine. An extensive collection of folk and popular music does exist from the early part of the twentieth century, and it reflects the *mestizo* character of Brazilian styles.[25] While many song styles reflect their Luso-European[26] origins, most popular (particularly strongly rhythmic) genres today demonstrate "a clear Bantu origin," incorporating pentatonic scales, flattened sevenths, and other features that connect them with their African roots.[27] Among the numerous Brazilian genres available today, *samba* is possibly the best known worldwide and represents well the results of continuous blending of cultural musics that occurred in South America during the last centuries. Its forefather is believed to be the *lundú*, a Bantu genre brought by African slaves from Angola in the eighteenth century. However, the word *samba* is probably more closely associated with the term *semba* from the *Kimbudu* ethnic group,[28] Indigenous influences are less prominent in Brazilian national

23. Behague, "Brazil," 222.
24. Behague, "Brazil," 222.
25. Behague, "Brazil," 224.
26. The prefix "*luso*" stems from the earlier name for Portugal—*Lusitânia*.
27. Behague, "Brazil," 224.
28. McGowan and Pessanha, *Brazilian Sound*, locs. 453–95.

genres but have left their mark through the use of the *reco-reco*[29] as well as the *maracá*[30] and certain dance and performance characteristics.

Behague's article on Brazilian music in *The New Grove Dictionary* describes the development of Brazilian genres as a "reverse acculturative process" in which the political power of the Portuguese did not determine the overall trend of popular music.[31] The resulting blended styles (the "real melting pot")[32] gave rise to genres which presented stronger characteristics from the cultures of those who were being subjugated.

3.2.2 Xerente Contact with Brazilian Genres

Along the centuries of interaction with the national society, the Xerente have presumably encountered multiple musical genres which they may have heard (and listened to) with or without interest, incorporated, or rejected altogether. For the purpose of this analysis the genres of interest are those which have influenced and become a part of the Xerente musical life as a whole or as a component of Christian fusion genres. Geographical proximity, the provision of electrical power, as well as radio and television programs that began to be followed by the Xerente, have all contributed to the development of today's genres. Attractive productions of popular central and northeastern music penetrated the daily life of the communities and became a part of the daily musical menu through the media. Consequently, it is probable that new preferences could have naturally been developed among the members of the villages, particularly among the younger people who would have listened to the national genres along with traditional ones in relative proximity.

The national genres most frequently encountered in Xerente villages today are *sertanejo*, *forró*, and *brega* (or *tecnobrega*). *Sertanejo*, a word derived from the Portuguese term *sertão* (the hot and dry area of the interior of northeastern Brazil), identifies a series of sub-genres such as the *baião* adapted and made popular by the singer and accordionist Luiz Gonzaga from the 1930s into the 1980s.[33] *Forró*, a term with an uncertain

---

29. McGowan and Pessanha, *Brazilian Sound*, loc. 230. The *reco-reco* is an idiophone originally made of wood. Also see Traditional Instruments of the World, "Reco-Reco."
30. Behague, "Brazil," 224.
31. Behague, "Brazil," 224.
32. McGowan and Pessanha, *Brazilian Sound*, loc. 208.
33. McGowan and Pessanha, *Brazilian Sound*, locs. 4245–64.

etymology meaning "a party or place to play dance music,"[34] refers to a faster-paced type of *baião* also introduced by Gonzaga. *Brega* (*Paraense*: from the northeastern State of Pará), "a pejorative label for unsophisticated romantic songs," is the basis of a more recent genre development called *tecnobrega* made popular by the *Banda Calypso* around the turn of the twenty-first century.[35] The musical features of the northeastern genres mentioned above will be discussed further in conjunction with the examination of Xerente fusion genres.

3.3 MUSIC IN THE XERENTE CHURCH

3.3.1 Brief Historical Overview of Church Music Styles

In the 1960s and 70s, Xerente evangelical Christians adopted the hymns from the *Cantor Cristão* (the standard Baptist hymnbook in Brazil at the time) with which the missionaries were familiar. Those hymns filled a need for worship expression through music from the onset of the earliest church plants. As this research has concluded, the missionaries simply offered the Xerente the music with which they were acquainted in their personal church worship practices, without necessarily attempting to restrict or even forbid local musical genres in church services on missiological, traditional, or theological grounds. Not long after the beginning of their missionary activity, Christian composers began to introduce choruses (*corinhos*) into Brazilian Christian congregations. These, too, were infused into Xerente worship services in their own language.

Pr. Rinaldo affirms that the Xerente never really rejected these "foreign" musical forms. There are a variety of potential reasons for this response. It may be a result of the centuries-old interaction with Catholicism which had imprinted onto them an expectation of a codified form of worship. It may also be reflective of the apparently stable character of Xerente traditional music which did not appear open for further development at the time. Likewise, as will be discussed in a later chapter, the acceptance of new forms by Xerente Christians may be due to their perception that traditional music would have still been too closely linked to Xerente traditional religion, at least in the mind of a segment of the population. Nonetheless, it is also equally possible that the most

---

34. McGowan and Pessanha, *Brazilian Sound*, loc. 4265.
35. McGowan and Pessanha, *Brazilian Sound*, loc. 4846.

important reason for the willing acceptance of Western hymnody in those early years is that the Xerente gained a new taste or preference. Musical elements such as rhythm, harmonic structure, and melody could have simply been more appealing to local individuals than the features of their traditional music. It is not uncommon to find subjugated cultures around the world with a low view of their own of their musical or artistic system and have struggled with defining the value of their cultural identity.

Notwithstanding this initial acceptance, according to Pr. Rinaldo, parallel to national movements of cultural preservation among indigenous people groups, people in the church became more interested in preserving their own cultural styles for Christian purposes. Since the 1980s, several Xerente Christian musicians have composed songs that retain features of the traditional cultures. He asserts, nevertheless, that no complete Xerente hymnody has been developed so far that utilizes exclusively traditional musical features.[36]

Among the village churches, various concurrent musical preferences exist. Certain ones have adopted the *forró* genre. Pr. Rinaldo and other missionaries among them explained that Xerente musicians feel that their traditional style is too slow and believe that the people generally prefer more movement. Pr. Rinaldo, although not forcing his opinion on the local people, expressed doubts about the musicians' evaluation of the people's preference. Yet, although musicians' preferences could possibly be overshadowing some wishes of other church participants, the general consensus about the fusion genres among musician and nonmusician interviewees is positive and does not indicate any resulting antipathy.

3.3.2 Introduction of Western Instruments in the Church[37]

The standard accompanists for the services in Xerente villages during the 1960s were Pr. Rinaldo de Mattos and a lady teacher by the name of Mrs. Tilda. Rinaldo played the guitar and she the accordion whenever she could accompany them to the village services. Electronic keyboards as we know them today were not yet accessible to the general public. The Xerente enjoyed music and were quick to learn many of the hymns. Their

---

36. Portugal, "Musical Choices," 88.

37. The bulk of the information for this subpoint comes from Pr. Rinaldo at my request. Although this is not a strict translation, the information here carefully reflects the content of his email on March 12, 2019. Translated portions in this section are marked with quotation marks. On file.

enthusiasm was such that they, at times, "held back" the missionaries until late at night requesting to hear various hymns.

Pr. Rinaldo explained that it was only in the 1990s, after a period of several years when he and his wife were not working in Xerente villages, that Armando Sõpre, a young man from the village of Salto "demonstrated interest in learning to play the guitar. Shortly thereafter, another young man from the village of Porteira close by, Tiago Wakuke, had the same wish." Pr. Rinaldo began to teach both around the same time and gave no more than ten lessons providing them with a method, chord charts, etc. He describes them as geniuses in their learning abilities. They developed their skills yet further on their own, began to actively participate in the musical activities of the church, and, soon after, assumed the responsibility for playing the guitar in their respective churches. After some time, the same young men wanted to learn the keyboard. Although Pr. Rinaldo felt unable to properly teach the keyboard since he did not play it himself, he provided them with a method book (by a well-known Brazilian music educator—Mário Mascarenhas) and organized ten introductory lessons for them. Once again, the two young men carefully applied themselves to learning and introduced the instrument to their churches. In time, other village churches observed the use of the keyboard and decided to adopt them also. It was taught by fathers to sons, or by friends and acquaintances, and no one, in Pr. Rinaldo's own words, "ever asked anything else about music from me." Today there is a great number of guitar and keyboard players in the Xerente village churches.

Pr. Rinaldo's concern with this development, however, was the absence of their own traditional musical instruments. He began to carefully encourage the use of the zâ (maracá) in the church, but it was not very well taken since, as discussed earlier, this instrument "belongs" to the shaman and is considered by the majority of Xerente believers to be "of the devil." Through various leadership training venues and continued encouragement of a few people, little by little some churches began to utilize the zâ, although many are still uncomfortable with the idea. The ethnoarts workshop in July 2017 with the musicians from around Cabeceira Verde, he believes, was a decisive step for the broader adoption of their own traditional instruments. Yet, the guitar and the keyboard seem to remain as their favorites.

3.3.3 Present-Day Genres of Church Music

The music workshop in Cabeceira Verde took place at the church meeting place at the entrance of the village. The structure is made of wood, about fifteen meters long by seven meters wide. It has a thatched roof and resembles the home structures in that village. Although a few villages make use of a cement building structure for church meeting places, this setting is characteristic of most villages where the church music genres are performed. As in other classic indigenous village life settings, the church structure does not provide any sound proofing, and those that participate presumably also have no expectation of sound isolation. In fact, the intention is to broadcast the sounds of the church service at a volume that the village residents can indeed listen to what is being said or sung within the church meeting place. Within this line of thinking, the Xerente musicians are not shy to make ample use of amplification.

Xerente Christian music has come to be performed with the electronic keyboards and acoustic guitars which proliferated since the 1990s. A typical keyboard contains dozens of rhythmic settings which help to animate the musical moment. None of the Xerente musicians encountered and interviewed for this research have so far endeavored to read Western music notation with great fluency although several of them have basic notions of musical notation. Methods, such as that of Mário Mascarenhas used by Pr. Rinaldo to teach the keyboard to the first students, do introduce the use of music notation, but also offer helps that allow the student to make practical use of the instrument's features while playing by ear.

Within this mode of learning many Xerente have become quite proficient in discerning the chord structures and progressions that have undergirded the harmonic features of their new compositions. During the composition portion of the music workshop, instrumentalists involved in the composition process readily reproduced the sung melodies on the keyboard or guitar, and developed arrangements with introductions and suitable accompaniment chords and rhythms for each of the songs.

Present-day Xerente Christian music is frequently sung by a soloist or a duet either in unison or with a second voice. The singing style resembles the general demeanor of the Xerente people: soft spoken and tentative. Full voices are typically only heard when a group participates in the singing. Singers use the microphones by placing them very close to their mouth, and when the microphones are not on a stand, they hold them close to their bodies.

Of the twenty-eight songs recorded during the workshop in 2017, I have transcribed ten for analysis and they serve to illustrate their general characteristics in this work. Appendix C contains their complete transcriptions. The five songs partially displayed and described in this section provide adequate indications of the components commonly found in this genre. The descriptions also entail aural and visual observations made during the recording sessions and the audio recordings themselves which the written notation cannot provide.

1. Ĩpkẽ wadkâ wa waza Jesus dawa by Lázaro Rowakro

Ĩpkẽ wadkâ wa waza Jesus dawa

Lázaro Rowakro

3—First page of the song *Ĩpkẽ wadkâ wa waza Jesus dawa*

Lázaro recorded four songs during the music workshop. *Ĩpkẽ wadkâ wa waza Jesus dawa* displays many of the typical characteristics encountered in Xerente fusion. In coordination with the young man playing the keyboard, an introduction was prepared that closely resembled the melodic line of the song. The keyboard used a setting mimicking an accordion or a harmonica, sounds which are typical of northeastern folk genres, such as the *baião*. The bass guitar is also a keyboard preset and it is rhythmically shaped as used for genres like *baião* or *tecnobrega*.[38] The first melodic phrase is repeated six times with varying lyrics (sometimes repeated). After a one-measure break, a slightly longer secondary melody proceeds, which is sung through only once. The whole song is repeated three times in the same format, each time with unique verses, and closes with the return of the first melodic phrase (six times) followed by an instrumental closing.

The practice of repetition is a frequent feature of Xerente traditional music, particularly that of the same phrase before presenting a contrasting one. Four of the new songs produced during the 2017 workshop were traditional melodies to which the participants added Christian texts. *Waptokwa Zawre dawarze* (Figure 4) is one such song that illustrates this typical feature of traditional song:

---

38. For a historical survey of the development of *brega* and *tecnobrega*, sites such as this are available in Portuguese: http://zinetribos.blogspot.com/2009/11/historia-da-musica-brega_17.html.

The Xerente and Their Musics

This is a traditional Xerente melody to which musicians in Cabeceira Verde gave a Christian text. The recording was made with about 15 people singing together, basically in unison, except for the addition of an alto line for the first half of the phrase at times. The accompaniment was simply the zâ or maracá. The score above is 'metered' as 2/4 since most traditional Xerente music is in duple meter. This often does not apply to the length of time between phrases. This group seemed to have consistently (based on the puxador) changed the last note of the chord into 3 beats - thus the change of meter.

4—Traditional melody with Christian lyrics—*Waptokwa Zawre Dawarze*

Lázaro's songs[39] make frequent use of intervals of thirds outlining a major chord at several instances throughout his melodies, although not often completing the chord in the same sequence. This characteristic, although by no means exclusive to Xerente melody, could demonstrate a reflection of other melodic ideas that Lázaro, as Christian composer as well as a Xerente elder responsible for leading traditional songs, may have naturally integrated into the new melodies. The traditional song *Arê Arê* shown in Figure 5 demonstrates the custom of outlining a major chord in Xerente melodies.

39. The greater part of the Cabeceira Verde songs' lyrics can be found in Appendix C. The audio recordings can be accessed through the B. H. Carroll Theological Institute Library or provided upon request: elsen.portugal@bhcarroll.edu.

Arê Arê

5—Traditional Song *Arê Arê*

On the other hand, *Ĩpkĕ wadkâ wa waza Jesus dawa* makes use of the 7th scale degree in a way that resembles northeastern melodies more than Xerente ones. The sequential character of the melodic structure of Lázaro's four recorded songs give evidence of his perception of potential underlying chord progressions and of a final cadence that could be defined as Western. These similarities, however, may not be an indication of a recent adoption of Western musical languages, but could be rooted in earlier incorporations of other musical systems. Traditional songs, such as *Arê Arê* in Figure 5, also display a potential for Western harmonization, raising a question as to the age of these melodies which could have been earlier adoptions from the music of the colonists in the surrounding areas.

The singing style used for this and several of the other songs, but not necessarily noted in the transcriptions, demonstrates the practices of scooping to a note—not unlike contemporary Western singing—as well as a characteristic fall from a pitch (particularly high ones) either anticipating the next pitch or falling lightly about a fifth before moving back up to the next main tone. This practice could be interpreted as "natural" from a positive perspective, or as "careless" from the point of view of the Western classical tradition. Without placing a value judgment on this practice, it is relevant for this discussion, however, to highlight the apparent lack of attempt on Lázaro's and other singers' part to imitate voice types from genres from which they borrowed instrumentation, rhythmic, and harmonic features. The maintenance of the Xerente singing character, which would be more clearly identified if the instrumentation were completely taken away, serves as a sign of the natural and authentic character of their song.

The lyrics of this song express the Christian's resolve to turn to Jesus in various situations of his or her life. Stanzas are modified primarily by changing the seasons of life ("when I am *sad/crying/worried/weak/sick*, I will pray to Jesus") as sampled below:[40]

Refrain

Ĩpkẽ wadkâ wa waza Jesus dawa zatô ĩm waihkânĩ
Ĩwwai wa waza Jesus dawa zatô ĩm waihkânĩ
Ĩpkẽ zako wa waza Jesus dawa zatô ĩm waihkânĩ
Ĩpakuwa wa waza Jesus dawa zatô ĩm waihkânĩ
Ĩhâze wa waza Jesus dawa zatô ĩm waihkânĩ
Ĩpahi wa waza Jesus dawa zatô ĩm waihkânĩ
Tô tanẽ dure tôka tô ĩsenã Jesus dawari
Zatô Jesus tôka aiwaihkâ nĩ are zatô dure tôka aipkẽtoinĩ

Refrain repeats

Tanẽ nmẽ mãtô Jesus kriĩ pê wazô sabunĩ
hêwa nsĩ wa mãtô wanõwa kriĩ pê mãtô wazô hrinĩ

Refrain repeats

Tanẽ nmẽ dure tôka dazakru Jesus dam sawidi
Tô dure tônmẽm hã akwẽ tô ĩsenã mãtô dasimã smĩstunĩ

Refrain repeats

---

40. This and the following texts with the translations were provided by one of the missionaries, Werner Seitz, on July 18, 2019.

2. **Kâ psêktabdi** by João Simrãmĩ

Kâ psêktabdi

João Simrãmĩ

6—Transcription of the first two pages of the melody of the song *Kâ psêktabdi*

Kâ psêktabdi can be translated as "Excellent Water." The song declares that God's good water saves. Therefore, the singer calls, "let's go to Him!"

> *Kâ psêktabdi Waptokwa datê hã tahã zatô wapkẽhi*
> *Kâ psêktabdi Waptokwa datê hã tahã zatô wapkẽhi*
> *Tanẽ nmẽ arê kba tô kbure tô tammõ wawahtu kwaba; Tô tahã tô ĩpsê tmẽ*

Tanē nmē arê kba tô kbure tô tammō wawahtu kwaba; Tô tahā tô īpsê tmē
Nōkwap sa tô tahā? Nōkwap sa tô tahā?
Tahā tô Jesus hā kātô dure Waptokwa
Nōkwap sa tô tahā? Nōkwap sa tô tahā?
Tahā tô Jesus hā kātô dure Waptokwa

This song is introduced and accompanied by the keyboard rhythmic setting for a bass guitar, an electronic keyboard using synthesized trumpet-like sounds, and the *zâ*. Its triple meter is unlike the duple meter of traditional music. Some melodic patterns are similar to traditional Xerente music (particularly the minor third jump—3rd to 1st degree) and use traditional patterns of phrase repetition, although not unlike Western folk music. It adds a refrain resembling Western hymn patterns and shifts the tonal center to the dominant of the song's original key. The melody also uses the 7th scale degree which is uncommon in Xerente traditional music. The recording, done after the accompanists had a very short period of acquaintance with the melody, probably does not harmonize as intended by João when the 7th scale degree is used. The location of the 7th scale degree in the melody implies a unique extension of the melody created by the composer that are not as common in Western compositional styles.

The repetitions found in João Simrãmĩ's song also display the expectation of a repeated first phrase before a contrasting one is presented, being repeated in the same manner as the first one. João sings in the same fashion as Lázaro and others and sets his song apart from traditional song primarily through the use of triple meter.

3. *Waptokwa Zawre damã danõkrêze* by Marcelino Kasuwamrĩ

Waptokwa Zawre damã danõkrêze

Marcelino

7—*Waptokwa Zawre damã danõkrêze*

This song is the only example of Marcelino's songs in the workshop recordings. It consists of a triple repetition of a single phrase, adapted each time to the structural needs of the lyrics followed by a short tag of three measures. The song has a few verses separated by a short instrumental interlude similar to the introduction, followed by an ending with the instrumental tag, which, once again, resembles the introduction. It is entitled "Hymn to God" and has a basic theme of laboring for God since the Christian has the Holy Spirit.

Waptokwa Dahêmba wakmã mārd mnõdi
Tanẽ nmẽ mātô dat wanõrī
Danīpī damã wat krdakmādkâ mnõ da

Tâkāhā dazakru mātô sā mnī
Tanẽ nmẽ Waptokwa dapkẽ toiti

Wasisu zahā krwanmrõ mnõ nmẽ
Tanẽ nmẽ wa tokto īpkẽ toiti
Waptokwa damẽ krinẽ mnõ wa

The melodic structure and the accompaniment created by the instrumentalists at the time of the recording are based on an aeolian mode (the pattern of intervals of a descending melodic minor scale) in A. The accompaniment consists of a keyboard's electronic rhythms as displayed in the simplified transcription in Figure 7, a guitar maintaining a semi-regular movement like the electronic drums, emphasizing every other beat, sometimes plucked instead of strummed, the keyboard's harmonic accompaniment with a simulation of an accordion sound, and a preset bass sound in rhythm.

Marcelino uses the frequent feature of repetition found in Xerente traditional music, particularly of the same phrase before moving to a contrasting one. As with Lázaro's song, *Waptokwa Zawre dawarze* in Figure 4 (and below as Figure 8) demonstrates this same typical traditional feature of Xerente songs.

8—*Waptokwa Zawre Dawarze*

As a traditional melody, this tune is immediately recognized by the Xerente community at large. Traditional tunes which were re-used for Christian purposes have not been fully accepted yet since some members of the community question the propriety of using the same traditional melodies (which could appear sacrilegious to both Christian believers and unbelievers). The new lyrics are a prayer to God. Albeit, they still maintain the common practice of addressing the audience present:

> 1. I have prayed to God
> I have prayed to God
> Always in the name of Jesus
> Always in the name of Jesus:

The Xerente and Their Musics

2. Lord, come help us everyday
Lord, come help us everyday
May we truly love you
May we truly love you

4. *Dazakru sĩm warewdêhu* by Ronaldo

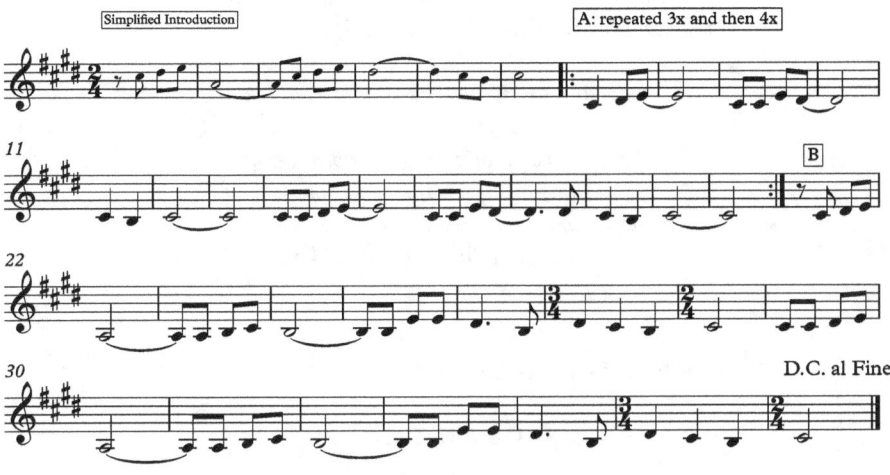

9—*Dazakru sĩm warewdêhu*

Ronaldo and a female vocalist recorded this song in unison, accompanied by a guitar strumming on the beats and the keyboard playing a trumpet imitation with accompanying chords. It has a ballad-like character using a short range of notes based on the Dorian mode. The lack of pre-programmed drums and bass line give it a mood quite distinct from the first three songs described above and could eventually be labeled as a distinct genre within the Xerente church. The melodic pattern, however, is not unlike other traditional melodies.

The song follows the same pattern of melodic phrase repetition common in Xerente songs. Phrase labeled as A displays a single repetition which has been transcribed for the purposes of this study, but the doubled phrase is also repeated three times for the first stanza. Phrase B appears only after this long repetitive exposition. It is also a doubled phrase which has been fully transcribed in the figure above. The song continues with a repetition of the instrumental introduction (simplified) followed by a second stanza which repeats the double phrase A four times, thus completing the song.

The lyrics of the song celebrate the deliverance from darkness that a village called *Warewdêhu* has come to enjoy. The initial verse says: "Earlier, in the Warewdêhu village, people walked in darkness, but now Jesus came for us and, because of this, all walk in the light. And his light will never end, and his light will never end."

> *Dazakru sĩm warewdêhu wa aire romzakrã wa kwanmrõ mnõze tô tazim si*
> *Are tokto mãtô Jesus kãnẽ waimã ĩmãntamĩnĩ*
> *tâkâhã hawi zatô mẽ romkuiwẽ wa kbure krdanõmrõ*
>
> *Are tô tahã romkuiwẽ za sikutõr kõdi (2x)*
>
> *Ambâ nõrĩ, pikõĩ nõrĩ, aikte nõrai zemã*
> *wasi bdâdi hirê watô smĩstu psênĩ*
> *tanẽ nmẽ wapkite snã wasisa ktab snã*
> *damẽ si tô ĩsenã snã wakmã kba*

5. *Aisi hawim hã nã* by Pasiku

Aisi hawim hã nã

10—Instrumental introduction and melodic line of the song *Aisi hawim hã nã*

While this song was transcribed with a 2/4 meter, it appears that Pasiku envisioned a longer time measurement in view of the extended notes. Due to certain irregularities in the recording, however, this time signature was chosen for reasons of proportion. The melodic phrase presents a longer idea than others described above. Harmonically, the accompanists begin with a I chord in measure 13, moving to V in measure 16, to IV in measure 21, returning to V in measure 24, and finally resolving to I in 28. The melody, although longer than usual, is similarly repeated multiple times. The text, as in other samples offered in this section, is a call to go in God's ways so that one can hear well what his plans are.

> *Waptokwa Zawre danĩm bdâdi nã*
> *wi tô wê aimõr wẽ nã*
> *aisĩm romãdkâ wẽ zawre*
> *wat wapar wẽ pibumã*

> **Refrain:**
>
> ***Tanẽ nmẽ***
> ***wi tô wê aimõr wẽ nã***
> ***aisĩm romãdkâ wẽ zawre***
> ***wat wapar wẽ pibumã***

> *Wapkẽhrikwa mãtô mnĩ*
> *aisaprõnnĩ*
> *aisĩm romãdkâ wẽ zawre*
> *wat kmãdkâ wẽ pibumã*

> **Refrain repeated**

> *Dazakru mba hã akwẽ nõrĩ*
> *Tet aisô danmĩpar wẽ*
> *aisĩm hawim hã nã wê*
> *aismĩ wẽ nã*

> **Refrain repeated**

> *Waptokwa Zawre zatô aipâ*
> *aimõ saprônnĩ*
> *tô nmãinnĩ aimõrze mba*
> *aipâ aisiwẽttê nã*

> **Refrain repeated**

3.3.4 Overall Observations

Gathering observations from the workshop discussions, from performance practices observed during the meetings and in the recordings, as well as from the various features of these and remaining songs studied for this section, the following characteristics could be highlighted:

1. The composers appear to envision a harmonic structure for their songs from the outset of their preparation.

2. The songs display a preference for duple meter characteristic of Xerente traditional songs. The only exception in the group of songs studied was *Hêwa nsĩm hã tô Waptokwai ktabi* by João Simrãmĩ.

3. The melodic phrase was repeated often multiple times. The pattern follows the common practice in traditional Xerente songs: AABB. However, the composers made use of the same melody as they wished, fitting new stanzas by adapting the melody according to the verbal construction they wished to incorporate.

4. Electronic instrumentation seems to be an accessible preference and is used in all of the songs except two that were traditional melodies with Christian words.

5. The melodic contour of the songs relates to Western harmonies in frequent instances, giving rise to the question of earlier influences since this characteristic is common to "traditional" Xerente songs and not a recent introduction into their musical vocabulary.

6. Melodic rhythm does not contain syncopation except occasionally when an eighth note is followed by a quarter and another eighth note. Faster syncopations and frequent anticipation of the note on the following beat are virtually absent. While these characteristics are found in many genres of contemporary popular music, including the northeastern genres, they may not suit the Xerente musical taste well.

7. Song lyrics are directed to the audience in the majority of cases. Hence, the songs could be called "worship music" if one understands "worship" in the broad sense of service to or for God through any of multiple ways of expressing or exercising one's faith. However, the lyrical content is *not* primarily intended as a "conversation" or monologue of worship directed to God himself.

3.4 THE XERENTE FUSION: NOT AN EXCEPTION

The trend to adopt external musical systems, genres, and singular features as their own is not unique to the Xerente. Historical parallels exist in other indigenous cultures in Brazil. A similar development occurred among the Makuxi (pronounced: Mah-Koo-´Shee) as reported by Felipe Munhoz Martins Fernandes in his 2015 thesis. The Makuxi, living in a politically divided situation on the border of Brazil and Guyana, adopted the *forró* genre as their own in the first half of the twentieth century through migrants from the northeast of the country.[41] However, they elaborated it in such a way that an eventual reincorporation of traditional rhythms also occurred and developed into a symbol of ethnic identity.[42] The ethnomusicologist Erich von Hornbostel was the first to analyze the traditional music of the Makuxi and other South American peoples in northern South America. As early as the 1920s[43] he identified traits indicating both intra- and extra-continental influences on Makuxi traditional music.[44] Along the same line of progression as countless indigenous peoples in the Americas, the Makuxi opted for rescuing their culture for political and identity reasons through select knowledge, as well as objects and practices.[45] "Without adhering exclusively to 'tradition,' . . . [they] leaned on them as a starting point for their cultural-artistic productions,"[46] all the while making internal choices (individually and corporately) that led to the integration and 'ownership' of new features. Felipe Fernandes's 2015 master's thesis demonstrates a musical trajectory from traditional genres to external ones, later recapturing some of the musical language from the internal genres of *parixara* and *tukui* and transforming the combined elements into "cultural performances" with political overtones. Like in this research, Fernandes's research seeks to identify the development of "significations and meanings attributed to different musical rhythms and repertoires of the Makuxi."[47] Fernandes's thesis demonstrates that musical genres have malleable borders that permit changes, restructuring, incorporation of external elements, along with other processes, all the

---

41. Fernandes, "Parixara ao Forró," 67.
42. Fernandes, "Parixara ao Forró," abstract.
43. Kuss, *Music in Latin America*, 54.
44. Fernandes, "Parixara ao Forró," 68.
45. Fernandes, "Parixara ao Forró," 94–95.
46. Fernandes, "Parixara ao Forró," 114.
47. Fernandes, "Parixara ao Forró," abstract.

while developing new internal or external functions (or fulfilling earlier ones) and attaining meaning in the community.

3.5 CHAPTER SUMMARY

Chapter 3 overviewed the musical world of the Xerente people, including an exposition of traditional musical instruments and locally acknowledged categories (or genres) of song. Musical categories in the Xerente context relate to their functions in community life. They are partners of life-cycle celebrations such as the naming of children and of cultural festivities that reaffirm Xerente identity.

This chapter has also considered the development of Brazilian musical genres and their links to Xerente society. Brazilian music of today owes its existence to the multiple interactions among Europeans, African, and indigenous cultures. Certain resulting genres have taken root in indigenous communities such as the Xerente and have either influenced or been adopted by them for internal use. Northeastern genres have found abundant space in Xerente society and have been integrated into the musical spectrum both of community and church.

Through a description and analysis of five recently recorded Christian songs by different composers, this chapter displayed the mixture of features present in current practice. The fusion of elements has produced a local style of Christian music that prevails in most church meetings and has indications of being imbedded in their communities as part of the Xerente Christian identity.

4

Fusion Genres

4.1 GENRE DEVELOPMENT OR FUSION

4.1.1 Definition of Genre

CHAPTER 1 INTRODUCED THE definition of the term "genre" as used in this book. "Genre" refers to a particular subset of artistic compositions—in this case a musical one—containing multiple distinctive characteristics, some of which are form, style of singing or playing, content, origin of composition, choice of performer, purpose, and audience. A genre's characteristics are not necessarily unique and are often reapplications from other genres in different combinations. Similarly, genres often consist of a great number of elements from a previous genre with the addition of "new" ones. Furthermore, factors including its cultural, geographic, and/or ethnic origin, as well as its function, audience, and form of dissemination could all affect the categorization of a musical event style as a distinct genre.

It is difficult to determine where a genre begins and ends. Practitioners themselves hold to different opinions on whether a song, piece, or other type of musical event belongs to a previously identified genre. Although I use the term for the Xerente church music styles, I do not presume to establish a precise label for them, nor to identify them as a single genre or as multiple genres. The Xerente—the "owners" of the musical style—will themselves be responsible for giving it a name, if they so wish. I am affirming, however, that a fusion—not simply copying—has indeed occurred in the music that is practiced by the Xerente Christians today and that one should consider their validity as authentically Xerente. Additionally, there are certain performance practices not specifically "musical" that can be identified as typically accompanying Xerente Christian fusion genres and can be factors in the identification of a genre.

4.1.2 The Rationale of Genre Development and Classification

Genre development has a dynamic character as demonstrable through historical examples of blends and fusion of elements from different cultures. The process, although not proof of the authentic character of Xerente music in and of itself, reveals the fluid nature of musical reality in human experience. The results of these mixing processes typically come to be accepted as a "genre" by at least a segment of a society, and often also by academic institutions and other social groups from within or without the original group that developed them.

Genres commonly take their cues from previously existing musical systems. Most of their characteristics have been inherited as norms (or rules) from previous genres and mixed together with a few new elements. Fabbri explains that the "new" characteristics "are only transgressions to the rules of other genres."[1] When a musical creation containing such "new" features achieves some measure of success, "these innovations are used as a model and become a rule."[2] The results, he states, are placed "in a sort of black box," and the "[transgressions] are codified."[3] New expectations are developed and the newly codified style of musical event becomes successful (which, he clarifies, "has nothing to do with aesthetic value") since it gives a response to these new expectations.[4]

In Western classical (or "art") music, genres can be categorized according to eras or historical periods (medieval, renaissance, baroque, etc.) since each period's musical production appear to display unique or distinctly combined features. Genres, however, often surpass any specific historical period. These examples of classical music genres can serve to clarify the term's application:

---

1. Fabbri, "Theory of Musical Genres," 6.
2. Fabbri, "Theory of Musical Genres," 7.
3. Fabbri, "Theory of Musical Genres," 7.
4. Fabbri, "Theory of Musical Genres," 7.

- *Opera*: a genre including solo and choral singing, as well as staging and the acting of a play. This genre has existed since the Baroque period and continues to be used by modern composers.
- *Choral Music*: music performed by a choir with or without instrumental accompaniment. This genre includes music as far back as the early medieval period. Its binding feature is the performance by a choir.
- *Orchestral*: music composed specifically for orchestral performance. This genre has existed since the organization of the Baroque orchestra and lives on today.
- *Tone or Symphonic Poems*: an orchestral genre (or sub-genre) suggestive of a storyline. Although originally developed during the Romantic period (nineteenth century) it continues in existence today even under other terms.[5]

Encompassing classical, folk, pop, and other large categories of genres, the "Music Genre List" contains around 900 terms, including numerous sub-genres.[6] The categories on this list mingle both popular and academic views about what can be considered a genre. Genres in this list owe their existence to their distinct venues (ex. Opera), era of composition (ex. Romantic period), origin (ex. Chicago House, a sub-genre of House), as well as to their purpose or intended audience (ex. Lullabies; Dance music).[7] The crowdsourcing character of this list, although not adding an academic authority for the existence of such variety of types and classification models, does illustrate the potential of sociologists Jennifer Lena and Richard Peterson's broad definition of musical genre. Lena and Peterson identify "two dominant approaches to the study of genre,"[8] one focusing on the "'text'[9] of a cultural object" and the other on a social context.[10] Even though "most musicologists employ this textual approach to identify genre as a set of pieces of music that share a distinctive musical

---

5. Johnson, "What Is a . . . Tone Poem?"

6. Music Genre List, "What Is a Music Genre?"

7. Chapter 1 contains Franco Fabbri's explanation of the nature of the guiding "rules" of genres: form, technique, semiotics (meaning), behavior, social, ideological, economical, and juridical.

8. Lena and Peterson, "Classification as Culture," 698.

9. "Text" as used here is not limited to the linguistic elements, but to concrete (tangible) language including a musical one.

10. Lena and Peterson, "Classification as Culture," 698.

language (van der Merwe 1989)," the authors "define music genres as *systems* of orientations, expectations, and conventions that bind together an industry, performers, critics, and fans in making *what they identify as a distinctive sort of music*."[11] This definition highlights "the set of cultural practices (Becker 1982) that a music community defines as a genre and view[s] its texts as the product of social interactions in a specific sociocultural context (Frith 1996)."[12] This perspective, therefore, allows for a wide variety of genre categories and potential ways one could classify musics, unbound by limiting classical or academic criteria.

Following the same broad line of thought, ethnodoxology advocates acknowledging local perspectives of categories as valid within their own social contexts. Along the course of this study, my colleagues, interviewees, and I observed that the Xerente categorize their song repertoire on the basis of their context of performance, the performers themselves, and the general purpose of the music. Differences in musical language (the "text" in the first approach discussed by Lena and Peterson) may play a part in some cases but seem to be less relevant for their classification as separate genres.

4.2 THE QUESTION OF ABSOLUTE GENRES

4.2.1 Culture and Music Are Not "Static"

According to Nestor Garcia Canclini, "all culture is the result of a selection and a combination—constantly renewed—of its sources . . . it is a product of a staging in which what is going to be represented is chosen and adapted in accordance with what the audience can listen to, see, and understand."[13] Music, as an element of culture, develops along the same lines. Canclini, citing Martha Blache, proposes that even traditional culture is not "an authoritative norm or static and immutable force," but rather "a mechanism of selection, and even of invention, projected toward the past in order to legitimize the present."[14] Carolina Bertolini, in her analysis of last century's joint identity of a few indigenous peoples living in the city of Manaus (the capital of the Brazilian State of Amazonas), cites Fredrik Barth explaining that "culture must always be generated

11. Lena and Peterson, "Classification as Culture," 698. Emphasis added.
12. Lena and Peterson, "Classification as Culture," 698.
13. Canclini, *Hybrid Cultures*, loc. 95.
14. Canclini, *Hybrid Cultures*, loc. 156.

in people by means through which [one's own culture's] learning takes place" and that "culture is in a *state of constant flux*, since the cultural materials are constantly *generated from people's experiences*, and it is not possible to consider them as traditions fixed in time and transmitted from the past, from generation to generation."[15]

Anthropology's contribution to ethnomusicological research has helped to identify "differences, diversity, and plurality"[16] of musical styles and norms among the peoples of the world. Countless musical ethnographies have been formulated as theses, dissertations, and book publications, validating the great diversity of musical systems in vogue around the world. Although genre classifications used by anthropologists and ethnomusicologists in their earlier stages may not have regarded developmental or transitional stages as classifiable or indeed regarded as less than valid,, this perception has progressively changed and brought into focus a "change as norm" as a reasonable and valid concept. Hence, this book questions the validity of potentially outdated, overly rigid ideas of genre classifications, especially when they are used as a basis for evaluating whether a musical event belongs or not to a given culture. Categories of genres as commonly outlined perform their best service as reference points for the comprehension of unifying musical features, rather than as systems limiting the privilege of "belonging to a genre" or the determination of its authentic character as demonstrative of a particular community. The malleable and fluid character of music manifestations challenges the idea that musical genres are closed and that absolute categories embody the "pure" (untainted by the influence of external features) elements of a particular style.

4.2.2 Brazilian Genres—Birthed through Fusion

The musics of the Brazilian national society are perhaps the most appropriate illustrations of how music adapts, changes, is categorized by stakeholders in a society, and then receives the status of genre. Although this progression has taken place throughout history and, presumably, all over the world, the development of the classical, folk, and popular genres of the Brazilian national society has a more natural kinship with the musical

---

15. Bertolini, "Performance Musical e Reconhecimento," 56. Emphasis added. Translation mine.

16. Bertolini, "Performance Musical e Reconhecimento," 141.

milieu of its indigenous peoples than other distant and foreign processes. In the following pages, we consider the initial fusion of musical elements along the history of Brazil, and in particular of two of the best-known Brazilian genres, *samba* and *bossa nova*, demonstrating the tendency towards a level of consolidation that curtails further "outside" influences.

McGowan and Pessanha's view of Brazil as "a real melting pot"[17] is supported through multiple descriptions of the rise of each of its musical genres. Their study is curiously indicative of the exchange of musical features within the country and the fact that Brazilian music has also had great influence on international popular music.[18]

Although an estimated two million indigenous people lived in what is now called Brazil in 1500, indigenous music did not make a great mark in the common musical genres of Brazil. Indians sang monophonically with the accompaniment of whistle- and flute-like instruments, using hands, feet, sticks, and drums to mark the beats, as many indigenous peoples do today.[19] As referenced earlier in the book, Jean de Léry, the Calvinist traveler who lived in Brazil during the time of the failed French attempt to establish a colony in what is now Rio de Janeiro, took note of the indigenous musical practices during his time in Brazil[20] and related that their songs did not have a particular "author" (composer) but that their singing was directly linked to their communal life, being performed indistinctly by gifted and not-gifted singers.[21] This integrated purpose of indigenous music may have hindered greater penetration of their musical features into the general Brazilian musical sonic world.

A purposeful incorporation of indigenous themes did indeed occur in Brazilian music when several Brazilian classical composers followed the wave of nationalism taking place in Europe and other parts of the world in the late nineteenth century. Composers such as Alberto Nepomuceno, Ernesto Nazareth, and the most famous Brazilian twentieth century composer Heitor Villa-Lobos, all integrated Brazilian themes and sounds including indigenous melodic ideas or exact quotes.[22] Among popular

---

17. The full quote is found in chapter 1 of this dissertation.
18. McGowan and Pessanha, *Brazilian Sound*, loc. 144.
19. McGowan and Pessanha, *Brazilian Sound*, loc. 222.
20. Léry, *History of a Voyage*.
21. Camêu, "Música Indígena," 4–10.
22. Villa-Lobos's *Tres Poemas Indígenas* (*Three Indigenous Poems*) of 1926 is a set of songs for voice and piano that illustrates this nationalist practice. His interest and use of indigenous musical or topical themes is discussed, for instance, in Moreira, "Estilo

genres, however, other than the use of the indigenous *reco-reco* (a scraper ideophone), the *maracá* (like the Xerente *zâ*), some choreography,[23] as well as some recent attempts at reviving indigenous sounds, national folk and popular music did not adopt a pronouncedly Indian sound, although some scholars identify its influence on vocal production features as well as certain religious ideas imbedded in some genres.[24]

During colonial times, the Portuguese introduced tonal music "as well as Moorish scales and medieval European modes."[25] The *Entrudo* brought by the explorers, for instance, would become an early celebratory form for *Carnaval*.[26] Portuguese syncopation and "brisk, complex rhythms,"[27] according to McGowan and Pessanha, would facilitate its blend with the African music which slaves would eventually bring to the shores of South America. An estimated four to five million Africans slaves were transported to Brazil between 1538 and the 1850s. Hundreds of thousands did not endure the voyage across the Atlantic Ocean as well as the abusive conditions, dying en route to South America. Despite their subjugated condition and frequently inhumane treatment, in time the cultures and musics of Africa would become key culture-makers in the developing Brazilian national society.[28]

As horrid as this reality is, Europeans and Africans had been enslaving each other centuries before the establishment of a colony in Brazil. On the flip side, the interaction between the conquerors and the Africans before their forced transport to Brazil did positively affect the tolerance level of the Portuguese towards African cultures.[29] It may have been an important factor in what Behague calls a "reverse acculturative process" that resulted in the "amalgamation" of musical features and in genuinely new "mestizo traditions."[30]

---

indígena de Villa Lobos."

23. Behague, "Brazil," 224.

24. McGowan and Pessanha, *Brazilian Sound*, loc. 229. Behague's article "Brazil" suggests that performance characteristics could also be traced to indigenous influence (p. 224).

25. McGowan and Pessanha, *Brazilian Sound*, loc. 257.

26. McGowan and Pessanha, *Brazilian Sound*, loc. 263.

27. McGowan and Pessanha, *Brazilian Sound*, loc. 263.

28. McGowan and Pessanha, *Brazilian Sound*, loc. 270.

29. McGowan and Pessanha, *Brazilian Sound*, loc. 287.

30. Behague, "Brazil," 224.

Historical approaches to the study of Brazilian genres, such as John P. Murphy's *Music in Brazil*, confirm their character as "blends of musical elements from within and outside of Brazil."[31] The musical panorama of Brazilian music known today would likely not exist had these mixtures not taken place. The static view of genres, commonly adopted (often unintentionally) by the general population, contradicts the very essence of their creation process. Murphy identifies the presence of a frequent pattern of blending followed by genre consolidation and a subsequent wave of protectionism in Brazil: "Once the blend has attained a distinctive form and become a symbol of national identity and pride, as *samba* did in the 1930s, further blending is discouraged by those who consider themselves the guardians of tradition."[32]

Some historians believe that the term *samba* derives from the Kimbundu (a people group from Angola) meaning "invitation to the dance."[33] Other origins have also been suggested, such as the *lundú* dance music. Precise derivation is further complicated through the use of the term in the nineteenth century to describe various Afro-Brazilian dances and to "designate parties held by slaves and former slaves."[34]

The genre took root and developed into the present form in the city of Rio de Janeiro. The process of change continued, however, through an influx of Afro-Brazilian persons migrating from Bahia (northeastern Brazil) where "neo-African culture had survived to a greater extent."[35] Early in the twentieth century, "the emerging style of samba gained influences from polka, habanera, and the lively genres of marcha and maxixe. From this rich matrix emerged a vibrant musical form distinguished by its responsorial singing and percussive interplay and a less formal sound than either maxixe or marcha."[36] Some *sambistas*[37] are credited with various modifications or additions to the form. João da Baiana introduced the *pandeiro* (a type of tambourine also played with a drumstick) to *samba* in the early twentieth century. The advent of the *escola de samba*

---

31. Murphy, *Music in Brazil*, 24.
32. Murphy, *Music in Brazil*, 24.
33. McGowan and Pessanha, *Brazilian Sound*, loc. 494.
34. McGowan and Pessanha, *Brazilian Sound*, loc. 494.
35. McGowan and Pessanha, *Brazilian Sound*, loc. 506.
36. McGowan and Pessanha, *Brazilian Sound*, loc. 525.
37. *Sambista* refers to someone who composes or performs *samba* as music or dance.

(samba school)[38] and its participation in the *Carnaval* parades brought about an increase in participants, both dancers and musicians. The musician Alcebíades Maia Barcelos (nicknamed *Bide*) "introduced the practice of playing the second beat of a 2/4 measure strongly on the *surdo* bass drum and using the *tamborim* in the samba percussion section."[39] Numerous musicians made adaptations to these practices along the decades and distinct styles became recognized as important sub-genres, such as *samba-canção* (samba song) and *samba-exaltação* (sambas praising Brazilian natural beauty).[40] By the 1950s, *Samba-canção* "had been diluted by contact with boleros, fox-trots, and cha-cha-cha."[41] The time was ripe for another development: *Bossa Nova*.

Bossa Nova offered a more harmonically intricate and softer version of samba rhythm. "It was full of unusual harmonies and syncopations, all expressed with a sophisticated simplicity."[42] Besides its acknowledged jazz connections—initial and ongoing—*Bossa* composers admittedly imported elements from classical music such as the compositions of George Gershwin and Debussy (Johnny Alf in the 1950s), as well as from twentieth-century composers including the Brazilian composer Villa-Lobos (Tom Jobim).[43] The two songs written by Tom Jobim and Vinicius de Moraes that launched the genre were recorded by João Gilberto and demonstrated a captivating combination of "unconventional harmonies, the apparently *strong influence of American jazz*, and Gilberto's unusual vocals."[44]

Bossa Nova made a successful entrance into the music scene of the United States[45] through a performance at the White House during John F. Kennedy's presidency. At the invitation of Carnegie Hall, a "legendary concert" took place in November of 1962 with "Brazil's Bossa hierarchy including Gilberto, Jobim, Sérgio Mendes, and Carlos Lyra" performing "alongside jazz musicians like Stan Getts and Charlie Byrd."[46] Some

38. *Samba schools* rose out of the need for recognition of poor segments of society that lived on the hillsides (a common feature throughout Rio de Janeiro) of *Estácio de Sá*, a section of town close to downtown Rio de Janeiro.

39. Murphy, *Music in Brazil*, 9.

40. McGowan and Pessanha, *Brazilian Sound*, locs. 648, 707.

41. McGowan and Pessanha, *Brazilian Sound*, loc. 816.

42. McGowan and Pessanha, *Brazilian Sound*, loc. 1552.

43. McGowan and Pessanha, *Brazilian Sound*, locs. 1574, 1601.

44. McGowan and Pessanha, *Brazilian Sound*, loc. 1528. Emphasis added.

45. SophyaAgain, "Brasil, Brasil," 7:20.

46. SophyaAgain, "Brasil, Brasil," 7:30—9:00. Also see McGowan and Pessanha, *Brazilian Sound*, loc. 1908.

Brazilian *bossa* musicians considered the result of this combination "a big mess." Yet, others believed the event was important for the ongoing dissemination of the genre since several Brazilian musicians signed contracts and remained in the US for a time.[47] The attractive new sounds of *Bossa Nova* spread through the country and even commercial products adopted the name (*Bossa Nova* washing machines, *Bossa Nova* haircomb, *Bossa Nova* shoes, etc.). *Bossa* musicians generally disliked these developments as well as the interminable influence of jazz on *Bossa Nova*.[48] In frustration, musicians such as Carlos Lyra decided to move away from the United States to Mexico. He believed that "there shouldn't be so much jazz" in *Bossa*. Even though its influence over *Bossa Nova* was important, he said, "it shouldn't be too much" and should just serve as "spice."[49] In response, Lyra wrote a song called *Influência do Jazz* (Jazz Influence) with these lyrics:

> *My Poor Samba mixed itself up,*
> *It was modernized and got lost.*
> *And the swing? Where is it? It's gone.*
> *Where is that jiggle that moves us?*
> *My poor samba, it changed suddenly,*
> *The influence of jazz.*[50]

Although it is beyond the scope of this study to relate a full historical account of the development of these or other Brazilian genres, the progression of genre creation through importation, blending, adaptation, and other similar processes is present in both *samba* and *bossa nova*. Some composers and performers seemed to be at ease with a continuing transformation of a genre. Sérgio Mendes, for instance, in his album "*Sérgio Mendes and Brasil '66* . . . mixed bossa, pop, and MPB[51] in a light, upbeat blend."[52] Carlinhos Brown, a songwriter from the State of Bahia

---

47. McGowan and Pessanha, *Brazilian Sound*, loc. 1942.
48. SophyaAgain, "Brasil, Brasil," 9:30—10:00. Interview with Tom Jobim.
49. SophyaAgain, "Brasil, Brasil," 10:00—11:00. Interview with Carlos Lyra.
50. SophyaAgain, "Brasil, Brasil," 10:20—11:00. The lyrics were originally in Portuguese. The translation above is my adaptation. In "Brasil, Brasil," cited above, Carlos Lyra discusses this and plays a sample of the song.
51. MPB stands for "Música Popular Brasileira"—Popular Brazilian Music—a term encompassing multiple Brazilian national musical styles from the seventies until the present.
52. McGowan and Pessanha, *Brazilian Sound*, loc. 2164.

"fused MPB and Rio samba with *axé* music and funk."⁵³ However, at least within some segments of society, including composers who made the genre popular (such as *Bossa* composer Carlos Lyra), a certain protectionism arose against musical forces that attempted to or did modify the genre as they envisioned it.

Northeastern popular genres, those closest to the people of interest in this study—the Xerente, have also resulted from multiple blends involving tonal production, tonal and modal scale patterns, rhythmic preferences, and many other musical and linguistic features. David Behague's *New Grove* article on Brazil paints an overall picture of musical features, suggesting origins of the genres or of specific musical characteristics. Behague states that "the majority of the many types of idiophone are of Amerindian and African derivation." African instruments such as *anzá, afoxé, caxixi, agogô, berimbau, conga*, and countless others, have been incorporated into the musical panorama of northeastern music. Northeastern genres have melodic lines demonstrating recitative-like characteristics derived from Gregorian Chant along with "rhythmic traits and melodic cadences related to chant."⁵⁴ The musician and scholar Antonio José Madureira also identified early Iberian musical modes, harmony, and other characteristics which they inherited from the Moors who occupied Spain and Portugal for about seven centuries.⁵⁵ Literary forms from Spain and Portugal also affected many northeastern musical forms.⁵⁶

The long centuries of interaction among African slaves in the South American continent tended to homogenize their styles. Thus, it is difficult to discern specific ethnic origins of imported musical traits.⁵⁷ Dance genres generally traced to African roots are plenteous. One of them is the *baião*, mentioned earlier in this book. The term is a dialectal form of the word *bahiano* which refers to things or people from the State of Bahia, one of the areas where African influence was the strongest. This genre—originally the name of a song composed by Luiz Gonzaga—was made popular by Gonzaga who sang and played his accordion, familiarizing the rest of Brazil with "the sounds and culture" of the Northeast for several decades.⁵⁸

53. McGowan and Pessanha, *Brazilian Sound*, loc. 2175. Emphasis added.
54. Behague, "Brazil," 226.
55. McGowan and Pessanha, *Brazilian Sound*, loc. 4404.
56. Behague, "Brazil," 227.
57. Behague, "Brazil," 240.
58. McGowan and Pessanha, *Brazilian Sound*, locs. 4236, 4183.

Baião

11—*Baião* by Luís Gonzaga[59]

 The 1960s and 70s brought a new wave of influences into the traditional sounding northeastern genres of *baião, xote, maracatu,* and *embolada*. Influenced by *bossa nova* and foreign performers from the era (ex. Beatles, Bob Dylan), these contemporary composers "added keyboards, electric guitars, pop arrangements, and other influences."[60] Popular performers such as Elba Ramalho and Gilberto Gil helped transform *forró* ("a speeded-up type of *baião*" used in dance parties) by using "electric guitars, basses, drum sets, and keyboards."[61] These mixes, along with *tecnobrega* and the *sertanejo* (or *forró*) *universitário*, have been penetrating into the Xerente aural world since the late 1990s and have left a mark on the people's apparent taste for electronic sounds and rhythms.

 59. https://image.slidesharecdn.com/luiz-gonzaga-baiao-150105165152-conversion-gate02/95/luiz-gonzagabaiao-1-638.jpg?cb=1420476798.
 60. McGowan and Pessanha, *Brazilian Sound*, loc. 4517.
 61. McGowan and Pessanha, *Brazilian Sound*, loc. 4691.

4.2.3 Fusion: A Worldwide Phenomenon

Although Brazil's musical development can possibly suffice as validation of the existence of such pattern of genre development, it is important to reiterate that this phenomenon is not unique to South America but can be recognized throughout the world. Examples of genre developments through the fusion of elements from various cultures are also not rare in the North American continent. In some cases, fusions have transcended their experimentation stage and have become recognized as established genres. In others, they are the fruit of local creativity, which, in time, may or not be identified as a distinct class of music.

Bluegrass, a favorite "southern" genre, popular since the twentieth century, is not a form developed without the influences of various cultures. Its roots are linked to "string band music"[62] in a variety of musics brought by Scotch-Irish immigrants to the American South in the seventeenth century.[63] It also includes elements of "African American gospel music and blues. In fact, "Africans that were sold into slavery brought with them many elements of their culture, one of which being the banjo, which is a central part of string band music."[64]

Furthermore, it is likely that its spread beyond the rural South is due to the advent of certain technological developments—the phonograph and the radio—in the early part of the twentieth century. Bluegrass is one branch of country music that was favored by these advances after World Word II. Price explains that "Kentucky native Bill Monroe fused elements of country, old-time string music, and the Blues to create another distinct genre that he termed 'bluegrass' in the late-1930s and early-1940s."[65] Monroe blended blues into the new style he was creating. "Like many forms of American music, bluegrass was an amalgamation of many styles of music, and it represented a unique blend of white and black cultures, as well as the relatively primitive Appalachian culture. Bluegrass was an instant hit because of this, as it had elements that could be related to by nearly everyone in the United States (whites and blacks alike)."[66] Bluegrass as a genre, therefore, exists in the present form (typically uncontested as an authentic musical expression of the southern United States)

---

62. Price, "Bluegrass Nation," 7.
63. Price, "Bluegrass Nation," 10.
64. Price, "Bluegrass Nation," 10.
65. Price, "Bluegrass Nation," 22.
66. Price, "Bluegrass Nation," 22.

precisely through a fusion of musical and instrumental elements brought together from multiple peoples—not all from the same continent or region—along various stages of its development.

Music bands often develop their own styles and, as in Brazil, often become emblematic of a new genre, or at least promote some genre's wider acceptance. In Australia, the Black Image Band is one such example. When it was organized in 1997, it consisted of five brothers who had grown up playing in their father's band. The family, of Gugu Yimithirr and Kuku Yalangi roots (Queensland aboriginal peoples), had listened to a variety of genres but favored the Australian Country. They have experimented with several genres in their performances, but also perform "their own original material."[67] They identify themselves as an "indigenous Rock band."[68] Black Image combines traditional aboriginal instruments with modern electric guitars and country and rock popular styles.[69] Whether their style has the breadth and ethnic identification to be called a genre in its own right would be the topic for another research. But they illustrate the freedom used around the world, particularly among musicians, to incorporate elements of their aural world into a single fused performance or to a group of compositions.

Another example of blended musical elements is found in the little-known Jewish-Jazz connection in New Orleans, Louisiana. Although the Jewish contribution to both European and American music (popular and classical) is generally acknowledged, one may find it "hard to imagine a serious Jewish influence on a music scene that's traditionally and predominantly African American."[70] Allison Good, however, notes that a "handful of Jewish entrepreneurs are reinventing the jazz scene in New Orleans, a city with a tiny and aging Jewish population but a strong musical tradition in which different cultures have long mixed."[71] The blend displays scale and patterns typically understood as pertaining to the European Jewish cultural musical world of the last couple of centuries as well as the commonly heard jazz sounds and rhythms.[72]

---

67. Black Image Band, "History," para. 1.
68. See https://www.abc.net.au/triplejunearthed/artist/black-image.
69. See https://www.abc.net.au/triplejunearthed/artist/black-image.
70. Good, "Jazz Messengers," para. 1.
71. Good, "Jazz Messengers," deck.
72. Echoes of a Friend, "Rebirth Brass Band - Why Your Feet Hurt," 1:30–2:30.

4.3 ACTIONS LEADING TOWARDS FUSION

Contemporary Xerente Christian music, although rising from a fusion of earlier and recently adopted elements from non-static genres, appears to be consistently identified as "of the culture" when described by the local population. The music does not entirely fit the molds of generally accepted classifications of either traditional or popular Brazilian genres. Yet, it appears to be accepted as a proper member of Xerente culture. It is performed in a community in which individuals (musicians and participant audience) choose to communicate Christian messages through genres that have roots from within and outside of Xerente traditional culture. The question of whether this blend has consolidated to the point that its guardians will defend the present form cannot be answered definitively. Intuition, ingenuity, and imagination, however, have simply led a good number of Xerente musicians along the same path of genre development that has characterized most musical creativity on Brazilian soil and around the world.

The move towards the present-day fusion of musical elements incorporates various actions or responses, exercised in different measures, that took place along the years and promoted the rise of new genres. Swee Hong Lim categorizes the "styling" of music through cross-cultural interaction in this fashion: the "Adopted Song," the "Adapted Song," and the "Actualized Song." The Xerente "Adopted Song," under this classification refers to the multiple Western hymns which have been incorporated into the musical world of the growing local churches by means of language translation. "Adapted Song" is applicable to the few traditional melodies which the musicians participating in the 2017 workshop in Cabeceira Verde transformed into Christian songs. These were recorded at the time accompanied only by the *zâ* but have since been frequently performed with instrumental accompaniment (guitar and keyboard) with preset rhythms.[73] One could potentially describe this adapted song as one of the new genres sprouting among the Xerente Christians. Lim's "Actualized Song" describes in part the fusion genre on which I focused in this research. This type of song "draws on the local culture for inspiration and

---

73. This information was obtained from the Bible translator and missionary Werner Seitz with whom I was able to spend valuable research time during the month of June 2019. I was also privileged to observe it during a night service in Cabeceira Verde on June 14, 2019.

idiomatic expressions," but, unlike Lim's description, *not* "at the expense of overt Western nuances."[74]

Although Lim's classifications are applicable and valuable, it is also possible to follow the process by reviewing the actions or events (in contrast to Lim's categorization of the product: the "song") that move towards the rise of new genres. The interaction of Western hymns with the Xerente community and the developing churches evoked a series of responses from the local population. The missionaries, who were deeply appreciated by the community for their effort to assist them in their health and social needs, presented to them the music of their culture and of their heart—the evangelical hymns. Those who received the message *adopted* these hymns into their sphere of aural experience as a testimony and affirmation of the faith they were receiving. One could say that the continual practice of performing and listening to these hymns caused the effect of *naturalization* of the forms and the following generations grew up hearing them as a part of their aural world. As the hymns were used in a church setting, a process of *adaptation* also took place. The vocal style used for their performance, although guided by the missionaries' practices and recordings of the hymns available at the time, underwent deviations that reflected singing and linguistic techniques native to the *Akwẽ*. The changes became *incorporated* into the regular singing styles leading to a *unification* with the original form.

The musical fusion present in the local Xerente churches reflects the presence of a variety of practices similar to hymn-singing practices. However, these are not necessarily unidirectional steps of change. At the present time, there are those who have *adopted* a style such as *forró* for the instrumental accompaniment but have *adapted* it to the listening preferences of the Xerente church. The vocal style of *forró* popular songs, which often deal with topics such as sensuality and drinking alcohol, from a national perception, displays a certain tone of aggression and arrogant affirmation of practices understood by local believers to be contrary to the Christian faith. The adaptation to a milder singing style, while possibly a natural reflection of Xerente traditional singing and linguistic features, could also be an intuitive response to the perception that the style of singing should reflect a responsible and humble attitude towards God and behavior that would be agreeable to the Christian faith. A similar adaptation occurred in the musical development of the Makuxi,

---

74. Lim, "Forming Christians through Musicking in China," 6.

who maintained only "the accordeon timbre, frequently emulated by the electronic keyboard, and the syncopated rhythm of compositions characteristic of variants of *xote* and *baião*."[75]

From traditional song, as the chapter describing the fusion genre(s) described, an intuitive or intentional *adoption* of melodic structure for many (not all) of the new songs has taken place. The same can be said for the melodic structure and overall form of the song. *Adaptation* of traditional features can be found in the marriage of these melodies with the electronic and guitar instrumental accompaniment which practically every interviewee mentions as the current Xerente (Christian) preference. By all accounts, the Xerente *like* the more animated music.[76]

4.4 GENRES AND THE XERENTE CHRISTIAN IDENTITY

Xerente Christians as well as missionaries and professionals in the areas of education, social work, and health made no suggestion in any interview that the Xerente church has chosen their present-day musical genres specifically for the purpose of ethnic distinction. On the contrary, particularly those of non-Xerente upbringing may be the first to regard these genres as an unwarranted development given the Xerente desire for cultural affirmation. Notwithstanding, music in this context may have aided the creation of a Xerente Christian identity.

Kathrine Morehouse addresses the Mandinka church preference for Western hymns in her 2017 article "They're Playing Our Song." After a presumably successful music workshop emphasizing local artists and the creation of Mandinka songs in the local traditional musical language, the community insisted on "maintaining their repertoire of the same poorly translated, badly performed Western hymns in church."[77] Morehouse comments that, despite the frequent insistence on using Western hymnody by missionaries throughout missionary history, "local agency is often the primary factor in a community's decisions to continue using Western hymns or compose their own songs, and this is often decided in relation to how these songs *function* in navigating local (intracultural) and global

---

75. Fernandes, "Parixara ao Forró," 121.

76. In Portuguese, "*Eles gostam de música animada.*" *Animada* refers, similarly to the English word "animated," to something or someone that is lively and suggests movement.

77. Morehouse, "'They're Playing Our Song,'" 1.

(intercultural) identities."[78] Xerente churches, unlike the Mandinka, have not given a honorary primary place to Western hymns in their repertoire, but have also not rejected them. It is likely that each genre exercises different spiritual and liturgical functions, all of which are part of the aural identity of the Xerente church.

4.5 FUNCTIONS AND MEANINGS IN MUSICAL FUSION

The development of Xerente Christian music is only one of the patterns of change among Brazilian Indians. Until recent decades when media communications reached unprecedented speeds, a people's radio reception capabilities, differences of location and non-indigenous interest in the area had varied effects on local indigenous musical tastes and practices. Indeed, the long-standing hegemony of Western musicology in Brazilian national society, as in other political or financial colonies of European/North-American contexts around the world, threatened the very continuation of indigenous practices in Brazil until recent decades.[79] The processes of adoption, adaptation, incorporation, along with the creative imagination of local musicians have been intricately involved in the development of new meanings for individuals and the community as a whole.

Music can play various roles in any given society. These roles (or functions) could have been present in earlier periods of its history or have been newly created through new circumstances, environments, or tastes. The meanings associated with the music strongly affect the relationship between the music's performance and the function of the musical activity. In the case of the Xerente church, hymns and other adopted songs have indeed developed meanings and fulfill various functions in the Christian community along with the newly created songs in fusion genre(s).

Among the functions identified by Morehouse for the use of Western hymns in the Mandinka church (safeguard against syncretism, filling an artistic void, separation or distinction from the community, sameness or a "sonic territorial marker," stylistic diversity, having an adopted/unified/traditional canon),[80] some correspond to the continual use of the hymns among the Xerente also. The contemporary wave of new musical compositions among the Xerente, which have been slowly replacing any earlier

---

78. Morehouse, "'They're Playing Our Song,'" 13. Emphasis added.
79. Bertolini, "Performance Musical e Reconhecimento," 23.
80. Morehouse, "'They're Playing Our Song,'" 14–19.

"artistic void," may be filling the other functions mentioned above as well as others not mentioned by Morehouse. It could also reflect distinct functions found in the Xerente church that the Mandinka opposed, as well as a spectrum of individual meanings that present contradictory perceptions.

Todd Saurman's dissertation identifies the importance of "three essential intergenerational components" for the revitalization of a community's music: "community ownership of the process, transmission of music knowledge, and active use of music as communication."[81] Although the development of Xerente Christian music as a fusion alongside the Western songs displays distinct characteristics from a revivalist movement towards the traditional, his three ingredients above resonate with Morehouse's observations and the Xerente reality: 1) both by contemporary conviction of the missionaries and the Xerente Christians' express wish, the Xerente community has taken ownership of the process; 2) local musicians, through public performance and recordings, have transmitted the new songs as well as taught others how to perform them; and 3) the new songs are actively used as communication, along with many beloved Western hymns. These factors favor the proposition that the new fusion genres are performing vital functions in Xerente Christian lifestyles and have integrated meanings deemed central to the spiritual health of the church.

4.6 CHAPTER SUMMARY

This chapter reviewed the concept of genre in classical and popular settings worldwide. Genres in this discussion are categories of an art modality—in this case, music—that display certain standard characteristics which have been acknowledged by a segment of society, or multiple societies, as belonging to a single kind or genre. However, the consolidation of these artistic features into a genre result from a human perception of unity and do not necessarily imply an unchangeable character. On the contrary, music as well as other arts follow the cultural processes of change, being influenced by internal creativity or necessity, as well as by one or more external features inserted into the musical world of a particular community.

Genres, therefore, are demonstratively fluid in character. Music is often found in what some may deem as transitional forms. It is the perception of absolute stages of genres, however, that causes such stages to

---

81. Saurman, "Singing for Survival," 2.

be deemed as "intermediary." The combination of musical features along known musical history often demonstrates that borrowing, adapting, blending, and other innovative modifications are part and parcel of the creation of genres. Indeed, without these interactions, the set of characteristics that determine the genre's parameters would not exist.

Brazilian as well as other musical cultures testify to this evolving and ever-changing combination of musical elements. The Xerente have followed along similar paths of musical development. Their musical world came in contact with Christian music through the Western hymns primarily. These and other external genres were either adopted, adapted, or blended in some fashion and helped shape the newer creations by contemporary Xerente musicians. The contemporary collection of musical sounds heard in the church meetings have aided in the development of a local Christian identity. According to local testimonies, the songs play vital roles in the life of its members and in the communication of the Christian faith in the Xerente territory.

Finally, considering the dynamic character of musical genre development registered in documents and recordings, particularly in Brazil in the last 150 years, it is reasonable to conclude that the natural fluidity of musical genre development speaks against confining musical expressions to closed genre systems which, in turn, determine their validity, genuineness, or authenticity. On this basis, the following chapters will give attention to the evidence of an authentic value of Xerente fusion genres based on their meanings and functions within the community, as well as on the competence and the exercise of local agency (control) applied to their creations and practices as attested by the Xerente Christian community, particularly those involved in leadership and in the process of musical composition and performance.

5

Musical Meaning Development in Christian Genres

5.1 MUSICAL SEMIOTICS AND MEANING DEVELOPMENT

5.1.1 The Place of Semiotics in Genre-Meaning Studies

IN VIEW OF THE vastness of the subject of semiotics, which the Finnish semiotician Eero Tarasti describes metaphorically as a "conceptual jungle,"[1] its application to Christian music may seem controversial or unnecessary. However, I address this topic in this book in confidence that the benefits of semiotics greatly outweigh its difficulty. The reward is a clearer comprehension of the process of meaning creation, and a subsequent graceful understanding for the value and views of those whose cultures differ from one's own in a variety of ways.

The thesis of this book challenges not only to the perceived closed character of musical genres, but also the assumption that musical enactments, styles, and genre categories are universal in their meanings and functions. Absolutist views of music's meaning have often been responsible for the imposition of foreign styles in cross-cultural exchanges around the world. Few voices in recent times (perhaps throughout history) have attempted to make sense of the evidence against this universality

---

1. Tarasti, *Theory of Musical Semiotics*, xiii.

of meaning in music. Early-twentieth-century author Vernon Lee, for instance, sought an answer for the variety of "emotional and imaginative" responses to music in psychology.[2] The idea of a single meaning for a piece or for musical genres regardless of the listener/participant's input, however, has persisted to this day through popular as well as educational channels and continues to challenge the varied reality. I believe that a deeper understanding that musics and their elements have a potential for limitless connotations can lead to a positive, culturally appropriate development of musical practices, including those of Christian communities, at national, communal, and denominational levels.

5.1.2 Foundational Ideas and Their Founders[3]

The field of *semiotics* has focused primarily on *language* as a sign system along its history. Its modern development can be traced to the work of Swiss linguist Ferdinand de Saussure[4] and of the American philosopher Charles Sanders Peirce.[5] *Music(al) semiotics* has been built upon the foundation laid by earlier linguists and semioticians along the course of the twentieth century unto the present time and incorporated research from the fields of ethnomusicology, psychology, and the social sciences.[6]

The semiotician Phillip Tagg states that "music is a matter of interhuman *communication*,"[7] a sign system that can deliver "meaning," whether it is intentionally designed by the composer to carry specific and invariable messages, moods, or feelings to individuals across national, community, and generational boundaries, or whether the information (perceived as a message) is a "value added" to musical material. Semiotics wrestles with the issue that the meanings perceived by music participant—a spectrum going from music composers with its performers to those who listen to it intently or hear it inadvertently—can differ

---

2. Lee, *Music and Its Lovers*, loc. 128.

3. A more in-depth discussion of musical semiotics as applicable to the development of meaning in music, Christian or otherwise, can be found in my article "Musical Symbol and Meaning: A Semiotic Approach to a Diverse Christian Musical Perception." On file, accessible upon request from elelportugal@gmail.com. The handout summary of this article is found in Appendix D.

4. Joseph, "Ferdinand de Saussure."

5. Atkin, "Peirce's Theory of Signs."

6. Tagg, *Music's Meanings*, 4; Salgar. "Musical Semiotics as a Tool," 2–7.

7. Tagg, *Music's Meanings*, 12.

immensely. Part of the reason for this reality is the presence of multiple layers of musical features contained in a given piece of music (such as tempi, harmony, timbre, etc.), any of which, as well as any combination of elements, can simultaneously direct the listener to a number of memories and meanings. Semiotician Thomas Turino explains: "Music has a great multiplicity of potentially meaningful parameters sounding simultaneously, and its status as a potential collective activity helps explain its particular power to create affect and group identities."[8] The observable diversity of—often contrasting—meanings suggest that musical fragments, interpretive elements, specific songs or pieces, or musical genres *do not* possess inherent meanings that are equally comprehensible by all humankind. Leonard Meyer, in his influential book *Emotion and Meaning in Music* (1956), identified "universalism," "the belief that the responses obtained by [musical] experiment or otherwise are universal, natural, and necessary," as an error.[9]

Presumably, certain universal features exist, such as the presence of a rhythmic structure, a commonality of major seconds in melodies, a tendency toward melodic descent at the end, to name a few.[10] Ethnomusicologists such as Bruno Nettl held to this view. Nevertheless, the existence of these similarities does not warrant a belief in a universal "meaning" for each of them. Philip Tagg, Laura-Lee Balkwill, and William Thompson suggest that features such as fast tempo, long notes, loud or soft volume, timbre, pitch range, and repetition could indicate the existence of "bioacoustic" universals.[11] Balkwill and Thompson's study, however, fails to demonstrate a universal character to such bioacoustic features for two reasons: their evaluation observes the responses of only two cultures, and the "ratings" (percentages) provided by the results only demonstrate that a majority of participants had "the same" emotional perception as the opposing culture does. Tagg, who terms these potential universals as "bioacoustics" in contrast to Balkwill and Thompson's "psychophysical," notes that their research indicates only a partial correspondence of emotional significance between two among thousands of people groups around the world.

8. Turino, "Signs of Imagination," 249.
9. Meyer, *Emotion and Meaning in Music*, locs. 179–80.
10. Nettl, *Study of Ethnomusicology*, 68.
11. Tagg, *Music's Meanings*, 15. Also see Balkwill and Thompson, "Cross-Cultural Investigation."

5.1.3 Charles Peirce's Trichotomies

American philosopher Charles Peirce's semiotic concepts have played vital roles in the research of numerous musical semioticians and authors around the world. Peirce systematized his ideas about the process of creating and understanding meaning (*semiosis*) by the elaboration of multiple trichotomies (or triads). Two of his most important trichotomies provide the basis of the approach used in this chapter to aid the comprehension of meaning development.

The first and central trichotomy of elements identified by Peirce involves the *sign* (also termed *representamen* in his notes), the *object*, and the *interpretant*.[12] Figure 12 shows a sketch of the relationship among these elements. For the purpose of this discussion, however, I have chosen to illustrate this trichotomy with a continuous line representing a "semiotic" movement from left to right: Object → Sign → Interpretant. The *sign* is the linguistic, pictorial, sonic, or other type of form that presents the object being signed, whether it is material or not. The *object* is that to which the sign refers, and the *interpretant* is the "sense made of the sign,"[13] which can also be described as the "perception" of meaning. This trichonomy places the stages of communication in a system demonstrating the trajectory of communication carried, in this case, through a musical medium. A composer may *intend* to communicate some particular idea, mood, or emotion (the "object") to an audience. For this purpose, he or she chooses a musical language, possibly with multiple layers, and creates a piece of music (the *sign*). The performance of this piece provides an opportunity through which "every individual 'negotiates' musical meaning in a different manner,"[14] aided by culturally induced cues and naturally imbedded perception skills.

---

12. Tagg, *Music's Meanings*, 102.

13. For a more thorough description of Saussure's Structuralism see Chandler, *Semiotics for Beginners*, "Signs," para. 38.

14. Salgar, "Musical Semiotics as a Tool," 3.

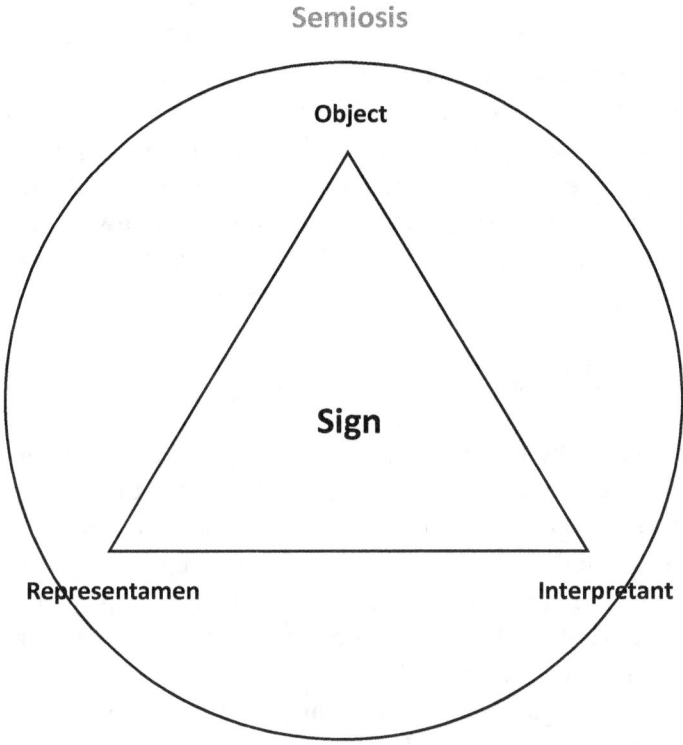

12—Peirce Trichotomy 1—Semiosis

Peirce's second trichotomy relevant to this analysis classifies the various types of signs: the *icon*, the *index*, and the *symbol*. *Icons* are "signs bearing physical resemblance to what they stand for."[15] This type of sign is more common in the visual realm, but certain musical elements can also resemble naturally produced sound and serve as *icons*. *Indices* are "signs connected [to the object] either by causality, or by spatial, temporal or cultural proximity, to what they stand for."[16] Tagg believes that "this sign type . . . is particularly important in music semiotics to the extent that all musical sign types can be considered as at least partially indexical."[17] Music can serve as an *index* through references containing partly iconic sounds (the effect of "sounding like" something recognizable) but it can

---

15. Tagg, *Music's Meanings*, 107.
16. Tagg, *Music's Meanings*, 108.
17. Tagg, *Music's Meanings*, 108.

also carry a connotation of a broader concept than the thing it sounds like. Peirce's *symbol* in this trichotomy, also called *arbitrary sign*, is applied to a specific category of signs and should not be confused with the colloquial and generic use of the term "symbol" or the process of "symbolizing." "A *sign* can be called *arbitrary* when its semiosis exhibits no discernible elements of structural similarity (*icons*), or of proximity or causality (*indices*), between sign and object/interpretant."[18] Music used as *symbol* is the *arbitrary sign* carrying an association between the object and sign which has arisen by "convention" or a conjunction of events. It does not depend on any clear resemblance to the object.

5.1.4 The Process of Meaning Development

In order to clarify the significance of the 2 Peircian trichotomies described above, some analogies and explanations may be helpful. The first trichotomy—Object → Sign → Interpretant—helps us understand that the interpretant (or the perceived meaning of a given sign) results from a trajectory involving various factors that can affect the interpretation of the sign, and can potentially move it away from the object, as well as amplify or diminish the content of the "object."

A linguistic example can help shed light on this trajectory and its resulting possibilities. Words in any language serve as signs for concepts which the speaker or writer wishes to communicate. Both the word *Wand* in modern German and *pared* in Spanish both mean *wall* in English. In each of the languages, a series of letters (likewise *signs* representing the spoken sounds) is combined to communicate a concept. As the German speaker hears or reads the word (the linguistic *sign*) *Wand*, an image or the concept of *wall* normally comes to mind (*meaning* or *interpretant*). Yet for each person, specific interpretations differ from those of others. One may envision a beautiful portion of one's house with attractive decorations. Another may imagine a falling wall. The wall could be conceived in all sorts of colors, shapes, and sizes. Furthermore, it may elicit memories that are specific to that person, carrying meaningful memories, both pleasant and disagreeable to the listener or reader. Even additional descriptive words (i.e., adjectives) could fail to carry the exact image of the wall the speaker or writer intended to describe.

---

18. Tagg, *Music's Meanings*, 109. Emphases added.

As in most *symbol* type of signs, words are a result of a long linguistic development which brought them into association with the objects they symbolize. There is nothing in the form of the letters, or the sounds they represent, that have any particular resemblance (iconicity) to the idea of *wall*. *Wand, pared,* or *wall* mean *wall* (the initial idea or "object") because they are associated to the concept by convention or by sociolinguistic processes, not because the group of letters or the sounds they represent actually "resemble" a wall. They also do not "indicate" a wall, neither by the forms of the letters, nor by the number of letters, nor by the sounds of a wall. This illustration also alerts us to the danger of reading an English meaning onto the sign form *Wand* in German, seeing that a *wand* in English is a very distinct object from the *wall* represented by the German word. Hence, the *interpretant* of any given sign can present a wide spectrum of possibilities that make it unlikely that a *sign* always signifies only one thing to the person who interprets it.

Applying Peirce's trichotomy of sign types to the world of music, one can say that its signs are not commonly of the iconic type. The generally unspecific character of musical signs (sounds or music) can indeed become associated with ideas through convention, but, like words, do not necessarily truly "sound like" the meaning the composer may have intended to communicate. There are indexical possibilities to musical signs. However, music can also be unclear as an *index* and often unable to give such "indication" if the listener (the actual interpreter of the musical sign) has not had any previous information about the sound of the *object* being signed by the music. If the sounds of a bird, for instance, were integrated into a musical piece played by a flute, its interpretation as *bird song* would only be possible if the listener had had previous knowledge of bird sounds. Given that it is unlikely that a hearing person anywhere in the world would not have heard a bird sing, one could assume that such flute sounds are iconic of birds or indexical of a nature scene in which birds would be heard. Nevertheless, the fact remains that previous knowledge is necessary for its recognition as bird song.

The musical iconicity described above, however, is actually atypical of most music heard in our societies. Indeed, with a few exceptions,[19] most music does not attempt to imitate either natural or artificial sounds of the society's aural world. Melodic lines, while possibly indexical of movement up, down, or straightforward, are not specific enough to

---

19. See Feld, *Sound and Sentiment*; see also Levin, *Where Rivers and Mountains Sing*.

describe a clear concept or physical object. Other musical elements are also weak in their capacity to reproduce everyday sounds. In the absence of direct iconic or indexical elements to communicate a message through music, songs and pieces serve as *symbols* or *arbitrary signs*. A genre, a style, an instrumentation, a piece of music, a riff, as well as multiple combinations of these elements and features develop meaning not because of their inherent resemblance to recognizable sounds, but by the association of events in one's personal life or culture which connect existing sonic works either temporarily or permanently with a given idea. A piece of romantic music heard by a married couple during an important date at an expensive restaurant, may *symbolize* their deep love for one another and a myriad of other memories associated with this love. The piece could or not have been composed for this purpose, but it can become associated with their love and have *come to mean* "love" for this couple. In the unfortunate event that the couple comes into an irreparable conflict and a contentious divorce, it is likely that the same piece of music would become connected to feelings of sadness, anger, and perhaps even hate in the perception of those individuals.

As this research attempts to demonstrate, the Xerente Christian community and their evangelical missionaries have varied perceptions of meaning connected to musical genres and specific songs. Musical features that are often associated with certain values in one generation or community subset may host contrasting and dissonant meaning to another generation or community subset. The interviews and interactions within the Xerente Christian community related later in this chapter showcase both similarities and contrasts in meaning, demonstrating that genre meaning is not absolute for all its practitioners and listeners, but develop meaning in the individual and the community at large (the *interpretants*) through the circumstances that surround it by association or convention (the *symbol*).

Despite the imprecise manner through which nonverbal sound communicates an idea or message, general concepts within the same community or society do tend to be more uniformly understood by its members. As will be noted at a later instance, there is a general consensus of significance among both Xerente fusion music composers, performers, and listeners in the community as to its general meanings and functions. This common bond, therefore, indicates the possibility that these contemporary genres are indeed speaking an authentic musical language of the community.

5.1.5 Emotion and Meaning

Texts on musical semiotics tend to intertwine the ideas of music's *meaning* and its power to evoke *emotions*. Since emotion is a common, verbally acknowledged response to music among the Xerente, this subject needs to receive concentrated attention.

The relationship between the affective (*emotional*) response to the musical stimuli and the creation of meaning is complex and even the most knowledgeable scholars have not yet completely understood it from a psychological perspective. Leonard Meyer, for instance, in his theory of the psychological effect of music addressed both topics in conjunction:

> From Plato down to the most recent discussions of aesthetics and the *meaning of music*, philosophers and critics have, with few exceptions, affirmed their belief in *the ability of music to evoke emotional responses in listeners*. Most of the treatises on musical composition and performance stress the importance of the communication of feeling and emotion. Composers have demonstrated in their writings and by the expression marks used in their musical scores their faith in the *affective power of music*. And finally, listeners, past and present, have reported with remarkable consistency that music does arouse feelings and emotions in them.[20]

Experts in the area of human response to musical stimuli do not present a unified authoritative model describing the perception of meaning and its relationship to emotion. Questions remain open as to whether the response to musical stimuli begins with emotion or with a cognitive idea related to meaning. It is also not established to what extent internal musical features as well as personal and cultural experience play a part in this development. In terms of Peircean semiotics one could say that the balance between the contribution of iconic or indexical musical features and that of the individual's previous experiences vary according to each situation.

David Huron, who has been studying listeners' response to music throughout his career, offered relational models[21] in his course on music and emotion to illustrate his belief that sonic stimuli evoke emotion first in human beings. Emotional response and cognitive perception of meaning (the "appraisal" of the slow and fast brains), according to Huron, frequently precede affectivity reflected in the visceral (intuitive and

---

20. Meyer, *Emotion and Meaning in Music*, locs. 181–85. Emphasis added.
21. Huron, "Models of Emotion." See also Huron, *Sweet Anticipation*.

potentially emotionally-driven reactions) and facial responses to the sensation of sound. Although his course materials are no longer accessible through the link used for this reference, his 2006 publication *Sweet Anticipation*[22] provides one of the most recent studies on music's potential for arousing emotions.

The work of twenty-first-century Swedish psychologists Patrik Juslin and Daniel Västfjäall identified six distinct brain mechanisms involved in emotional response to music:

1. Brain stem reflex—a response reflecting a perception of urgency.

2. Evaluative conditioning—prompted by earlier pairing of the musical stimulus to either positive or negative experiences.

3. Emotional contagion—whereby the listener perceives emotional content and "mimics" it internally, this, in turn, leading to personal emotion.

4. Visual imagery—when the listener creates mental pictures which interact with the musical stimulus.

5. Episodic memory—when the music evokes a memory from the listener's life due, presumably, to a musical instantiation simultaneous with an event.

6. Musical expectancy—when a musical feature violates, delays, or confirms how the listener expects the music to continue.[23]

There is a correlation between the six mechanisms above and Peircean sign types demonstrating the creation of meaning. "Evaluative conditioning" (2), the pairing of earlier experiences from the past with the musical stimulus, closely describes what occurs through a *symbol*-type of Peircean sign. Memories of emotionally charged events can be evoked through an earlier synchronous instantiation of the genre, piece, song, or musical fragment. An "emotional contagion" (3) may also take place if the listener "perceives the emotional expression of the music,"[24] internalizes it through mimicry, and adopts the emotion. This perception of emotion, however, would presumably require a certain cognitive

---

22. Huron, *Sweet Anticipation*.

23. Juslin and Västfjäall, "Emotional Responses to Music." More in-depth discussion on the topic of music and meaning can be found in my article "Musical Symbol and Meaning." A condensed version in handout form can be found in Appendix D.

24. Juslin and Västfjäall, "Emotional Responses to Music," 570.

familiarity with musical features of a musical language, as well as stylistic tools, which could be intentionally utilized to elicit emotion. Thus, a certain level of inculturation is necessary for this process to take place. Sonic stimulus leading to this kind of brain mechanism would serve as an *index* sign type and could be responsible for stirring the emotions of an individual, who would, in turn, formulate meaning.

The Peircean *symbol*, which this study suggests is the most common type of sign that music can provide, relates closely to the fifth of the above brain mechanisms: the "episodic memory." This mechanism, which Juslin and Västfjäall describe in distinct form from "evaluative conditioning" (possibly due to a rather immediate assessment as positive or negative), has been regarded by some music theorists as less "musically relevant."[25] The authors, however, state that recent evidence suggests that *it could be one of the most frequent and subjectively important sources of emotion in music* (see Juslin et al., in press; Sloboda & O'Neill 2001)."[26] "Episodic memory" could be the most common mechanism responsible for the development of 'meaning' in an individual or community. It provides support for a reasonable explanation for the wide range of perceived meanings attached to the same musical stimulus.

5.1.6 Collective Meaning

According to Charles Kraft, some of the functions of a culture's worldview are the "patterning of interpreting and evaluating," and that these patterns are related to the "assignment of meaning." Kraft insists "that meaning is assigned by people. Meaning is not inherent in the vehicles we use to convey it."[27] As mentioned earlier in this study, Turino discusses music's potential as a "collective activity" and it possesses "power to create affect and group identities."[28] Xerente church genres also present a number of simultaneous musical layers and characteristics. Combined, they have attained a regular place in Christian circles whether in church gatherings or in private settings. As interviews have helped to detect, the

---

25. Turino and Tagg doubt the strong frequency of the *symbol* type of sign in music. I propose that it is actually the most common type of sign for the reasons delineated in this section of the chapter.

26. Juslin and Västfjäall, "Emotional Responses to Music," 573. Emphasis added.

27. Kraft, *Anthropology for Christian Witness*, 60. Reference for all quotes in this paragraph.

28. Turino, "Signs of Imagination," 249.

music identified with contemporary evangelical Christianity in the Xerente territory displays characteristics of identity markers of the collective body of Christian practice within the culture. As it happens with the development of individual meaning for the genres and particular songs, the performance of contemporary Xerente Christian music also develops corporate meaning, highlighting spiritual and emotional responses as well as a local Christian identity.

5.2 PERCEIVED MEANINGS AMONG LOCAL CHRISTIANS—AN ETHNOGRAPHIC REPORT[29]

5.2.1 Testimonies of Pastors

The overwhelming majority of Xerente evangelicals are connected with congregations established by the Baptist missionaries on which this research has been focused. Among the Xerente, denominational lines are porous, and Christians associated with the Foursquare Church (*Quadrangular*) and Assemblies of God regularly interact with each other. Indeed, this could be said of most evangelical movements among indigenous peoples in this generation.[30] Besides these denominations, there are pockets of influence among the Xerente from the Seventh Day Adventist Church and the *Congregação Cristã* (Christian Congregation), an originally Brazilian denomination. These latter two groups hold to views and practices that conflict with the other three and do not typically participate in events led by the others.[31]

As of 2019, among the congregations established by members of the Baptist denomination, three pastors had been ordained to Christian ministry. Two other Xerente leaders were being prepared for meeting

---

29. Information of perceptions of meaning and emotion in Xerente music included in the remaining portion of this chapter derives from my personal interviews and conversations with members of the community. In the absence of formal written or oral records that support this evidence, such as the case with these interviews, I provide my own testimony of the evidence that I obtained through participant observation and interviews to support the validity of this information.

30. Conselho Nacional de Pastores e Líderes Evangélicos Indígenas (CONPLEI), http://www.conplei.org.br/. CONPLEI communicates with the various indigenous ethnic peoples of Brazil and other supportive audience primarily through media such as WhatsApp and Facebook.

31. This information is based on various explanations of the church situation in the territory provided to me by the missionaries Pr. Rinaldo, Pr. Mário, and Pr. Werner who are daily involved in these matters.

with a council of pastors in preparation for ordination in late 2019. I have met and discussed music matters with all three ordained Xerente pastors and interacted and interviewed two of them at length. These pastors have been Christians for many years and have a diachronic understanding of the establishment of evangelical Christianity within the Xerente territory since the late 1980s.

In January of 2017, during my first visit to the Xerente work, I met Pr. Sinval Waĩkazate who leads a small Xerente-language church in the city of Tocantínia, on the outskirts of the actual Xerente territory. Although this meeting was brief, and my acquaintance with the Xerente genres was minimal at the time, he offered his observation of the church styles highlighting the presence of varied preferences of music among the Christians. There were those who had come to faith in the early years of the mission and had become very attached to Western hymns. Likewise, there are those who have come into the church since the turn of the twenty-first century who express strong preference for genres similar to the Brazilian northeastern genres. Concerning the revival of traditional styles for church music, Pr. Sinval thought, at least at that time, that it could have the potential of unifying church people since they are all generally appreciative of traditional Xerente music.

In June 2019 I interviewed both Pr. Pedro Waĩkainẽ, who leads the church and works as the schoolmaster in the village of Porteira, and Pr. Silvino Sirnãwẽ, the pastor of the church in the village of Salto and also a teacher at a more distant school. Both men have been church members for about three decades and have a good testimony of service in their respective communities. On June 14, Pedro met with me at the house of one of the missionaries to give his perception of the development of Christian music among the Xerente as well as the existing issues and hopes he has for the future.

In the early years of the Xerente church it was difficult for them to create in their styles. Pedro attributes the acceleration in the practice of composing new Xerente songs to the Quartet CD (2012)[32] composed of musicians from the villages of Salto and Porteira.[33] Although he does not

32. The Quartet CD, mentioned here a few times, was produced by local Xerente Christians. The four men who headed the project were not a 'quartet' in the literal musical sense. They sang mostly as soloists. This production included Christian music in northeastern styles which these men deemed appropriate and attractive to the local Christians and potentially communicative to the Xerente community at large.

33. The two villages have close interaction with one another since they are only about 7 km apart from each other. See Figure 13.

play any instrument or sings as a performer, Pedro is fond of (*gosta de*) the new songs others have composed, particularly with the use of musical instruments (referring to the guitar and the keyboard). His preferred songs are the new compositions recorded by Lázaro in 2017 (see chapter 4) and the hymns translated by Almir from the village of Brejo Comprido. The people, he believes, not only like but connect deeply with God through music and view the musical practices of the contemporary Xerente church as essential to their meetings. He expects that the upcoming project of incorporating the new songs into a new hymnbook will greatly help in the participation of the congregation in corporate singing, since the lyrics of the new songs are still unfamiliar to most church members.

Pedro expressed his concern about some of the musicians who participate in the Vigils (addressed later in this chapter). While these events provide opportunity for ample participation for musicians and speakers (evangelists) to share a message through their particular medium, they have also allowed musicians who are not regularly participating in a local evangelical congregation to perform for those who attend. The desire of musicians to share their music through these venues are a testament to the attractive power of music in the Xerente consciousness, but the lack of participation in regular church services also reflects a misunderstanding on the part of some concerning the importance of musical ministry and a consistent Christian testimony.

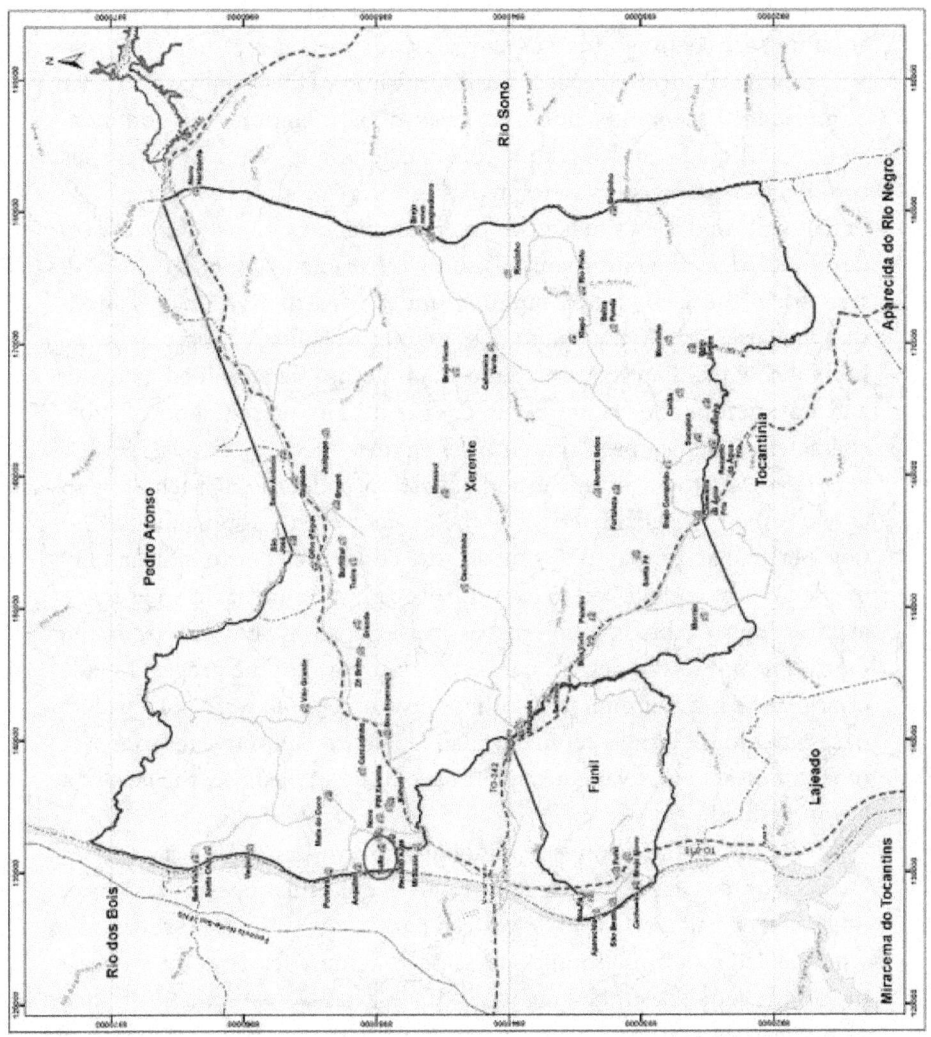

13—Xerente Territory and Population (2 parts: T. I. Xerente and T. I. Funil)[34]

Pastor Silvino leads the church in Salto. This village had been the seat of the Xerente Quartet to which Pedro referred. Silvino also sang several of the songs in that recording. His perspective includes his experiences as a singer and as the pastor of a people who respond to the music on a regular basis. Besides my first meeting with him in January of 2017, I

34. Layanna Giordana Bernardo Lima, "Os Akwẽ-Xerente no Tocantins, território indígena e as questões socioambientais" (The Akwẽ-Xerente in [the State of] Tocantins: Indigenous Territory and the Social-Environmental Questions) (São Paulo: Universidade de São Paulo, 2017), 175.

had an opportunity to hear his thoughts on Xerente music under various circumstances between June 18 and 20 of 2019.

Silvino confirmed most of the impressions of the essential character of music in the Xerente church that Pedro had mentioned. A comment from Pr. Rinaldo and Silvino's conversations and some spontaneous comments as the leaders were preparing for a Wednesday night service in Salto allowed me to make two interesting observations. On Wednesday, June 20, as the pastor and his son were placing "*o som*" (the sound system) in the new church building under construction, they realized that the large amplifying sound box was not working. That evening, the keyboard which had its own speakers, could not be amplified as usual, and no microphones could be used. A children's presentation of Bible characters had been prepared for a *desfile* (des-'fee-leh, "parade") for the congregation. It was a competition of costumes identifying each of them as a specific Bible character. Since the *desfile* would presumably need to take place unaccompanied by music, the children's coordinator had expressed doubt and wished to cancel it at the last moment. In spite of the awkwardness of this situation just as the service was about to begin, the pastor's response and determination to continue with the program made clear that he himself understood that music and *o som* were not absolute necessities for holding a service as planned, but the intuitive responses of others indicated this vacuum might have been an obstacle; the lack of a key ingredient.

The use of the Xerente traditional rattle *zâ* in church services has been a contentious issue as reported to me by missionaries and local musicians, particularly in this western part of the Xerente territory. Silvino participates in the traditional (non-religious) feasts of the Xerente in various capacities including as a rattle player. Nevertheless, he is one of the leaders who is most uncomfortable with the idea of using it in the church service as an accompaniment to Christian music. His position possibly reflects a personal consciousness of the instrument as of shamanic property. This attitude towards the *zâ* differentiates the villages in the area around Salto from those around Cabeceira Verde (some 60 km of difficult dirt road driving to the east) at least as perceived by the missionaries and musicians interviewed. In contrast to Salto's present stance, in Cabeceira Verde during the 2017 workshop the participants held a dedication service (a short prayer meeting) in which all who were present took part, clearly acknowledging the propriety of the use of the traditional rattle for the glory of God, understanding that it was not the "property" of the shamans any longer.

Both Pedro and Silvino affirm that music in Xerente churches connect with people in meaningful ways. They expressed it mostly in simple sentences such as *"eu gosto"* ("I like them") or *"eles gostam"* ("they like them") without feeling compelled to elaborate on these statements to emphasize the point. Yet, it appears that different groupings of Christian songs have distinct levels of appeal to church members and the community at large. As Sinval had identified for me in 2017, the distinct appeal of the different styles of songs are likely often linked to the music that was in use in Christian circles at the time of their conversion. This connection of the music style with the moment or time of decision suggests the conclusion that genres have become *symbols* of more than the immediate textual message among Xerente Christians.

5.2.2 Musicians, Meaning, and Emotions

Tiago Wakuke was one of the first young men who learned to play the guitar and the electronic keyboard among the Xerente, as explained in chapter 3. He continues to live in the village of Porteira where I interviewed him on June 12, 2019. He is now one of the teachers at the primary school as well as the *cacique* (village chief). His mother, Dinalva, is a Brazilian (non-Xerente) from the former State of Goiás who had come to the Xerente decades ago and married a Xerente man. Tiago is one of three grown sons. He is married and has five children.

Tiago's early involvement in music served as something of a model for other prospective music practitioners in Xerente communities. He was raised in a Christian home and has been a church member since his early teen years. Although he received a small amount of music theory instruction, Tiago continued to play mostly by ear and is reportedly very discerning of chord structures and their appropriate placing in songs. Around 2009–10, as he stated, there was a "revolution" in music production among Xerente church musicians. He believes he and others were "freed up" by composing their own songs. Up to that time, most of the songs at church had been translated from Portuguese and not many had been written—words or music—by the Xerente. They were bound to the older songs they had been singing for a long time. "We expected it only from the missionaries,"[35] he said.

Tiago is articulate in Portuguese and was able to provide the details of musical characteristics as well as his analysis of people's responses, wishes, and needs within the Xerente Christian communities. He said he listens to various Christian music genres including *forró*, *samba*, and *pagode*. Although few contemporary Brazilian genres would surpass these as controversial for use in Christian contexts, Tiago affirms that he "senses" the Spirit of God in these songs, too. Yet, he believes the Xerente really "like" (*eles gostam*) *forró* best of all. He described the Quartet CD, of which he had been an integral part, as mostly in *forró* style. He does not believe that slower songs, such as the popular MPB[36] multifaceted genres, are attractive to the Xerente. Although more "conservative" Christians may question the use of *forró* stylization for their music, he feels the *ambiente* (environment) in which they live makes this choice important.

On the other hand, he believes that the (fusion) genres as described in chapter 4 are quite different from secular *forró* due to the inflection and linguistic habits of the *Akwẽ* language itself. The primary connection to secular *forró*, in his perception, is the use of its rhythm and instrumental foundation. The singing itself has more to do with the linguistic features of their language. It is, in his mind, a fusion of elements.

At this stage of interaction with the outside culture and its musical styles, Tiago believes it would be difficult to change the direction of their church music. Regional music continues to influence the tastes of those both within and without the church. Conversely, he recognizes the dynamic character of both culture and music, and that their culture is not monolithic. Different people listen to different styles of music. Likewise, there is room for some slower music during times like the Lord's Supper for which he would not compose a song with a fast tempo. The varied spectrum of musical preference and meaning in the relatively small population of Xerente that Tiago identified is not uncommon.

---

35. Interview with Wakuke in the village of Porteira, June 12, 2019.

36. MPB stands for "Música Popular Brasileira" (Popular Brazilian Music). In spite of the apparent bland meaning of this phrase, it is the standard term identifying an eclectic grouping of Brazilian styles (a "musical rainbow" as described in Brazilian Sound, frequently ballad-like, used throughout Brazil). The term arose as a reaction to the large number of foreign genres that were penetrating Brazil's media in the sixties and seventies and promoted the advancement of national musical creativity and more widespread use of Brazilian genres. McGowan and Pessanha. *Brazilian Sound*, locs. 2228–3230.

Unlike sociology, which, according to Canclini attempts to "homogenize" society,[37] anthropological studies demonstrate that this breadth of variation can be found even within small communities.

From a semiotic point of view, Tiago's observations demonstrate that traditional hymns that had an endearing character for the missionaries and early converts, are "too slow" or not "very animated" for the following generations who grew up on a musical diet of continuous percussive beats and rhythms. Furthermore, the northeastern Brazilian rhythms, *symbolic* of worldliness and wild parties for those who have been imprinted with this association and, at times believed to be inherently unredeemable for Christian usage, have perhaps become *symbols* of life and energy for the younger generations of Christians eager to be expressive and intense in their actions.

In the village called *Aldeia Nova* lives another musician by the name of Janio. He has been a Christian and involved in church services for two years and now plays the guitar at Bible studies and church meetings on a regular basis. He attended the Baptist School in a city nearby (now an independent school not connected with the Baptist Convention)[38] and received his initial guitar instruction from one of its teachers. Since completing his studies, Janio has continued to play and to try to improve on his own.

Janio enjoys many music styles, but the contemporary styles of Xerente Christian music are the ones that most move him spiritually and touch him emotionally. He believes the Xerente people have developed a taste for new songs and that they enjoy listening to them even if they are not singing along. Songs with short texts, he said, are more readily learned and would likely be the best ones to spread among the people.

Referring to the songs recorded during the 2017 Cabeceira Verde workshop, he thought the ones written and sung by João Simrâni demonstrated an excellent balance, using Xerente characteristics and *forró* rhythms without exaggeration. Concerning the four songs which reutilized traditional Xerente melodies for Christian lyrics, he expressed approval along with some critique. He reported that there had been some criticism of them among the Christians, in particular about the vagueness of the songs' lyrics—a critique with which he agreed. On the other hand, those traditional songs (whether because of their character or due to the

---

37. Canclini, *Hybrid Cultures*, loc. 95.

38. This information was provided by local missionaries Werner Seitz and Mario Moura.

memories they evoke) lead them to "travel in their imagination."[39] Some musicians, he said, have been using one the songs (he did not specify which) that had been originally recorded with the simple accompaniment of the *zâ* and have been adding electronic instrumentation. Since the song has become "more animated,"[40] the people have enjoyed it more than before when only the *zâ* was used for accompaniment.

Janio told me of a song he composed and recorded in MP4 on his phone at a time when he was feeling lonely and in a state of depression. His song expressed his trials as well as his hope in God through this stage of life. While he hoped that if he shared it with others, they would understand that they were not alone, he was pleasantly surprised when, after sharing his song with family members and acquaintances, someone from another village contacted him about going to perform it at a vigil. Although he was not able to attend that vigil, someone else learned and sang the song. He related to me that he heard that one of his cousins was profoundly touched and brought to a greater joy when she heard it. Janio did not specify if his song, which he had recorded only with a guitar accompaniment, had been performed with an additional keyboard with rhythms in that instance.

He spoke with certainty about the meaningful impact that locally composed songs have on Xerente Christians without necessarily making absolute distinctions among the genres, classifying them only as hymns (translated Western hymns), new Xerente compositions (incorporating songs with more or less Xerente linguistic and vocal features), and the traditional melodies transformed into Christian songs by newly created lyrics. Through his emphasis on meaningful connection with the people, he highlighted the importance of lyrics with personal testimony and the call for people to follow God. Nevertheless, he also reiterated the drawing power of rhythmic *animation*. Considering the widespread absorption

---

39. Interview with Janio at Aldeia Nova, June 13, 2019.

40. Interview with Janio at Aldeia Nova, June 13, 2019. While I am aware that connotations in each of the languages are different for the word *animado* or *animated*, the Portuguese expression *mais animado(a)* has been intentionally translated in a fairly literal manner as "more animated." The Portuguese word *animado* would probably be best translated as "lively" if it were used in a generic fashion. However, the repeated use of this word in this context refers to specific attributes including instrumentation as the local community envisions it. In the strict sense of "lively," Xerente traditional music could also be "lively" if the participants sang it enthusiastically, with a slightly faster tempo, and with joyous bodily movements. However, this is not what the Xerente are referring to with *animado*, but rather the specific combination of electronic and percussive sounds that typically accompany their music and other northeastern genres.

of external musical tastes by the Xerente, the *animated* sounds could signify ideas of connection with the national society, feelings of celebratory atmospheres, hope, or a number of other concepts. Songs with deeper emotional textual content may tend to speak to individual situations in direct ways. But they may also become *symbolic* of other aspects of life through its musical and, specifically, rhythmic features.

Between June 14 and 17 of 2019 I accompanied Pr. Rinaldo to Cabeceira Verde where he led a leadership training seminar. Several of the participants of the 2017 music workshop also attended this event. They gathered from the local congregation as well as from surrounding villages. In this context, I was able to converse again with several of the musicians I had met before, as well as with others whom I met for the first time, about the questions addressed in this dissertation.

Maciel was one of the singers I had not previously met. He has a college degree from a state university and works at a Xerente school a few kilometers from Cabeceira Verde along with two other participants at the seminar. Maciel attended the meeting with his wife and child and participated in song twice singing a duet with Denilson, who also works/teaches at the same school. He participates in a congregation linked to the Foursquare Church and demonstrated a musical flavor somewhat distinct from those I had previously met. During the days of the seminar, the few that had come from the Foursquare congregation played and sang translated songs from the national contemporary Christian music scene in Brazil, in particular songs by the Brazilian Christian singer Fernandinho.[41] Maciel has been involved in *forró* (secular) throughout his life and was once invited to become part of a professional band being organized in the Xerente area. He declined the invitation since he felt he would be trespassing his personal Christian convictions if he were to allow himself to participate with the secular scene to that extent. He also translates songs into *Akwẽ* and showed me a notebook replete with lyrics of songs he had translated. He was keen to attribute his translations to God's gift in this area, declaring that in two cases he dreamed of the translation and then wrote them down. According to Maciel, these translated songs have been well-accepted. He stated that one song in particular has been "a blessing to people, and [that] they have been moved to come closer

---

41. See Fernandinho's official website at https://fernandinhooficial.com.br/. Fernandinho is a well-known worship song leader in Brazil. He is the Brazilian voice singing the Portuguese version of the theme song of the Christian film *God's Not Dead*.

to God through it."[42] Maciel looks forward to another workshop/course like the one held in Cabeceira Verde in 2017. He is eager to learn and develop his musical skills to become even more effective in his musical ministry. His friend and singing partner, Denilson, also plays the guitar. He showed a greater appreciation for "slower songs" and a closer affinity to Brazilian worship songs than others I met during this research.

The origin of Maciel and Denilson's connection to the contemporary worship music may be their life outside of the Xerente reservation when they attended college and attended Brazilian Christian congregations. They both declared themselves in favor of using a variety of genres, even within the Xerente Christian community. However, they are aware and respectful of the present musical choices of Xerente churches, acknowledging that the musical features of these genres (ex. the use of electronic instruments and preset rhythms of northeastern styles) are part and parcel of the affective power of music among them. People become, in their own words, *emocionados*[43] when they listen to the songs.

Lázaro, the composer of several of the songs recorded in 2017 in Cabeceira Verde, was also present at Pr. Rinaldo's seminar in June 2019. He greeted me warmly when I arrived and proceeded to tell me with excitement about his and others' plan to organize a musical and arts group that would evangelize in various Xerente villages through music, drama, dance, and preaching. On the basis of his experience and personal impressions, Lázaro has come to believe that music can and should be used as a tool to soften the hearts to hear the gospel message.

During this seminar, Lázaro took the opportunity to honor Pr. Rinaldo (who was present) and Pr. Guenther (whom they call Pr. Carlos, not present) for their service along the course of the last six decades. For this short memorial time in the afternoon of June 16, Lázaro sang (accompanied by the local guitar and keyboard players) an improvised musical story of the two missionaries' service to the Xerente. He chose a tune which he repeated multiple times and improvised the lyrics retelling the story. It was an emotional experience to all who were gathered and particularly to Pr. Rinaldo whom several of them later embraced and with whom they cried for several minutes after the conclusion of Lázaro's song.

Among the participants of the seminar mentioned above was a singer by the name of Valmir. His story has been of one of struggle to

---

42. Personal conversation with Maciel on June 15, 2019.

43. *Emocionados* literally means "emoted." In English this state could be best described as "touched emotionally" or "emotionally moved."

make a firm decision to follow Christ faithfully. Valmir had become a Christian around two years before I was introduced to him in 2017. Soon after his conversion, he became immediately involved in music ministry in Xerente congregations. He lives in Brejo Comprido, a village about 20 kilometers from Cabeceira Verde, and attended the workshop there in 2017 when he also recorded several hymns he had translated. He has now translated over forty traditional Western hymns which could likely become part of the upcoming revised Xerente Christian songbook. At first glance, his acquaintance with and appreciation for the hymns appears anachronistic—although he also sings the hymns with the electronic rhythmic keyboard accompaniment. However, his journey until his recent firm decision to be a disciple of Christ was not at all distant from Christian communities. He had "joined" the denomination called *Congregação Cristã* many years before, but without a firm or sincere commitment to follow Christian principles. A feeling of regret for his indecision earlier in life could account for his special connection to the hymns. In some way, the hymns that surrounded his experiences during that period of evading his need to change his life's direction, may have achieved *meaningful* and *emotional* links to his former frustrated desire to walk upright paths. They may have become *symbols* of a life for which he longed and has finally come to experience.[44]

---

44. Although I first met Valmir in 2017, I was not made aware of Valmir's life story until 2019 through two of the missionaries late during the visit. Hence there was no further opportunity at that time to discuss this proposed connection directly with him. These thoughts are personal attempts at understanding his preference for the older hymns, but they also reflect Pr. Mario's opinion. Pr. Mario is the missionary who has been personally discipling him since his 2017 conversion and baptism.

14—Picture taken during the 2017 workshop.
Workshop leaders Héber Negrão and Elsen Portugal with singer Lázaro Rowakro

In Cabeceira Verde and in Salto, other musicians briefly expressed their deep connection to church music styles, particularly in the forms currently being produced. The preference of the Xerente for a layer of northeastern rhythms is made clear by those who appreciate the blend as well as those who dislike it. A great number of people, either verbally or through consent, deem the loud sound from the amplifiers to be indispensable, regarding this as a "necessity" in similar ways as the pulpit has been considered essential for a preacher to the point that the word "pulpit" can be used as indexical for "message" or "leadership." Emotion through music is also a common topic of conversations. About half of the people interviewed, or briefly inquired, relate emotional responses to specific songs in all genres present, but frequently those in the contemporary Xerente fusion genres.

5.2.3 Perspective of Missionaries

Among the missionaries there is general agreement that the Xerente Christians should be encouraged to make their own choices regarding cultural matters related to Christian practices. They are available for advice and do voice their opinions as partners in the local Christian community but always strive to allow the Xerente to have the last word.

Four Baptist missionaries have been working closely together in the Xerente areas studied here in the last few years. These are the ones with whom I had the closest interaction. Naturally, they all have personal perspectives, customs, and preferences concerning music and the Xerente modes of musical expression. Pr. Rinaldo's long-standing relationship with the Xerente places him in a position to look at the situations from a variety of perspectives. His opinions reflect much of his own tradition and preference, but they are perhaps often restrained as a result of his great respect for their culture and understanding of the communicative potential of cultural forms for the community's members. As a musician, he was able to provide me important insight about the practices and significance of both traditional and contemporary genres. Pr. Guenther, the contemporary of Pr. Rinaldo, is responsible for the development of the translation of the New Testament. He and his wife Vanda have lived in villages as well as in the city of Miracema. Pr. Werner Seitz is a recent addition to the team of missionaries, focusing on the continuation of the Bible translation project started by Pr. Guenther. He is a gifted violinist and linguist. He and his wife sing together for church meetings when opportunity calls. Pr. Mario has been with the team for over a decade. He and his family have served multiple villages with services and Bible studies, but he concentrates on the area around Cabeceira Verde where he has built a house.

It is not uncommon among the missionaries to perceive the loud amplified sounds as an unnecessary feature considering the small size of the meeting places they construct for this purpose or utilize from the community. From a Western perspective, such amplification serves the primary purpose of aiding hearing comprehension in large settings. Although this principle may seem to be ignored even in Brazilian urban settings, it may be only partially back of this technical choice. Undeniably, Xerente Christians are not meeting in hiding and have a cultural sense of community that is not greatly concerned with problems with neighbors for using loud sounds (music or speech). The fact that the surrounding houses and possibly the whole village can hear the musical and spoken messages proclaimed inside the meeting place could be the main stimulus for the use of microphones and amplified instruments. However, the amplification, as suggested earlier in this chapter, could have communal meanings related to celebratory feelings of joy and hope.

Some of the missionaries also express hesitations as to the quality of the music production of these fusion genres. In contrast to the missionaries' musical training, Xerente music levels of precision raise questions concerning their instantiations but not necessarily of the sincere character of this music. For instance, when performing fusion genres (as well as traditional Western hymns) some musicians have a flexible understanding of precision and meter, a fact easily noticeable by trained musicians and nonmusicians familiar with Western musical practices. However, accuracy or quality control of musical performance is not necessarily a characteristic of every cultural musical environment. Bruno Nettl demonstrates this variation in his comparison of the practices of North American Navajo and Pacific coast peoples, for whom practicing was "essential" and whose "mistakes were punished,"[45] with those of some peoples from the Northern Plains. The latter nations "took a less formalist attitude"[46] towards musical accuracy. He explains that "since music was primarily a personal and individualistic activity and experience [for these cultures], practicing was not done systematically to any large extent, and not much heed was paid to the accuracy of performance."[47] Although exactness of rhythm can be identified in many of the more advanced musicians, it does not seem to be a primary preoccupation. Another characteristic of Xerente musical practice is the relative lack of precise beginning and endings of songs. Apart from recordings that underwent musical scrutiny among the Xerente, open performance of songs in church settings may begin with the keyboardists looking for the best preset rhythm to apply to that particular song, a process which could last a few to as many as forty-five seconds before a clear introductory line is played. The Xerente singers' patience along this process correlates to traditional Xerente styles. In traditional song, a *puxador* typically starts the first phrase of a song before the remaining participants begin. They do not function as a chorale led by a conductor that indicates when every singer or accompanist should start singing or playing. There is a

---

45. Nettl, *Study of Ethnomusicology*, 430.
46. Nettl, *Study of Ethnomusicology*, 430.
47. Nettl, *Study of Ethnomusicology*, 430.

transactional period when the participants listen for the sung cue of the *puxador*. Along the short history of church musical practices among the Xerente, a cooperative leadership including the singer as *puxador* and the accompanist has developed. The outcome appears to lack a visceral necessity to "start altogether."

The above issues of precision and amplification, although not points of contention with the people, are the primary negatives that missionaries have conveyed to me in our conversations. Musical instruction for the musicians and the publication of a larger songbook including the newly composed songs are also topics at the forefront of their discussions, but they do not contrast with the Xerente musicians' expressed ideals. They appear to have a broad base of support from missionaries as well as from Xerente musicians and church members. In spite of some of the misgivings about this particular musical fusion, the missionaries are openly supportive of the musical initiatives of Xerente Christians.

5.2.4 Hopes for Improvement

Xerente Christians express a broad consensus that music is an integral part of their church life, communicating meanings which they value as individuals and community. Along with this positive perspective of music, however, they do express concerns and hopes for the future that can potentially affect the continued development of their Christian musical repertoire.

Musicians with experience ranging up to around twenty years, such as Tiago Wakuke, have seen the transformation of musical practices within their territory and more specifically within Christian congregations. Tiago shared with me his desire to see their musicians continue to improve in the composition of new songs, and that they aim at producing good lyrics that blend well with the music. Demonstrating a certain disappointment that people do not know the lyrics by heart, Wakuke wishes they would develop a practice of singing on their own during the week.

Those musicians who have had little training so far express great interest in developing their skills in the future. Many singers, though not instrumentalists, described their need for help in order to complete songs they begin to compose. The missionaries and local Xerente musicians hold frequent conversations about how to help the furtherance of the musical composition movement among the Xerente. They fully expect that this advancement will benefit the indigenous community in social relations and spiritual growth. Although they wish the Quartet had continued to work together, they realize this vacuum could serve as an opportunity for new ideas to be implemented that would encourage the creation of new songs and that they would penetrate the lives of Xerente communities even more than they have so far.

5.3 VENUES AND OTHER CHARACTERISTICS

5.3.1 Church Services and Vigils

Church meetings are vital in Xerente Christian practice, as it commonly is around the world. The *culto* (worship service) provides the regular opportunity for Christians to gather, hear teaching from the Bible, and receive encouragement through music and prayer. Xerente services, unlike many Christian communities around the world, are not usually thoroughly preplanned. It permits and encourages the participation of the congregants in areas of their ability without constrains of time. It is not uncommon for services to last two hours even in small congregations.

Typically, the leader of the service initiates the meeting by either bringing a word to the congregation or inviting someone to sing or pray. At times, as in Cabeceira Verde where one of the leaders is the *cacique*, the leader calls out through the sound system inviting the village to come to the church a few moments before the beginning of the meeting. The service continues by allowing for individual participation until the leader decides it is time to close, or if no one else wishes to offer a contribution of song or message. As a rule of thumb, someone is scheduled to be the main speaker, but this does not necessarily imply that this speaker is allowed more time than anyone else. Each person is at liberty to proceed as long as he or she feels is necessary. An offering may be taken at some point in the service but does not appear to have a specific place in the order of service.

The vigils mentioned earlier in this book provide another venue for Christians to gather and to present a song—new or old. They began a number of years ago at the suggestion of Tiago Wakuke as a substitute for other feasts. In the northeastern region of Brazil, as well as within the Xerente communities, Catholic traditional feasts have been held through the centuries. These feasts, however, have mostly lost their religious meaning and are now characterized by dance balls heavily accompanied by the consumption of alcoholic drinks. Through the night people engage in openly dissolute behavior which commonly turns into fights and ongoing feuds. People are often physically hurt and subsequent deaths have ensued. Committed Christians who have identified the environment of such feasts as inappropriate and inadequate for them, avoid any involvement with these events. Years ago, Tiago reportedly commented that if non-Christians can spend all night dancing and drinking "for Satan," then Christians can spend all night in prayer to God.[48] He then took the initiative of organizing a night of prayer in his village, scheduling the event precisely on a night when the regional feast was taking place not far from there. Soon, another village followed the idea and organized a vigil at the house of a church member near a creek. The movement grew and became a new tradition in which most Xerente churches participate. Typically, one congregation organizes the event and invites other churches. According to Pr. Rinaldo, some of these meetings have gathered representatives of more than twenty churches from the Xerente area, and there have been more than 300 participants in a single event.

Vigils have reportedly been fertile ground for the circulation of new ideas and, pertinent to this study, new musical compositions. In spite of the concern expressed by Pr. Pedro that some who wish to sing in the vigils are not committed to serving in their local congregations, these venues have provided a form of exchange that is likely responsible not only for the accelerated distribution of new songs, but for instigating or at least encouraging others to write down their lyrics, match it with music, and present them.

5.3.2 Technology

The introduction of technological resources into Xerente culture clearly affected subsequent choices among the people. Technology became a part of Xerente life, however, through a variety of interactions, not only with the church (in the case of the electronic instruments) but with governmental and other parties which have intersected with indigenous life. TVs are not uncommon in Xerente huts, sound systems playing either secular or Christian music can be heard in the villages, and cell phones are ubiquitous especially among younger people. The sound amplification

---

48. The story of the rise of these vigils has been documented by Pr. Rinaldo de Mattos and constitutes part of Appendix E in this book.

of instruments and voices for services also result from this general introduction and interest in technology among the Xerente. Nestor Canclini explains that "these new technological resources are not neutral, nor are they omnipotent. Their simple formal innovation implies cultural changes, but the final sign depends on the uses *different actors assign* to them."[49] Among the Xerente, these technological tools of communication have now taken root and become part of daily life. The "different actors" among the Xerente assign meaning and function to the various gadgets and utilize them in ways that makes sense to them and could potentially benefit them and their community.

WhatsApp is a tool of communication used by practically every owner of a cell phone in Brazil. This application has helped Brazilians by-pass the complicated system of cell phone providers which often limit free calls and file transfers to numbers served by the same provider or raise the cost significantly if interchanges occur between providers. Without constant care, these charges can become extremely high. WhatsApp functions as an application of communication using the data of one's phone (in some cases not even adding to the typically limited data usage service plan) and has become a preferred tool of communication. Hence, it has opened new venues for sharing songs along with any voice or written messages. Until recently, cell reception in the villages had still been limited since few of them have antennae that locally amplify cell phone signals. Internet has been available only at a few locations, particularly in schools. Nevertheless, the Xerente make use of the communication system by going to other villages or nearby cities, or by using Bluetooth technology.

Technological advances can become points of contention, especially when they induce quick transformation of the customs of any given society. Modern urban societies also face changes in meaning and rise of new functions by the development of technologically advanced tools and devices. The last three decades, for instance, have brought about multiple changes in modes of communication by the development and popularity of the internet and the accessibility of information for the society at large. Although it could be argued that the manifestation of technology among urban societies is something of a natural and internally developed change, it is pertinent to note that modern technological tools used around world in urban societies have not necessarily been developed by that same

---

49. Canclini, *Hybrid Culture*, loc. 226. Emphasis added.

society. Technological advances are often made by comparatively few scientists and engineers in a particular country and are subsequently marketed worldwide. Although this distribution is interpreted as cultural interference by some, its adoption is perhaps mostly regarded as a positive move. The adoption of technological tools by the Xerente and other indigenous peoples may strike human perception as having a different character, or as a negative change, due to the brisk pace of this development. This incursion, however, may have become or may still become incentives for Xerente creativity in technological as well as artistic areas.

5.4 CONCLUSION: LOCAL MEANINGS AND FUNCTIONS

This chapter introduced key concepts of musical semiotics based on two trichotomies developed by Charles Peirce in order to lay the groundwork for the recognition of local meaning in Xerente music, particularly that of fusion genre(s) studied in this dissertation. Music serves as a sign system that can deliver "meaning," whether intentionally designed or as "value added."

The first of Peirce's two trichotomies addressed in this chapter demonstrates the trajectory of meaning development and highlights the importance of the *interpretant* or the meaning that the receiver of the message actually interprets as the message. The interviews demonstrated that the Xerente genres and the performance practices associated with them connect deeply with local Christians and have meanings both for the community as a whole and for individuals. The use of preset northeastern rhythms as an accompaniment to these songs, often deemed inadequate for those who hold to aesthetic concepts of the Western tradition (their *interpretant*), not only help define the characteristics of the fusion genres under development among the Xerente, but also communicate the identity of Xerente Christian community or "the church music sound" as well as other potential meanings. Music allows the performer or listener the opportunity to negotiate musical meaning in manners that may be unique[50] to the individual or community by means of culturally-induced cues and naturally-imbedded perception skills.

Peirce's trichotomy of sign types reveals that musical signs seldom serve as icons or indexes of ideas without some previous knowledge of the object (or idea) being signed. As I have come to understand it, music

---

50. Salgar, "Musical Semiotics as a Tool," 3.

functions primarily as *symbol* of an idea through its connection with personal or cultural events, either temporarily or permanently. Furthermore, emotion has a regular presence in Xerente cultural life, as verified by the comments by Xerente Christians during the interviews. Although the question of whether the emotional message of a song first affects the listener, or whether the cognitive memory and connected idea lead to the emotional affect, is not something to be easily resolved. Their frequent simultaneous appearance makes the investigation of the process difficult. Emotion, however, whether consciously or not, can also be evoked through music's association with events or ideas.

Through the venues and means of communication available to or developed by Xerente Christians, their new musical compositions are taking root in the community—sometimes also heard among non-Christians—bearing meaning and fulfilling functions in the society that are often unique to its population. As of 2023, I continue to hear reports from the missionaries that the musical ministry is growing, and that there are newer and younger composers continuing these practices. Given the observations made as a result of this research, I propose that the internal perception of meaning and function should take precedence in the evaluation of character and authenticity, and that external meanings which do not match those perceived by the Xerente should not quench the impetus of these enthusiastic musicians as they develop styles and genres which communicate well within their contexts.

6

Signposts of Authenticity

6.1 INTRODUCTION

THROUGHOUT THIS BOOK I have mentioned the four indicators that I have come to believe can identify local authenticity of a particular community practice, especially of a musical or an otherwise artistic expression. While chapter 7 discusses the concept and the merits of authenticity at length, this chapter brings together four types of cultural and sociological demonstrations–termed "signposts"–which can be indicative of the authentic character of a cultural manifestation.

On the question of who has the authority to define the authenticity of a cultural experience, I agree with Hodgson that the local culture and its sociological characteristics are best suited to indicate what is truly authentic.[1] Within this view, a community acknowledges an artistic expression as "their own" based on its connection to its cultural milieu in a variety of ways which will be discussed in this chapter. This posture, I believe, flows out naturally from the core values of ethnodoxology regarding human agency and locally grounded methods.[2]

Beyond the musical features closely identified with traditional form and style in the fusion genre(s) as described in chapter 4, the following signposts represent sociocultural phenomena among the Xerente which indicate deep levels of integration of the Xerente fusion musical genres in

1. Hodgson, "Perceptions of Authenticity," 57.
2. Global Ethnodoxology Network, "Core Values."

the community, particularly those involved in evangelical congregations. The four signposts are as follows:

1. *Meaning*—the presence of significance for individuals and the community, including associated emotional content and the potential to help form identities through the practice of the genres.
2. *Function*—the presence of roles for a music genre integrated into the life of the community (or church) in indispensable ways (or so perceived by the community).
3. *Competence*—the ability of local musicians to envision a combination of features that fuse as a genre, as well as the competence to compose and reproduce music in this genre.
4. *Agency (Control* or *Administration)*—the local community's decision-making practices concerning the local genre's performance within church services; the presence of local administration of a genre.

Interviews with musicians, missionaries, and other Christians presented in chapter 5 demonstrate the strong presence of these signposts in relationship to the fusion genres. This chapter considers all four of the signposts and integrates discussions with Pr. Rinaldo on his anthropological perspective of the four signposts. His long-standing and profound knowledge of Xerente society derives from his personal experience as well as from perspectives from three key anthropologists who studied the Xerente culture throughout the twentieth century: Curt Nimuendaju, David Maybury-Lewis, and Agenor Farias. They provide valuable support for the validity of these signposts.[3] Pr. Rinaldo was personally acquainted with Maybury-Lewis and Farias and assisted them with logistics during their research in at least one instance. His practical and academic experience allows him to provide some deep insights into Xerente consciousness, practice, and demeanor based on his interaction with the people since the early sixties.

---

3. Schroeder, "Política e Parentesco," 55–65.

6.2 MEANING AS A SIGNPOST OF AUTHENTICITY

6.2.1 Communal Meaning: Ethnic Identity

The conversations and interviews with Xerente Christians related in chapter 5 gave evidence of the significance of fusion genres for the community as a whole. The sounds of this class of music have become a type of identity marker of the body of Christians at least during the last decade. Similar to the situation of the Maninka church described by Dr. Morehouse, music—and in particular fusion genres—has helped construct the Ethnic Christian Identity (ECI) of the Xerente.[4] Morehouse believes that the traditional hymns used by the Maninka church "are deeply rooted, have become 'traditional', and are viewed as *authentic* indigenous expressions of worship."[5] Likewise, the youngest generations of Xerente demonstrate evidence of having incorporated a variety of musical elements not previously present in Xerente life and these have become "traditional" in the sense of "adhering to past practices or established conventions."[6]

Xerente society as it stands today does not show characteristics of a having a consistent orientation towards communal practice. Individuals and clans, according to the opinion of some of the missionaries, come into conflicts because of the level of individualism present, and the society often fails from benefitting from a participatory or collegial enterprise in business due to this characteristic.[7] Nevertheless, many practices have value and meaning that maintain an enduring connection among the individuals of the society, even if contemporary practices are organizationally in their community development. Cultural feasts, although not practiced as regularly as they had been in the past, do have collective meaning and imprint identity on the members of the society. For older people, the feasts represent an intergenerational method of transferring the identity of their people to the younger generation. By the same token, meaning for music and other cultural expressions is not restricted to individual perceptions but spreads rather through the interactions among individuals and develops a communal sense of meaning. Fusion genres of Christian music, not unlike other interactions in Xerente society, have

---

4. Morehouse, "They're Playing Our Song."
5. Morehouse, "They're Playing Our Song," 22. Emphasis added.
6. Merriam-Webster Dictionary, "Traditional," entry 3.
7. This observation from three of the missionaries was obtained through personal conversations in June of 2019.

developed collective meaning signaling the character of Christian faith and a valid form of transmission for its message.

As I elaborate on the presence of *meaning* in Xerente fusion genres, it is important to acknowledge that an absolute distinction between *meaning* and *emotion* as well as its interplay with the second signpost—*function*—is often impractical from an emic point of view. When attempting to attend to the specific questions of this research, the responders seek to use the terms used in the question. However, the constant interplay of the three concepts—meaning, emotion, and function—raise the question of whether a definitive distinction among the three is warranted at all. Not only in Xerente society, but in human experience in general, music meaning interacts with emotion at a deep level. Its function can either be a natural response to the meaning already present or serve as a cause for the production of meaning.

Rinaldo de Mattos remarks that the "sentiment of the Xerente towards music, . . . [their] feeling towards music"[8] is unlike that of the average member of Western culture. It is an essential element of *all* their traditional ceremonies, including the naming of boys and girls. Therefore, it has been inconceivable for them to think of holding a church service (*culto*) and not have music. Although today they are more likely to ask: "*Vai ter culto hoje?*" (Will there be a church service today?), it was customary in the earlier days when the missionaries Rinaldo and Guenther went to a village to be asked "*Debsa A'isõkrẽ?*" (Are you going to sing?) which meant for them: "Are we going to have to come together and sing?" Pr. Rinaldo believes that the Xerente were thinking mostly about the music than the other parts of the service. The meaning of music and the practice of "holding a service" are deeply attached to each other. He is certain that this is one of the strongest reasons behind the great amount of singing that takes place during services and why they are now composing so much new music. Vigils, for instance, consist primarily of music when compared to other potential church service elements.

As an essential component of a Christian service, music in the Xerente society is a spontaneous response and culturally imbedded. Pr. Rinaldo believes that the music they are creating now stems from an ethnic sentiment (feeling) of recovering[9] something from the past, a rhythm [of life] that had been forgotten, even though the musical rhythms have only

---

8. Interview with Rinaldo de Mattos, Village of Salto, June 18, 2019. All translations of the interviews are mine. On file.

9. *Resgatando* literally means "rescuing" in Portuguese.

recently entered their society. Potentially, even though the northeastern musical rhythms applied to the contemporary Xerente genres were not part of their earlier tradition, the very action of choosing genres to which they have grown accustomed in their society at large (unlike the hymns which are only sung by Christians) may be meaningful to them as an effort to rescue what is innate (in their conception) to their general society and apply it to Christian service.

The introduction of Western hymns as a regular part of the service may have had the effect of hiding their musical intuition, their creativity, and their ability to compose for a period of time. When the missionaries understood that this previously unseen ability was available and they started to analyze the lyrics of their new songs, they began to encourage them to continue composing. One of the songs that made an impression on Pr. Rinaldo as to their contextualized content says that Jesus "fixed for us a piece of land to which He will take us," connecting the indigenous struggle for land rights as symbolic for the heavenly home to which Christians expect to come. Tiago's interview in chapter 5 revealed some of the same sentiment Pr. Rinaldo addressed in this conversation. Tiago identified a long-standing dependence on the missionaries for their music. Since about 2010 when many new compositions appeared, as he explained, the Xerente have experienced a freedom which they had not sensed before.

Northeastern rhythms have a collective identity within the region the Xerente inhabit. This sense of belonging (once again recalling the struggle for land rights they had faced) is likely to be a subconscious affirmation brought through the use of the rhythms of local genres. The regional connection appears to supersede other Brazilian national sounds that could have become emblematic of their sense of belonging within Brazil. Genres generally popular around Brazil, such as *samba* and *bossa nova* are not commonly used in the area. From a musical perspective, *bossa nova* has a level of dissonance which the Xerente do not tend to prefer. On the other hand, Pr. Rinaldo believes that the harmonic structure, the melodic flow, as well as the duple meter of *forró* matched traditional Xerente music well and became easy to assimilate.

Emotion is a natural part of Xerente ceremonies. This emotional connection with their culture and the significance of their feasts was stated by several Xerente musicians that attended the 2017 workshop. Several musicians also referred to the emotional appeal of their preferred music during interviews in June 2019. As such, these associated features of meaning and emotion relay an equivalent (or comparable) sense of belonging to a special culture (in this case, that of the Christian church).

The loud sounds in the small meeting places have puzzled the non-Xerente since they seem to lack purpose and to contradict earlier customs. Pr. Rinaldo explained that the tendency to have loud sounds was not inherited from traditional culture since nothing in their earlier tradition, as far as their memory and records register, is ever "so loud." However, the Xerente have been bilingual and bicultural for several decades. Their children are born into the two general cultures (Xerente and national Brazilian) and they listen to the other genres as a natural part of their aural world. As a community, musical genres like *forró* have gained the privilege of becoming natural members of their society and provided substitutive or additional meaning to their community.

Given the presence of internal community meaning in artistic expressions indicated by the responses among Xerente Christians to their music, the relationship of these characteristics to ethnic identity and even ethnogenesis should be explored briefly. In his comprehensive overview of theories of ethnicity, German author Josef Joachim Sprotte reaffirms one author's explanation that group identity is not limited to those "endowments and identifications which every individual shares with others from the moment of birth by the chance of the family into which he is born at that given time in that given place" (Isaacs 1974: 26)," but by enculturation also receives "a personal, familial and group identity."[10] Thus, the community and individual perception of identity is not confined to early stages of identity formation as a group or in individuals. Rather, identity continues to be shaped along life through a continuing process of enculturation. This progression is akin to the process of ethnogenesis which Jonathan Hill describes

> as a process of authentically re-making new social identities through creatively rediscovering and refashioning components of 'tradition', such as oral narratives, written texts, and material artifacts. Understood in these terms, ethnogenesis allows us to explore the cultural creativity of indigenous and non-indigenous peoples alike in the making of new interpretive and political spaces that allow people to construct enduring social identities.[11]

---

10. Sprotte, *Hurons*, loc. 934.
11. Hill, *History, Power, and Identity*, abstract.

Although the topic of his research, which focuses on the broad development of new indigenous identities in Latin American cultures since the sixteenth century, cannot be fully discussed in this book, Hill provides relevant observations which support the idea of a genuine or authentic[12] character of the rediscovered and refashioned components, including the incorporation of non-native elements, in a process of developing "new interpretive and political spaces" and "enduring social identities."[13] From this perspective, it could be said that Xerente Christian music represents a rediscovery of an innate ability in musical creativity and demonstrates a refashioning of musical elements with the incorporation of new (external) musical characteristics. Together with numerous other cultural modifications along the last six decades, the Xerente are "authentically re-making" a new social identity through their new compositions and performance practices.

6.2.2 Individual Meaning: Emotion

The discussion of meaning as a signpost of potential authenticity of Xerente Christian music above gave initial priority to a group identity. However, a group identity and the potential ethnogenesis occurring among the Xerente cannot be completely segregated from the perceptions of the individuals without which no "group identity" would develop. Although the significance of group meaning and identity relates primarily to a sense of belonging or connection with the community, the perception is found *in* and identified *by* individuals. That is, group consciousness is composed of corroborative individual consciences of identity and cannot, in fact, exist on its own.

Xerente individuals, however, have reported meaningful and emotional experiences attained through music that were not primarily related to the group identity but were connected to their own personal spiritual experiences. Emotion appears to rank high among the Xerente as a marker of significance. Although the emotional expression of Xerente Christians may often appear subdued in comparison to other cultural areas, they do not seem to refrain from overt displays of emotion out of a sense of embarrassment. When relating an experience, they frequently

---

12. Although "genuine" and "authentic" are not identical in meaning, I believe they coincide in this application.

13. Hill, *History, Power, and Identity*, abstract.

tell the listeners that they were emotionally moved. These emotions, as chapter 5 describes, are sensed by individuals in connection with memorable events or ideas significant to their personal lives. Leonard Meyer's classic work *Emotion and Meaning in Music* suggests that music can function "as a kind of catalytic agent,"[14] enabling but not controlling or shaping the experience of emotion in the individual. Meyer suggests that "tendency" ("automatic response patterns, whether natural or learned")[15] and expectation in music are some of the key motivations in the process of emotional stimulation. He identifies multiple musical elements, individually or combined, which can also aid the intentional or circumstantial evocation of emotion. But he admits that "often music arouses affect[16] through the mediation of conscious connotation or unconscious image processes."[17] "Music may give rise to images and trains of thought which, because of *their relation to the inner life of the particular individual*, may eventually culminate in *affect*."[18] Other researchers like Vernon Lee and Max Schoen[19] have likewise attempted to provide an analysis of psychological processes involved in the stimuli of emotion and meaning. Although the sciences cannot describe the exact methods through which emotion is evoked in the individual, they generally agree that the inducements can somehow touch one's deepest being, his or her actual and authentic self.

6.2.3 Evaluation

"Music presents a generic event, a 'connotative complex', which then becomes *particularized in the experience of the individual listener*."[20] This "connotative complex" found in music and described by Meyer consists, at the very least, of meaning and emotion within individuals. That is, because music connects on superficial, cognitive, and frequently experiential levels with the listener/participant/performer of musical

---

14. Meyer, *Emotion and Meaning in Music*, 8.
15. Meyer, *Emotion and Meaning in Music*, 24.
16. In our modern usage of the English language, "affect" is an infrequent noun. It denotes "the conscious subjective aspect of an emotion considered apart from bodily changes." Merriam-Webster Dictionary, "Affect," entry 2.
17. Meyer, *Emotion and Meaning in Music*, 256.
18. Meyer, *Emotion and Meaning in Music*, 256. Emphases added.
19. Meyer, *Emotion and Meaning in Music*, 8.
20. Meyer, *Emotion and Meaning in Music*, 265. Emphasis added.

instantiations, it is interpreted as meaning and emotion. The meaning(s), and the accompanying emotional content, that arose from the development and practice of these fused genres give evidence of the genuine connection to individuals, particularly Christians, and to the society. The eager acknowledgment of Xerente Christians that their new music is emotionally appropriate and significant can thus serve as signposts for the presence of authenticity in the character of the Xerente fusion genres, seeing that they are meaningful for individuals and the community, and contain the potential to help form identities.

6.3 FUNCTION AS SIGNPOST OF AUTHENTICITY

6.3.1 Introduction

Since traditional music in Xerente culture and social interactions fulfill obligatory functions in the consciousness of individuals, it is reasonable to suppose that the newer compositions are not simply decorative but have also come to play integrated roles within the society. Whether the meaning and the emotion carried by the music opens up space for the establishment of its permanent role (*function*) as communicator, or whether the existence of a function for the music aids the creation of meaning and the stimulus of emotion is not a determinant issue for the purposes of this research. On the other hand, meaning and function appear regularly in the same context as constant interactive companions. Furthermore, concerning 'utility' or function, Canclini suggests that "human beings have always made art out of concern for something more than its pragmatic value—for example, for the pleasure it gives us or because it seduces or communicates something of ourselves."[21] That is, function is not found exclusively in externally visible or practical ends but includes roles aimed at the satisfaction of the individual through its communicative actions.

6.3.2 Social and Cultural Functions

Volgsten identifies as an important function of music the creation of identities.[22] His study focuses on Western musical genres with which

---

21. Canclini, *Hybrid Cultures*, locs. 77–78.
22. Volgsten, "Music, Culture, Politics," 2–3.

segments of societies of various countries have identified themselves. He suggests that the preferred global genres of music (i.e., rock, jazz, etc.) are capable of becoming a "limit-transgressing and unifying link at both a collective and individual level."[23] The formation and the expression of identity (both individual and corporate) are connected with meaning as addressed in the previous section. Volgsten's thesis suggests a functional capacity in musical works that can aid the creation of identity both within and without a particular culture. Presumably, Xerente fusion genres are doing both. They are creating a Christian identity within Xerente society as well as a common identity with the region of Brazil in which they live. Furthermore, Volgsten highlights a potential misunderstanding of identity as a given or unchanging characteristic of individuals or societies. Citing another author, he affirms that "we don't have identities, we *do* identities. An identity is something we perform by *acting in particular, culturally accepted, ways*."[24] Once again, as indicated through the discussion of ethnogenesis, identity is not a matter settled once for all at the beginning of a person's life, but continues to develop and change through adoption and adaptation of varied or entirely new practices. Xerente contemporary music genres exemplify this change serving either as catalysts or as expressions of the process of ethnogenesis. They function, therefore, either as collaborative designers or demonstrators of the identity development occurring within the Xerente consciousness.

Morehouse's study of the Maninka church's use of Western hymns gives relevance to the way these hymns function socially. Briefly stated, they function as connection to a "longstanding tradition," they "fill an artistic gap," they attempt "to protect the community from syncretism," and "provide stylistic diversity."[25] Although the Maninka's present-day preference of Western hymns for Christian services differ from Xerente choices in many ways, there are certain parallels between the functions of the respective musical preferences. Fusion genres among the Xerente may indeed be connecting them to their own tradition in the musical traits of their compositions but they have also not attempted to eliminate the hymns that had initially been introduced. The Xerente compositional initiatives are functioning as outlets for newer artistic creations, filling the gap of earlier years, and providing opportunities for local creatives to flourish through the use of their musical and literary gifts. The indigenous

---

23. Volgsten, "Music, Culture, Politics," 1.
24. Volgsten, "Music, Culture, Politics," 6.
25. Morehouse, "'They're Playing Our Song,'" 25–26.

hymns of the Maninka in Morehouse's research, which she and others had hoped would find a regular place in their churches, were supposed to exercise some six social functions which she describes in the following paragraph:

1. Provide a sonic bridge to connect with the local people; a sense that this music, this religion, and this God is "ours."
2. Fill an artistic gap, allowing the local community to create relevant socioreligious musical commentary and song styles that speak straight to the heart.
3. Encourage the community to focus afresh on scriptural and theological themes, specifically relevant to their current needs and vantage points.
4. Utilize local creative culture and artistry that encourage and support the arts in community at large and in the church.
5. Convey a coherent, cohesive message (the text of a song), which is imperative if music is going to be used by the local church for doctrinal teaching, evangelism, or encouragement of believers.
6. Foster a sense of agency and self-sustainability in the local church, which stabilizes the church in society as a legitimate, locally rooted religious community.[26]

Contemporary Xerente Christian compositions function on socially in several of the ways described by Morehouse. The Xerente openly testify that new compositions are connecting with the local people through a preferred genre which, in turn, creates a sense that the Christian faith is "theirs." Using Morehouse's terminology, the "artistic gap" is being filled through songs that "speak straight to the heart." Giving witness to this function, during the Cabeceira Verde workshop in 2017 one of the musicians rose up after a message on Ps 40:3[27] and said: "Music is like an arrow that crosses our heart!"[28] Moreover, the endeavor to create new songs functions as a catalyst to encourage musicians and lyricists to think about Scripture and theological themes in ways that are relevant to their needs and vantage points. The opportunity to create in these fused styles has

---

26. Morehouse, "'They're Playing Our Song,'" 25–26.
27. "And He put a new song into my mouth, *even* a hymn to our God; many shall see *it* and fear, and shall hope in the Lord." Ps 40:3. Logos Bible Translation.
28. Negrão, "Música," para. 10.

also fostered support for the arts in the community and in church, as well as "a sense of agency and self-sustainability," a signpost discussed later in this chapter. Of these six functions, the only one that may be dubious at this moment is the fifth in Morehouse's text. Although musicians and pastors do intend for the local compositions to have a "coherent, cohesive message (the text of a song)," some musicians, such as Tiago, realize that this is often not the case. However, even within this situation, the ideal of a "coherent, cohesive message" (and, in their opinion, one that matches the music well) *is* present in their minds and it may simply need a process of internal sifting of "good compositions" from the increasing number of songs being created.

In traditional Xerente ceremonies, music serves as an *autentificador* (certifier), as Pr. Rinaldo describes it. In the mind of the Brazilian national society the practice of *autenticar* (roughly translated as to "certify") is imbedded as a bureaucratic step indispensable for the validation (the official stamp of a clerk's office declaring the "authenticity" or truthfulness) of documents. In Xerente society, in which written records have traditionally only been important when they relate to the national society, the certification or validation of a birth or marriage is executed through rituals. When a girl receives a name, there is clasping of the hands and a circle is formed. At this point the group sings the name as a way of "sealing" the name, or else certifying that it is the girl's name. As the interview with Pr. Rinaldo was taking place in June of 2019, he himself came to the consideration of this particular function exercised by Christian music within the church for the first time. He came to recognize that music in the context of the service has likely been an irreplaceable feature since the beginning of the missionary work due to the cultural perception of certification or validation with which music endows the spoken words as well as accompanying activities. As the absence of music in a traditional ritual has the effect of incompleteness, so the absence of music in the church context could indicate in the minds of the Xerente believer that worship has *not* taken place at that moment. Music validates, it certifies the act of worship and edification of the church in the Xerente context.

6.3.3 Individual and Spiritual Functions

Within the discussion of meaning and emotion it was noted that they pertain to the realm of the community primarily on the basis of individual perception. That is, if individuals do not perceive meaning and sense emotions, there is not an abstract "community" spirit that holds to these perceptions. Likewise, the various social functions music can fulfill, and that are indeed present among the Xerente, are perceived by individuals who are able to acknowledge such functions. Additionally, music can play vital roles in the life of individuals that others in the same community may not recognize as relevant to themselves or at least have not yet experienced.

Through the corroborating sources presented in this work, music has been demonstrated to participate both in the development and the expression of identity within a given society. This identity is acknowledged by the community but perceived by individuals within it. For the individual, music can perform the function of bringing him or her into the common identity shared with others. Arguably, people can be drawn into Christian identity through a musical act, when they individually connect with the musical genre or song they hear. As in the first social function of locally created songs indicated by Morehouse, the individual has the sense that "this God is *mine*."[29] Likewise, music functions as a musical commentary speaking to the heart of individuals. It is oftentimes relevant to the current needs of individuals. Individual musicians are encouraged to create and develop their gifts, taking initiatives that affirm personal agency, supporting the local community.

More particular to the individual, however, are spiritual functions which the contemporary musical genres can fulfill in a Xerente Christian's life. Spirituality and faith, although frequently addressed in terms of community, rest foundationally in individuals. That is, from a biblical perspective, it is the individual who chooses to believe the tenets of the Christian faith, not the community for him. Those listening to spiritual themes addressed by musical instantiations, not unlike through public preaching, respond to them on a personal level. Individuals demonstrate their faith through confession, public acts, or other Christian practices. Hence, it could be argued that spiritual meaning as well as function in music is primarily identified at the individual level, since spiritual fervor in a given community or church is not verified through abstract ideas only, but rather through the demonstrations of spiritual sincerity and fervor in individuals, who, in conjunction with others of similar spirit, constitute an aura of spirituality within the community.

29. An individual application of Morehouse's statement. Morehouse, "'They're Playing Our Song,'" 25–26.

On the basis of the observations above, there is no lack of evidence of spiritual function in music in the lives of individual Xerente Christians and non-Christians. Although Xerente musical genres address different biblical themes through their lyrics, as Pr. Pedro indicated in his interview, the lyrics are frequently addressed to those outside the church as an invitation to receive the gospel. The songs manifest the evangelistic spirit that pervaded the ministries of earlier and contemporary missionaries. Through them the Xerente Christian demonstrates concern for fellow members of the society who have not yet responded to the gospel through faith. Music provides an outlet or creates an opportunity to speak a Christian message to the surrounding neighbors through a culturally acceptable medium of communication.

Although centuries and cultures apart from the Xerente contemporary fusion genres, the potentiality of a proclamatory power in music was likewise a topic of debate, or an affirmation of reality, among Lutheran leaders and cantors in the seventeenth and eighteenth centuries.[30] Gottfried Scheibel, Georg Motz, and Caspar Ruetz, for instance, defended not only that music had such a power, but "that the role of music is . . . of equal importance to the sermon."[31] Scheibel went so far as to advocate "explicitly . . . that the same musical affections cultivated in opera be carried into church music as a means of evangelization."[32] In this Baroque form of contextualization, the use of musical elements from opera (a popular genre of the day) may have been founded on naturalistic methodology and possibly on the Baroque doctrine of affections. Nevertheless, Scheibel along with Motz and Ruetz demonstrate something of the significance of the question of the proclamatory function of music. For Xerente communities, who have likely never heard of any of these German musicians, proclamation is also one of the principal functions performed by music. By means of a contextualized musical medium, Xerente Christians declare their faith and evangelize their community.

The emotional response of individual Xerente Christians to the music they hear or sing is more than a psychological reaction to musical sound. The very reasons given by interviewed Xerente Christians for the presence of emotions when they hear certain songs or music styles relate to memories of moments of spiritual devotion, or of repentance for unfaithfulness to God and to the Christian faith. Although such responses

---

30. Begbie and Guthrie, *Resonant Witness*, locs. 917–71.
31. Begbie and Guthrie, *Resonant Witness*, loc. 974.
32. Begbie and Guthrie, *Resonant Witness*, locs. 961–62.

and functions are not unique features of the fusion genres addressed in this research—given that individuals have personal meaning perception for different styles or songs—the testimonies given by the Xerente interviewees related primarily to the fusion genres of locally-composed songs. Thus, functions of spiritual practice and of spiritual reminders can be identified in these genres and have been implanted into common practice in church and recognized as characteristic of Christian practice by the Xerente communities.

6.3.4 Evaluation

The exploration of functionality in the newly composed Christian music of the Xerente has revealed its significant roles, particularly in the life of the Xerente church. Music functions in important social and cultural areas, but also provides a medium for individuals to connect spiritually with the church and the community at large. Moreover, the consensus of the missionaries is that the application of music for evangelistic purposes derives from the practices of the missionaries practice handed down to Xerente churches. In their creative acts of musical composition, this exercise arises as a prominent function of new compositions.

The composite number of functions performed by these musical fusion genres offer substantial evidence of their integration into the cultural setting of Xerente society. Therefore, it is reasonable to consider that these functions serve as markers or signposts that an authentic, purposeful practice is taking place among them.

6.4 COMPETENCE AMONG MUSICIANS AS SIGNPOST OF AUTHENTICITY

6.4.1 Xerente Musicianship

Christian musicians among the Xerente have been composing new lyrics and music at unprecedented and, according to the missionaries' reports, at accelerating rates during the last decade. Although training has been and continues to be sparse, many of them have taken in hand to learn to play the guitar and the keyboard by observing one another or watching instructional videos. Competence, in the case at hand, can be found in some musicians more than others. To be sure, some eager composers face difficulties bringing a song to completion and express a desire to learn more from formal teachers or one another. By their own admission, several musicians and hopeful lyricists see their shortcomings and would not consider themselves completely competent in the area of musical composition. However, competence in the creation of fusion genres is demonstrated through their joint efforts. The combination of melodic outlines containing typical Xerente linguistic and musical features with the electronic accompaniment of harmony and rhythm, at times also with a guitar, frequently takes place during a practice session. The accompanists freely improvise an introduction based on the melody of the song (which they may have only heard briefly) and musically indicate to the singer that his/her entrance is approaching. Following a cue, the singer begins the song and gives space to the accompanist for potential interludes between verses.

Masterful competence to compose and reproduce music of this genre may not necessarily be a quality presently found embodied in individual musicians, although some are able to sing and play at the same time.[33] Christian music among the Xerente is generally characterized by combined efforts. A fair assessment of competence in this case may, therefore, require a consideration that this characteristic is demonstrated primarily in terms of community.

Improvisational skills and creativity among the Xerente are greater than they themselves recognize, according to Pr. Rinaldo.[34] He retells a story of a time in 2014, after he had been sick and hospitalized for fifty-five days, had to undergo five surgeries, and was then received with honor in a ceremony in a Xerente village. His family and the Xerente had lost hope of his recovery. Nevertheless, he recovered and became relatively strong again. He relates the event:

> The MC chose a traditional song that told about the birth of the Son of God . . . I didn't know they had it. I was astounded. So, he took that music with the lyrics: "Let's meet at the plaza because our father will be arriving." They made the circle. . . . In the ceremony the last woman that had a child stands in the middle representing Mary, and an Indian comes bringing an offering

---

33. During the periods of interaction with the Xerente no case of singers who also played the keyboard at the same time was encountered, but guitar players appear to do this regularly.

34. Personal interview with Pr. Rinaldo at his house in a Xerente village on June 18, 2019.

representing the Kings. They made a new place for me to sing. They sang that song but adapted to refer to me. They improvised the lyrics at the moment. The melody was known, but he had changed the words.[35]

Similarly in June of 2019 during Pr. Rinaldo's leadership training in Cabeceira Verde, Lázaro improvised new lyrics to a melody honoring the missionaries among the Xerente through a retelling of their stories. In the words of Pr. Rinaldo, "we are working with a musical society."[36] These two illustrations, although not primarily samples of musical or melodic creativity, demonstrate nevertheless the innate creative abilities and the inclination to utilize and reshape elements already present in their cultural environment. In fact, four of the songs the musicians recorded in 2017 also involved the reutilization of an existing traditional melody, adapted to new Christian lyrics. Although their choice of using existing melodies brought a certain initial disappointment to the non-Xerente contributors, they are illustrative of the practice described by Pr. Rinaldo above.

Even though they recognize this potential among their musicians to a certain extent (and do make use of it), Pr. Rinaldo says that "they do not admit that they created it. If you ask an MC how he composed, he will say it was God that gave it to him. He thinks he is just repeating what God gave him."[37] Similar statements were made to me by several musicians, both in 2017 and 2019, that confirm Pr. Rinaldo's report. He also emphasizes that instrumentalists can easily transpose to other keys and learn well by observation, a common practice in Xerente culture. This innate capacity found in numerous Xerente members, however, does not prove they are already musically competent. Competence is a developed skill, one which individual musicians among the Xerente are attempting to achieve through educational means to which they have access.

6.4.2 Competence and Authenticity

The value of local or cultural competence and agency as indicators of authentic expression is not a novel observation. Beth Conklin's article

---

35. Personal interview with Pr. Rinaldo at his house in a Xerente village on June 18, 2019.
36. Personal interview with Pr. Rinaldo at his house in a Xerente village on June 18, 2019.
37. Personal interview with Pr. Rinaldo at his house in a Xerente village on June 18, 2019.

on aesthetics and authenticity in indigenous Amazonian activism brings to light how these factors weigh in for the evaluation of authenticity. She points to the anthropological celebration of the "possibilities implicit in turning Western technology to locally empowering grassroots purposes,"[38] in which case "the emphasis is on indigenous competency[39] and control."[40] Indeed, "the appropriation of complex Western technologies by indigenous people *challenges views that equate authenticity with purity from foreign influences.*"[41] Moreover, if one restricts a respect for authenticity within indigenous nations to that which is essentially untouched by foreign elements, then, in essence, a different measuring stick is being applied from the one which nation-states use among themselves. Nation-states, while concerned with the maintenance of ethnic or national distinctions, typically welcome cultural exchanges as a form of development and growth for its citizens. They may even procure training at a foreign location for the betterment of the practice in one's native soil. Still, these elements frequently become naturalized, being adopted and adapted to local needs and themes.

Along the journey of adoption and adaptation of external musical elements, there are certainly increasing levels of competence for which one can aim. Musical competence among the Xerente in reference to the evaluation of musical authenticity in fusion genres is not necessarily guided by Western classical musical standards or even by the mastery of traditional and regional genres. What the evidence demonstrates is that music is indeed being composed and performed in these styles through the capacity and competence of Xerente musicians and not by external players, even though instruments have been obtained from outside and other Brazilian sounds have been incorporated into this music.

---

38. Conklin, "Body Paint, Feathers, and VCRs," 6.

39. Although *competency* was used in the original springboard resource for this signpost, this variant of *competence* tends to be associated with 'professional' ability attained through training, as well as with academic markers of achievement. Therefore, the term *competence*, not intending to imply any significant level of mastery in professional or academic terms, has been chosen to indicate a general ability to create and perform in the genres associated with this research.

40. Conklin, "Body Paint, Feathers, and VCRs," 6.

41. Conklin, "Body Paint, Feathers, and VCRs," 6. Emphasis added. A comical representation of this dilemma is Gary Larson's "Anthropologists! Anthropologists!" in his famous *The Far Side* strip.

6.4.3 Evaluation

Xerente Christian musicians freely acknowledge their need and desire to obtain more intensive musical training. Nevertheless, competence is present as a combined characteristic of ensemble work. The evidence indicates that this internal independence in composing and performing in their chosen styles is a signpost of the genres' authenticity, seeing that the Xerente themselves are capable and responsible for the production of this music for the primary use of their own community.

6.5 AGENCY AS SIGNPOST OF AUTHENTICITY

6.5.1 Historical Development

The development of Xerente-style songs in recent years represents a new stage in the growth process of the Xerente church. Pr. Rinaldo retells that at the beginning of their work, the missionaries had little idea of the importance of considering ethnic identity and culture. He and Pr. Guenther, along with other collaborators, adapted to their newly gained anthropological information little by little. But since the missionaries were "in charge" of such church decisions, they unwittingly implanted in the Xerente mind that they were to be responsible to introduce everything to them. Later, Xerente Christians took greater initiative by translating the lyrics of the hymns into their language. The missionaries encouraged that effort and published the translation of the hymns for use in church services. Although a few new hymns were also composed, they resembled the Western hymns in most aspects. Today, Xerente musicians demonstrate an awakened consciousness towards their heritage which they are now attempting to recover.

Historically speaking, Pr. Rinaldo sees the administration of musical choices as a mixture of local and missionary agency. The very discovery of their musical potential may have come as a result of the missionaries' influence. The missionaries grew in this area throughout the years and have been willing since then not only to support the Xerente's initiatives to strengthen their cultural expressions, but also to rethink the missiological principles which guided their work. Through the encouragement of the use of local musical forms for Christian worship, the Xerente have come to recognize their own potential. As they began to develop their own music, it is possible that they also considered the option of using their own musical styles as contrary to the perspective of church leadership and may have hesitated to make such a move out of respect for them. Indeed, other denominational works present in the Xerente territory are still very resistant to local forms, and could remain so for the foreseeable future, according to Pr. Rinaldo.[42]

6.5.2 Performance Demeanor and Local Agency

New musical material is being spontaneously produced by Xerente singers and instrumentalists at the present time. Individuals create songs and manifest their desire to share them with a congregation at regular church services or vigils. At such venues, it is certainly possible that they will be denied an opportunity due to a lack of time in the service, but according to the general testimony of the Xerente and the missionaries, this is a rare occurrence. The use of the accompaniment of a keyboardist or a guitarist is an implicit matter by all accounts. In every situation which I personally observed, the singers have been patient with their accompanists as they elaborate an introduction or an accompaniment to a new song they are presenting. During the Cabeceira Verde recordings, for instance, singers and instrumentalists were accommodating to one another as well as to the needs of the music editor for the sessions, Héber Negrão, when silence was needed for adjustments. This even-tempered demeanor is characteristic during musical presentations in church services.

The choices of music to be sung in a service come in part from the pastor or congregational leader but are not exclusively theirs to make. Reflecting the Pauline description of a church meeting in 1 Cor 14, the Xerente implicitly accept that several people within the congregation may contribute to the service (songs, biblical messages, and prayers). This participatory approach which Xerente churches have adopted along the decades has had the effect of distributing the practical administration of service elements, particularly of musical contributions, among several of their members.

The church community, in the use of music and the overwhelming prevalence of fusion genres, has become the principal voice for the advancement and establishment of these genres. The specific song choices performed at each instance are made by individuals within the church, primarily the service leader and a singer (or singers) presenting a song.

---

42. Personal interview with Pr. Rinaldo, June 18, 2019.

The interviewees of this research expressed their motivations for their choices in terms of how a song had significance for themselves, and that they believed the words and musical style of the song will be appreciated. Understanding that the regional rhythms that have blended into their aural environment have the potential of communicating with the listeners on multiple levels, the choice of accompanying rhythm is generally maintained as previously heard or may be left to be decided by the accompanist in the case of a brand-new creation. Therefore, local agency in this case study still demonstrates characteristics of being a truly communal practice, although, reportedly, other areas of Xerente life have suffered because of conflicting individualistic practices.[43] The weekly administration of musical choices in Christian practice, which now shows preference for locally composed fusion genres, lies in the hands of the local congregations, especially those derived from the framework of Baptist missions.

The presence of local agency in musical choices, however, has not eliminated the potential participation of outside voices (such as those of the missionaries) in the decision-making process. As of 2019, Xerente church leaders, together with Prs. Rinaldo and Guenther, were forming a committee to evaluate the new songs that have sprung up during the last few years, and will decide which ones will become part of the new songbook scheduled to be published in 2020. This collection should contain 150 to 200 songs, including traditional Western hymns and choruses as well as many of the newly composed songs. The committee, consisting primarily of Xerente leaders, will make these decisions, yet weigh in the opinions of the missionaries which may differ from the majority for a number of reasons.

6.5.3 Evaluation

The question of agency in musical choices is multidimensional. In fact, historically, such choices were made by the missionaries and largely accepted by the Xerente as normative. Progressively, the local musical culture became viewed with more serious interest by the missionaries who encouraged the local believers to use it for Christian practices. This joint agency has probably influenced the local musical perception to a great extent along the decades. On the other hand, the Xerente churches are

---

43. Such situations of conflict were related to me by several interviewees during this author's visit to the Xerente territory in June 2019. Among them were the missionaries and Xerente pastors.

now the deciding voices that are "controlling" (allowing and encouraging) the proliferation of preferred musical styles. The potential for opposing voices from within or from outside the community still exists. However, it would be accurate to state that the administration of Xerente fusion genres is primarily in the hands of local people. Local agency, then, signposts the authentic character of Xerente Christian fusion genres through the demonstration that their own musicians and leaders, aware of the music's emotional and meaningful connection to individuals and to the society, regard it as appropriate and implement it in church services without dependence on external administration. Bertolini's case study in the Amazon region affirms the value of autonomy in the process of musical creation:

> On the basis of field work, I was able to verify the constitution of an autonomous process of musical production in which the social agents that were being studied manufacture their own musical instruments, compose their own songs, pen their own lyrics, perform the arrangements themselves, organize choreographies and present them publicly. The musical performances are, to a certain point, an emancipatory element, a product of this autonomy.[44]

This emancipatory element is made visible among Xerente Christians also, who, with the exception of manufacturing their own instruments—a skill that is also not usually required of Western musicians—are displaying similar autonomy through their fusion genres.

---

44. Bertolini, "Performance Musical e Reconhecimento," 168. Translation mine.

15—Recording sessions during the workshop in Cabeceira Verde, July 2017

7

Considerations of Authenticity in Xerente Church Fusion Genres

7.1 THE MEANING OF AUTHENTICITY

THE LITERATURE ADDRESSING QUESTIONS of authenticity uses the term focusing mainly on three contexts. As a sociological and psychological focus, authenticity studies address questions of the true identity of individuals, sincerity, and autonomy of choice.[1] Another group seeks to identify authenticity in performance of local genres in tourist settings or media-related programs.[2] A third group deals with the anthropological identification of material culture or the genuine manifestations of cultural practices.[3]

The approach in determining authenticity in this book does not primarily focus on issues of sociological identification of individual personality, although much of the character and value of Xerente fusion genres does relate *to* individuals. Questions as to whether individuals themselves are being "authentic" or "true to themselves," therefore, are not considered here at length. On the other hand, studies of tourist-oriented performances or the use of classic ideas of indigenous characteristics in

---

1. This context was of interest to philosophers such as Sartre, Freud, Kierkegaard, and others. See Varga and Guignon, "Authenticity," sec. 2.

2. Other authors exemplify this concern for authenticity in relation to tourism and are discussed by Beth Conklin and Renata Hodgson.

3. For instance, see Nezhad et al., "Definition of Authenticity Concept."

relationship to outsiders,[4] as well as those related to material culture, do provide insights into the identification of authentic expression as viewed either by insiders or outsiders and are considered in this chapter. As I have previously stated, the evaluation of potential authenticity as the genuine character of Xerente Christian musical fusion genres gives greater weight to the perceptions of the local Xerente communities. The purpose of this chapter is to correlate the concepts behind the various definitions of authenticity in the literature to the signposts (or criteria, as addressed by certain authors) as valid markers of an authentic character. The multiple definitions of *authenticity* encountered along the course of this research incorporate crucial ideas that can be considered foundational for identifying cultural expressions as authentic. Among them are autonomy of choice, the identification of insiders with these expressions, their truthful correspondence "to one's own personality, spirit, or character,"[5] and "the condition of significant, emotionally appropriate living."[6]

Considerations of authenticity in the preservation of material heritage also provide a set of ideas that support the criteria (the signposts) for a positive evaluation of authenticity proposed in this research. Three Iranian writers, Somayeh Fadaei Nezhad, a professor in the School of Architecture in the University of Tehran, along with two cowriters, published an article furnishing a list of international documents from 1964 until 2011 that address concerns of authenticity in the preservation of cultural landscapes around the globe.[7] The content of these documents reveal a progressive broadening of the perception of authenticity, although a "duality of meanings and terms"[8] continues to persist. From an earlier concentration on tangible characteristics of an architectural work of art, later documents recognized the importance of intangible features for a correct assessment of authenticity.

The earliest of these documents, labeled *The Venice Charter*, identified as "authentic" that which was historical and sought ways of slowing down the "heritage property erosion process."[9] In 1978, the World Heritage Committee elaborated four criteria of authenticity, "'design',

4. For this research, Conklin's (1997) and Hodgson's (2007) publications were particularly helpful.
5. Merriam-Webster Dictionary, "Authentic."
6. The Oxford Dictionary of Philosophy, "Authenticity."
7. Nezhad et al., "Definition of Authenticity Concept," 96.
8. Dushkina, "Historic Reconstruction," 92.
9. Nezhad et al., "Definition of Authenticity Concept," 94.

'materials', 'workmanship', and 'setting',"[10] continuing the focus on the tangible aspects of a cultural heritage. In 1994, however, the Nara Conference on Authenticity[11] broadened the scope of the concept by considering "the importance of intangible and associated aspects of heritage."[12] Natalia Dushkina, a Russian representative at the Conference argued in her paper, that "things that have tangible and material aspects (form, setting, techniques) and things that have intangible and immaterial aspects (function, use, tradition, spirit) "used to be *the bearers of authenticity* in a monument" that "they transmitted authenticity to us and thus *are relative to it*."[13] In another article, Dushkina cites Jukka Jokilehto who had come to understand authenticity from a broader perspective that included creative choices:

> Being authentic refers to a specific event; it describes someone or something acting *autonomously* and not depending on others, *having authority* and deep identity in form and substance, *being original, creative*, unrepeated, unique, *sincere, true*, exceptional or genuine. "Being identical," however, does not refer to a specific event, but to "universal" in the sense of being representative to a class with the same material constitution, properties, qualities, or meaning, e.g., identical reproduction, replica, copy, reconstruction.[14]

The World Heritage Convention in 2005 introduced a "test of authenticity" that advanced the concept of authenticity as "the capability of the property to transmit the cultural significance of a place."[15] The criteria listed are "form and design; materials and substance; *use and function*; traditions, techniques and management systems; location and setting; *language and other forms of intangible heritage; spirit and feeling;*

---

10. Nezhad et al., "Definition of Authenticity Concept," 94.

11. International Council on Monuments and Sites, "Nara Document on Authenticity (1994)." "The Nara Document on Authenticity was drafted by the 45 participants at the Nara Conference on Authenticity in Relation to the World Heritage Convention, held at Nara, Japan, from 1–6 November 1994, at the invitation of the Agency for Cultural Affairs (Government of Japan) and the Nara Prefecture. The Agency organized the Nara Conference in cooperation with UNESCO, ICCROM and ICOMOS" (see credits for this document).

12. Nezhad et al., "Definition of Authenticity Concept," 94.

13. Nezhad et al., "Definition of Authenticity Concept," 94–95. Emphases added.

14. Dushkina, "Historic Reconstruction," 91. Emphases added.

15. Nezhad et al., "Definition of Authenticity Concept," 95.

Considerations of Authenticity in Xerente Church Fusion Genres   169

and other internal and external factors (UNESCO, 2005: paragraph 82)."[16] Nezhad observes that the concept of authenticity "has moved beyond the physical aspect of heritage and [the properties] have been proposed as *social and intellectual structures.* As Jenny Kidd has pointed out, that "the concept of authenticity is of course *socially constructed.*"[17]

Clearly, not all architectural aspects suggested in the citations above could have absolute correspondence to musical elements, and the lists above are not intended to be directly applied to the evaluation of musical authenticity. However, the relevance of the evolution of the concept of authenticity throughout the last six decades is that it demonstrates a trend towards the admission of intangible considerations as key aspects of authentic expressions. Equally relevant is Jenny Kidd's concept of authenticity as *socially constructed.* This perspective supports the concept that the evaluation of authenticity is best demonstrated through aspects that are considered valuable within the Xerente social context rather than through those of outsiders.

Unlike architectural works, music is essentially intangible in the strict sense of the word, apart from written scores and musical instruments. Nevertheless, for music, "tangible" could also refer to form and other features which may be systematically codified or to actions confirmed through external observation, as indicated by the *competence* and *agency* signposts. One can, for instance, evaluate the musical competence and the community's agency in administering the use of the music by analyzing the skills of the musicians and leaders in their overt actions of playing and leading. Intangible aspects such as *meaning* and *function*, however, typically puzzle outsiders in regard to their cultural authenticity since they refer to qualitative indications that can only be verified through testimonials of those involved in the art. Simply stated, meanings (and functions to a certain extent) of a particular genre cannot simply be identified through observation but require subjective exposition and explanation from those who make use of the genre.

The four signposts I have proposed as potential markers of authenticity in Xerente music fusion genres incorporate, but are not limited to, the various definitions and the criteria suggested by other authors. They are not viewed as exclusive parameters by which authenticity should be evaluated but are offered as relevant and ascertainable markers of

16. Nezhad et al., "Definition of Authenticity Concept," 95. Emphasis added.
17. Nezhad et al., "Definition of Authenticity Concept," 95. Also see Kidd, "Performing the Knowing Archive," 25.

its presence in the genres. *Meaning* and *function* can demonstrate that the genres correspond truthfully, genuinely, or authentically to the community's and the individual's own, present-day, "personality, spirit, or character," as well as their value as "emotionally appropriate, significant, purposive, and responsible mode[s] of human life." *Competence* supports the practice of *agency* by allowing certain members of the community to autonomously create and utilize their compositions. The four signposts also take into consideration a wider view of valuable expressions, including recent blends of cultural elements, unchained from the dichotomy of traditional versus modern. Finally, they seek to provide a balanced perception of authenticity that includes both tangible and intangible aspects of this musical expression.

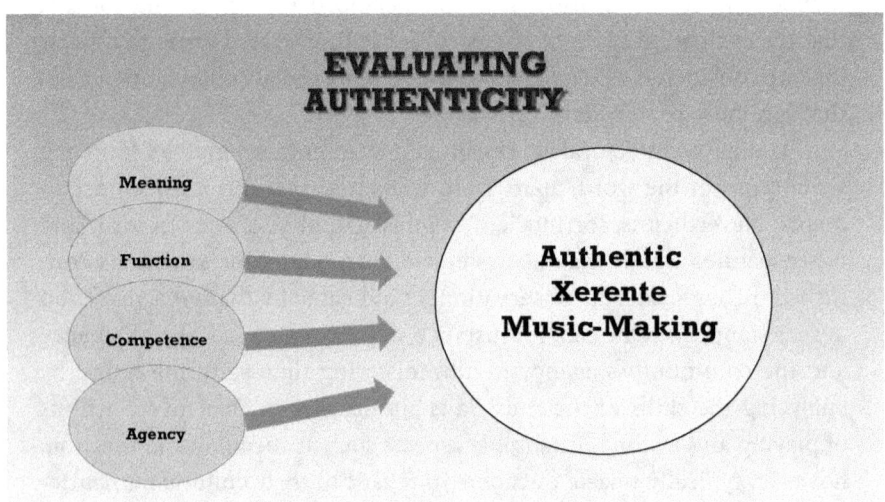

16—Model of Signposts of Authenticity

7.2 SIGNPOST OF MEANING

Throughout this research I have indicated that the meaningful communication among members of the Xerente community through the medium of its Christian music fusion genres is a potential indicator, or signpost, of Xerente authenticity. This indication is an intangible aspect that has been collected as evidence through the testimonials of individual members of Xerente churches.

The study of semiotics demonstrates the wide spectrum of "understandings" (or interpretants) which can develop through the catalyst of even a single song, let alone a whole genre. On the basis of Peirce's semiotic principles, I have affirmed that music's meanings are found primarily in the receptors who "register" the actual message they perceived, even if it differs from the intent of the communicator or from the typical connotation of a genre. As such, the meaning(s) considered crucial and of interest as indicators of authenticity in Xerente Christian music are those registered by members of the Xerente community, by whom and for whom the music is being created and performed.

The sounds of Xerente fusion genres could easily lead an outsider to the conclusion that the common meanings of the "borrowed" regional rhythms are the same set of meanings within the Xerente church and community. The evidence obtained through the interviewees among the Xerente, however, indicate that many of the presumed meanings have been modified as they were introduced to the local churches and may be anchored both in traditional and modern aspects of their society. Canclini suggests that the patrimony of hybrid cultures is not well represented by the dichotomy of traditional versus modern, but rather by a classification of "the archaic, the residual, and the emergent."[18] The emergent patrimony of such cultures "designates *new meanings and values, new practices and social relations*."[19] New Christian music compositions, while making use of regional rhythms and genres not normally associated with traditional church practices (and at times even associated with practices contradictory to Christianity), have been assigned or have developed new meanings in the hearts and minds of Xerente community members through their application in church settings. This fusion created by Xerente Christian musicians illustrates the "mix of continuity and change" discussed by Schrag in *Creating Local Arts Together*: "Cultural dynamism happens when artists masterfully use the most malleable elements of their arts to invigorate the most stable."[20] It has allowed for an infusion of "new energy into the stable structures,"[21] which in this case consists of the energy of the adopted electronic instruments and sounds into the singing styles and forms of earlier local traditions.

---

18. Canclini, *Hybrid Cultures*, loc. 138.
19. Canclini, *Hybrid Cultures*, loc. 138. Emphasis added.
20. Schrag, *Creating Local Arts Together*, 61.
21. Schrag, *Creating Local Arts Together*, 61.

Within the context of the current Xerente cultural revival and renewal path, in conjunction with the Christian message and significance communicated by these songs, the new genres represent one aspect of the process of "authentically remaking" an identity rather than a "made-up identity."[22] The case of the Makuxi trajectory from the strictly traditional, to the musical adoption of *forró*, to the subsequent reworking of their traditional music into a new whole, reaffirms the possibility of internal reassessment of cultural meanings in an authentic manner. Their stylistic journey "is an *integral part of their ethnic identity* . . . in the process of their constant reformulation."[23]

Outside observers may or may not fully comprehend how or why the emergent fusion genres communicate with Xerente Christians as they report. However, considering that the general participants in Xerente churches attach meanings to their musical fusion genres broadly *as intended* by their composers and performers, it is reasonable to consider that it is an authentic and culturally appropriate form of communication. The genres function *symbolically* (in the Peircean sense) as transmitters of spiritual connection and provide a sense of belonging and cultural vitality. They serve as emotional reminders of individual spiritual experiences and are not suffering any significant amount of codal interference[24] as communication moves from subject to interpretant. The significance of the close identity between the intended communication of the music "producers" of Xerente genres and the perception of their meanings by listeners demonstrates the presence of a relatively clear pathway which authentic (genuinely cultural) musical expressions generally enjoy. That is, in an ideal scenario of communication, communicators wish their audiences to understand their messages correctly, even if the communication simultaneously creates a variety of connotations that are not contradictory to the core of their message. It is reasonable, therefore, to infer from the Xerente musical interaction, that a mode of musical communication is being used that transfers the core *meaning* intended by

---

22. Hill, *History, Power, and Identity*, 27.

23. Fernandes, "Parixara ao Forró," 145. Emphasis added.

24. *Codal interference* is a concept introduced by the semiotician Philip Tagg (cited elsewhere in this book), which refers to the modification of the meaning of the "code" (the commonly used mode of communication being used) through the interference of some event or new association with the capacity to create a meaning distinct from that intended by the communicator.

composers and performers to the participants in a culturally appropriate—hence, *authentic*—way.

Roberta King's dissertation on Senufo Christian music acknowledges the complexity of affective, cognitive, and behavioral dimensions within the "pathway of communication."[25] The communication is effective and appropriate, however, when the songs "bring awareness of the past experiences and/or current life-situations of a song participant, creating *relevance* to a specific situation."[26] Relevance, as I perceive it, can be demonstrated through the presence of meaning as identified by participants and performers alike in Xerente contemporary genres.

In sum, locally perceived meanings signpost the contemporary Christian fusion genres as authentic on the following grounds: 1. a reassigning of meanings has occurred for genres adopted from Brazilian national genres; 2. local meanings are broadly understood by participants within the Xerente community as intended by the composers and performers; 3. the songs are relevant (or meaningful) by bringing awareness of past experiences and/or current life-situations in the lives of participants.

7.3 SIGNPOST OF FUNCTION

It is broadly accepted that artistic expressions, including music, perform functions within any given social situation or in individual lives. Volgsten, for instance, who states that "music can function as an identity marker,"[27] does not attempt to justify his assumption that music plays roles in various situations. In architectural art, both the 1994 Nara Statement and the 2005 Convention for the Safeguarding of the Intangible Heritage list *function* as an integral part of the concept of authenticity.[28] Music, as a usual mode of expression, normally demonstrates functionality in societies that have been studied by anthropologists up to the present time. The ethnomusicologist Bruno Nettl not only affirms this functionality but, considering its importance and the various approaches it requires, dedicates a whole chapter of his classic collection of articles, *The Study of*

---

25. King, *Pathways in Christian Music Communication*, 165.
26. King, *Pathways in Christian Music Communication*, 199. Emphasis added.
27. Volgsten, "Music, Culture, Politics," 4.
28. Nezhad et al., "Definition of Authenticity Concept," 95.

Ethnomusicology,[29] to this topic. Nettl finds little relevance in the earlier distinction made by the ethnomusicologist Alan Merriam between "use" and "function," although he closes his reply to Merriam's distinction by agreeing with him on this point: that music "is clearly indispensable to the proper promulgation of the activities that constitute a society."[30] He affirms his belief that music has two fundamental functions: "to control humanity's relationship to the supernatural, mediating between human and other beings, and to support the integrity of individual social groups."[31] In essence, according to Nettl, the specific functions (or uses) of music are linked to spirituality and identity. If this is true, then it is reasonable to conceive of the functions of music as intimately related to authentic spiritual experience, and authentic identity.

Furthermore, specific musical genres, styles, pieces, and features can all exert some influence—play a role or perform a function—on someone or some group of people. This "power" detected in musics of all sorts is largely acknowledged by scientists and lay people as a unique phenomenon of the human race. From a neurological perspective, Oliver Sacks discussed some important effects of the power of music such as coercion through cultural habit or volume, restoration of motor abilities in parkinsonian patients, emotional journey into one's self, visible physical responses, mental repetition of tunes, hallucinations, and many more.[32] Indeed, he stated that "our auditory systems, our nervous systems, are tuned for music."[33] Music has this capacity because of its "emotional power," its "affective impact by which [it] in its very specific way becomes a felt experience in time."[34]

Function in this study, however, does not refer simply to the presence of influential power. It denotes primarily music's *roles* as an established aspect of a given community, whether by intent or as a practical consequence of a cultural practice. The functions performed by Xerente music, in particular the genres emerging through a fusion of external and internal elements, have been identified in the previous chapter and are demonstratively connected to the spiritual life of the church and of its individual members as well as to both corporate and individual Christian identities.

29. Nettl, *Study of Ethnomusicology*, chapter 18.
30. Nettl, *Study of Ethnomusicology*, 273.
31. Nettl, *Study of Ethnomusicology*, 278.
32. Sacks, "Power of Music."
33. Sacks, "Power of Music," 2532.
34. Sacks, "Power of Music," 2532.

Considerations of Authenticity in Xerente Church Fusion Genres   175

The functions performed by this music demonstrate signs of deep integration into the local community and are distinct from those of the secular community that surrounds Xerente Christian churches. As such, through a re-elaboration of the functions of regional genres from which the music has been adopted, I consider them to be demonstrative of the authentic character of fusion genres, seeing that they have not been simply copied, but developed internally to represent aspects of a proper and responsible type of Christian spirituality unlike the regional perception.

7.4 SIGNPOST OF COMPETENCE

Musical competence, although dependent on the individual's capacity to learn and develop this art's skills, is usually not achieved without some degree of instruction and continuous practice. Talent, and at times genius, often distinguishes some music pupils as especially suited for the musical profession. Competence among the Xerente is varied just as in other societies. That is, some have a stronger aptitude to learn musical technique and often more interest in performing and composing than others. Consequently, the claim of competence among the Xerente is not meant to imply that the entire community can perform and/or create in the styles addressed in this book. Although such ability may be, at times, attributed to the society as a whole, it is found, in practice, among the musicians that are part of the Xerente community.

There is not one single, universally present, set of musical expectations in every society. This conclusion is a corollary of the idea that music is not a universal language. Expectations of how music is to be played, what elements belong and those that should not be included, are inherent components of what one terms a "genre," however fluid that may be. The reviews of performances, preferences, and opinions among Xerente Christian musicians reveal the awareness of internally accepted genre preferences and the capacity to create and perform in ways that concur with these expectations. Other indigenous groups have indeed adopted regional elements (ex. the Makuxi) and there may be similarities in the final combination of musical features, especially if they initially incorporated elements of northeastern popular styles in ways similar to those of the Xerente. Nevertheless, there are unique properties that identify *this particular fusion of elements* as a Xerente mixture, distinct from a Xavante, a Cayapó, or a Makuxi mixture. It is in this class of genres that

Xerente Christian musicians have attained a level of competence. Non-Xerente musicians who live among them or even commute to them from time to time (such as I) bring other expectations and competencies with them. If invited to perform or create in their genres, these would likely not be able to match their style without being willing to adopt and intentionally take on the expectations and practices of Xerente musicians. This fact signposts the internal competence as uniquely Xerente. Undeniably, their musicians initially learned from outsiders how to play the guitar and the keyboard. However, much development since then has been left to their own initiative, and the subsequent musical fusion was internally, not externally motivated.

The internal character of Xerente competence in creating and developing the genres is the basis of its value as a signpost of authentic practice. This music's existence as a total genre (or genres, if subcategories were attempted at this stage), while created from the adoption, adaptation, and incorporation of external elements into those previously present, owes its present-day character to Xerente creativity. Furthermore, the church members rely on their own musicians, trusting in their capacity to operate within the realm of musical sound they have adopted.

7.5 SIGNPOST OF AGENCY

Differing perceptions of authenticity can sometimes lead to situations where the enactors of a particular cultural expression perform in ways that are less than authentic. Conklin finds irony, for instance, in the possibility that indigenous performances may become a "staged authenticity": "Dean MacCannell nicely captured an aspect of this problem in his concept 'staged authenticity.'" This term refers to the staging of local culture to create an impression of authenticity for a tourist audience." Reflecting "pro-Indian" policies currently in vogue in contemporary politics, Conklin warns that "by insisting that native Amazonian activists must embody 'authenticity', it may force them to act 'inauthentically.'" That is, Indians are expected to portray themselves fashioned in manners that outsiders expect to see in them. Through body paint, feathers, and other visual or aural cues which in fact, have been modified through the adoption or adaptation of internal and external features, they could be displaying a cultural milieu that is no longer the norm. Thus, as Conklin's suggestions indicate, *authenticity exists in that which is commonly practiced within*

Considerations of Authenticity in Xerente Church Fusion Genres   177

a culture, rather than in the preservation of nostalgic ideas in the minds of outsiders concerning forms that are no longer extant, or that have been transformed in some way.

The importance of autonomy or self-determination (or local agency, as addressed in this work) is also reinforced by Conklin's article:

> Even more ironic is the fact that, at the same time that indigenist rhetoric champions Indian self-determination, this media-oriented reification of exotic body images devalues the choices of people like the Wari' and Awa, who have strategically chosen to downplay their visual exoticism in order to preserve some degree of cultural autonomy.[35]

In this complex inter-ethnic situation Conklin praises the strategy of indigenous peoples who, while submitting to the media request for exotic images to a certain extent, had downplayed them in favor of the maintenance of "some degree of cultural autonomy."[36] By exercising its power to administrate how their communities were to be portrayed, they also endeavored to portray a public image that was more compatible with their present-day reality.

The question of authenticity in Xerente Christian musical fusion genres, however, does not involve performances created for outsiders, a factor which could weigh in favorably towards the value of local agency as a signpost of the genres' authentic character. The practices of music within the environment of the villages and their churches, while observable by outsiders, do not happen because of their presence. They are local musical expressions created and performed by Xerente and primarily addressing the needs of, and communication to, a Xerente audience.

When it comes to matters of local agency and administration of musical choices, the question of who has the authority to define the authenticity often leads to conflicting answers. Throughout this text, I have confidently maintained that the local community and those who live among them are best qualified to give the most accurate answer to this question since they can express internal meanings and functions, as well as demonstrate competence and exercise agency. This aspect of agency, however, does not exercise complete control over opinions, neither of insiders nor of outsiders. The fact that varying "perceptions of authenticity"

---

35. Conklin, "Body Paint, Feathers, and VCRs," 728.
36. Conklin, "Body Paint, Feathers, and VCRs," 728.

can develop on the basis of differing expectations demonstrates the limits of this potential application.

In this research, however, agency has been primarily connected with the idea of the presence of internal choice in favor of the musical fusion genres as shown in earlier chapters. The ever-growing competence of Xerente Christian singers and instrumentalists in musical composition and performance appear to indicate an increasing autonomy in the administration of their musical practices. Beyond the uses of new Xerente music compositions in their church services and vigils, they not only actively participate in music events promoted by missionaries but make their own plans for Christian music events that bring musicians together from across the territory. This initiative and execution of projects that affirm the character of their culture and Christian worldview are indicative of internal motivation. As such, the presence of agency can be an indicator of a genuine or authentic interest in advancing and developing the genres that have become meaningful and functional in present-day churches.

7.6 THE SIGNIFICANCE OF AUTHENTICITY FOR SPIRITUALITY

A substantial portion of this book has given special attention to musical or otherwise artistic technical features involved in the structures and character that define the Christian music genres of the Xerente. It has also considered factors expressed by the musical participants, both producers and listeners, in terms of how the genres relate to them through meaningful functions of their church and society. Furthermore, it has considered their actual ability to create, perform, and administer the use of the genres addressed. Superficially, these points of study may appear to overemphasize humanistic, psychological, and administrative manifestations of a society undergoing profound cultural changes. However, these musical expressions also contain a level of spiritual implications which could otherwise be overlooked. Not only are these musical compositions replete with spiritual meanings and emotional connections, but they also perform spiritual functions as communication of sincere worship, as personal testimonies designed to edify the church members, and as carriers of the gospel to other members of their community,

One could argue that, since the Xerente did not always have the modern means to create and perform in the manner found in the fusion

Considerations of Authenticity in Xerente Church Fusion Genres   179

genres, the absence of these means had also not weakened the Christian community. To deny or confirm such a proposition would be difficult and require a historical study of individual Christians' personal lives to which this focused research cannot give attention. Nevertheless, it may be an unfair comparison to speak of *the* Xerente as if this indigenous ethnic group were static and its demographics did not suffer under aging factors or if it never multiplied its members. Mature Xerente adults of today, although intrinsically linked to their past and land, possess a different set of cultural heritage ingredients than those of their fathers and forefathers. As was discussed earlier, the youngest generation has grown up with new technology and sounds, has developed different expectations, and has become accustomed to newer forms of expression.

Ethnodoxology often supports the idea that authentic biblical worship[37] "is in and of itself transformative in nature."[38] Sooi Ling Tan suggests that ethnodoxologists' role is to be "in step with the transformative movements of God and to be in tune with the substance of worship as God has ordained,"[39] as well as "with the times and seasons of the societies . . . to be contextually in tune with the sound of their musical cultures."[40] If indeed the Xerente fusion is an authentic expression of their present day Christian identity, then it is likely to facilitate an unhindered expression of one's faith. Presumably, an authentic expression is less likely to create barriers or inhibitions. It could penetrate the deep thoughts and feelings of an individual to the point of guiding one's soul towards the perceived musical message. To admit that musical or artistic communication has such an aptitude does not signify a neglect of divine activity. It simply recognizes the instrumentality by which spiritual affirmation and renewal can be brought about.

7.7 THE DICHOTOMIES CHALLENGED

I have confronted the inadequacy of dichotomies such as *traditional v. modern* and *internal ("native,"*[41] *indigenous) v. external (foreign, imported)*

---

37. The term *worship* here refers to its broad application, which includes all expressions of honor to God through service and praise.

38. Tan, "Transformative Worship," locs. 4904–6.

39. Tan, "Transformative Worship," locs. 5084–85.

40. Tan, "Transformative Worship," locs. 5090–91.

41. Although the term "native" has developed negative connotations in recent times, it is used here solely as descriptive of that which is "natus" (born) in that same

was confronted by the reality of musical blends and fusions addressed earlier in this book. In chapter 4, I challenged the supposed closed character of musical genres was challenged by the evidence of fluid forms and constant interaction with features that had not previously been included as integral to them. In fact, genres may incorporate elements of both traditional and modern music, as well as of earlier internal and external genres. Likewise, the criteria to define the cultural authenticity of an artistic expression transgress the boundaries of what may be commonly defined as traditional, internal, or indigenous.

Authenticity, as emphasized in this work, depends considerably on the definition and understanding of the community in question. The character of each culture is malleable and can display contrasting characteristics, concurrently as well as diachronically. It is fair, therefore, to assume that the culture's own perception of authenticity can be variously defined within distinct groups and in distinct periods of time.

Bruno Nettl, in agreement with Charles Seeger, questioned the wisdom of using "age and stability" as indicators of authenticity.[42] Seeger "accuse[d] ethnomusicologists of practicing *ethnocentrism in reverse* and chide[d] us [ethnomusicologists] for the application of preconceived ideas as to what is worthy of study."[43] In this spirit, ethnomusicologists sought out for a long time that which most contrasted with Western music, looking for "the supposedly pure, unpolluted style of the folk or tribal community."[44] Nettl also alerted to the fact that "the concept of a pure music," an idea prominent in the nineteenth century, "has continued into the late twentieth century."[45]

In time, ethnomusicologists came to accept Nettl's warning. I have also heeded this warning and allowed it to expand the scope and expectations of this research. Refraining from the evaluation of authenticity on the basis of the "age" of the musical features found in the traditional music of Xerente culture when anthropologists first studied them in the early part of the twentieth century, as well as on the supposed "stability" of those traditional genres (which could also not be proven to be centuries old), my study focused on present-day indicators or signposts of an authentic character. I believe there is some truth to Seeger's suggestion

---

country or land, that is, not of foreign origin in relationship to the local culture.

42. Nettl, *Study of Ethnomusicology*, 405.
43. Nettl, *Study of Ethnomusicology*, 405. Emphasis added.
44. Nettl, *Study of Ethnomusicology*, 405.
45. Nettl, *Study of Ethnomusicology*, 405.

that ethnomusicologists could inadvertently practice *ethnocentrism in reverse* by insisting that a local "traditional" culture be maintained in the forms found at the time of initial contact with researchers. In such cases, the "external" ideas may again affect the local culture in a way that contradicts that which is *presently* authentic for them. As suggested earlier in this chapter, ethnomusicologists could lead a culture to actually behave "*in*authentically" for the sake of the outsider.

7.8 CHAPTER SUMMARY

In this chapter I have argued for the validity of the signposts of meaning, function, competence, and agency as demonstrative of authenticity in the practices of Xerente Christian musical fusion genres. They represent a broad contemporary view of authenticity that is not restricted to evaluations on the basis of the age or presumed stability of a cultural expression. The proposed view acknowledges local, socially constructed perceptions of authenticity including both tangible and intangible norms of evaluation, and tries to reach a cohesive, culturally truthful, and holistic assessment. This view is in harmony with an earlier quote from the *Akwẽ Xerente* acknowledging the "irreversibility of the contact with the white world," a development which has required them "to rethink the conditions of existence and ethnic continuity, not in order to disavow them, but to update them according to their own wishes and desire."[46] Therefore, affirming one of the principles of ethnodoxology that calls for the valuing and encouragement of heart musics and arts in worship, those which *reflect the various and multiple cultures in their communities*,[47] the process of evaluation which I have applied to Xerente musics leads to a conclusion that it is proper and truthful to permit the locally identifiable signposts used in this research to provide a trustworthy valuation of present-day musical expressions.

---

46. Wewering, *Povo Akwẽ Xerente*, 38.
47. Harris, "Genre," loc. 3065. Emphasis added.

8

Applications and Conclusion

8.1 XERENTE CONTEXTUALIZATION

THE CASE OF THE Xerente is a microcosm of the process of transformation that has occurred in South America along the last 500 years. I believe it could be demonstrated that many cultural assumptions, modi operandi, and trends observed in this Brazilian experiment have also been determining factors in historical intercultural encounters all along the history of the world. While the changes that have occurred in Xerente society have specific characteristics, they are not atypical. Through a combination of countless potential forces—physical, political, psychological, etc.—cultures manifest changes on a regular basis both in superficial and deeply grounded aspects of their society. It was not the goal of this research to evaluate whether changes and their resulting variations are mostly positive or negative. Indeed, some of them can be beneficial while others detrimental to the society and its individual members. Rather, the theoretical groundwork which this study has incorporated and laid down as principles underscores the fact that cultures, and consequently the features of their artistic expressions, are undeniably fluid or malleable in nature. Such malleability implies that the conscious and subconscious perception of reality may (and does) change along the history of a community and its members. It allows the individuals from a subsequent generation to view their story and experience as genuine or authentic, not only when they are close reproductions of past practices, but also when they result from influences or alterations in thinking to which community members found a connection. The community may also perceive the very process of change as a key element of its cultural identity, possibly unlike earlier generations. For outsiders, particularly those expecting rigid lines of traditional patterns, such malleability may be confusing and could produce a negative qualitative impression in the external observer. It could, at a minimum, suggest that the newer productions of this hypothetical community are too distinct from the culture's earlier character to be considered appropriate, genuine, or authentic.

This research avoided pronouncing value judgments on methodologies used when external cultural elements were introduced into the indigenous community, or on the internal or external motivations that led to their adoption. This does not mean that such evaluations are unimportant or illegitimate. Rather, any interpretation of methodologies and motivations provided in this work has come from an understanding of its importance for future intercultural exchanges. In view of this importance, these considerations are addressed in this chapter.

The musical journey of the Xerente, specifically that of evangelical churches during the last sixty years, demonstrate an initial level of submission to national ecclesiastical practices and later a growing interest in reviving certain elements of traditional music. By the end of the twentieth century the spread of the media among the Xerente appears to have developed a taste for certain external regional musical elements which have been progressively incorporated into the aural atmosphere of the villages. Eventually, these elements combined and tilled the fertile ground of Xerente creatives, giving rise to a habitual practice of integration of earlier (traditional) musical practices with the new sounds they had come to enjoy.

The Xerente musical fusion contains aspects of their traditional and Western (both popular and sacred) musics. One could see the relationship between these musics by means of "metaphors related to DNA, family traits, and ancestral family trees,"[1] as Robin Harris alerts. Viewing the new genre(s) through these lenses gives proper latitude for their distinct features while at the same time maintaining certain commonalities, or "shared 'genetic traits.'"[2]

---

1. Harris, *Storytelling in Siberia*, loc. 1701.
2. Harris, *Storytelling in Siberia*, loc. 1701.

The question of whether the Xerente fusion should be considered a single genre or many has been left open throughout this study. Traditional Xerente music classification, as described in this work, tends to categorize music types based on their purpose, application, or the "owners" (users) of each kind. It is possible that a classification of fusion Christian music is already under development in their minds or even in group discussions, but it has not yet come to the surface. Therefore, I have made no attempt here to create solid genre distinctions based on traditional (or Western) classification practices. I believe the people will be able, in time and if so perceived, to produce their own genre classification in accordance with their customs. For the time being, the emphasis remains on the consideration of the musical practices of the Xerente Christian Church as sufficiently consistent and identifiable to warrant acknowledging them as musical units, not of imitation, but of creation. Contemporary Xerente Christian musics, therefore, not conforming to previously "canonized" genre categories present a challenge to the dichotomy of traditional and Western forms, as well as to other closed systems of art classification, may be deemed as *new artistic entities* instead of simply receiving the label of "transitional" (the in-between form from the perspective of fixed genre categories) or "invalid" for not being subservient to academic or commonly revered forms.

8.2 IMPLICATIONS OF THIS STUDY

8.2.1 Fusion and Its Significance for Ethnomusicology

The ethnomusicologist Bruno Nettl, whom I have referenced and cited at various instances, voiced a sharp critique of members of the ethnomusicology community in reference to their hesitation to accept or acknowledge musical forms that exist outside of their assumed dichotomy of "traditional" versus "Western":

> Ethnomusicologists sometimes appear to be hypocritical. They claim to wish to study all of the world's music, on its own terms, and to introduce only those values that are held by the culture investigated. But their writings frequently show their inability (or unwillingness) to avoid injecting certain of their own values.[3]

---

3. Nettl, *Study of Ethnomusicology*, 404.

... Ethnomusicologists have from the beginning been concerned with the stratification of music within a society, imposing models such as the folk music–art music dichotomy or the folk-popular-classical continuum, sometimes buying into Adorno's E and U (serious and entertainment) categories, and—sometimes unwisely using these templates—trying to determine the hierarchical taxonomies of other cultures.[4]

Nettl's review of the tendency to apply Western standards and norms to all societies accurately describes paradigms which have been applied in academic research in the past. External norms have often been unduly applied to instances of musical expression that seem to lay outside of the parameters of the cultures from which they emanated and have been enforced onto cultures for which they were not originally designed. Ethnomusicologists in various parts of the world may still face this dilemma, especially if they operate under constraints of a local anthropological framework that holds to a narrow (old/traditional) view of authenticity.[5] *Without a broader understanding of what constitutes cultural authenticity as it is discussed in this work, instances of recently developed fusion within somewhat isolated indigenous communities may suffer from an inappropriate application of external paradigms.* Such examples of fusion may thus be denied the proper respect as genuine expressions of a culture.

Nettl also confronted the limited interpretation of authenticity in this academic field: "The concept of the 'authentic' for a long time dominated collecting activities, became mixed with 'old' and 'exotic' and synonymous with 'good.'"[6] In an essay, Nettl highlighted the prejudices of Western and non-Western ethnomusicologists who tended to dismiss as "bad" any admixture that displayed recent introductions of Western music styles, whether in the Americas or non-Western contexts like the Middle East.[7] Although resistance to such hybridity is no longer prominent in the field of ethnomusicology as at the time of Nettl's writing,

---

4. Nettl, *Study of Ethnomusicology*, 389.

5. This point is not further elaborated in this book, but, for confirmation of this framework in Brazil, I suggest observing Conklin's explanation of the insider/outsider view, Monteiro's discussions on *indigenismo*, as well as noting the stances of the contemporary governmental organization in Brazil (FUNAI) and other NGOs operating in among indigenous groups. I have followed the reports of conflicts resulting from this framework through private connections with participants in "The Third Wave" since 2015 until the publication of this book.

6. Nettl, *Study of Ethnomusicology*, 404.

7. Nettl, *Study of Ethnomusicology*, 406.

the older perspective may still direct the mindset of cross-cultural arts advocates who have grown up and studied through models created through "stereotypes of cultural purity,"[8] and who have not kept pace with current academic views. From my perspective, the earlier dichotomy addressed by Nettl still holds sway over many students of indigenous Brazilian music, as well as the general population of Brazil.

It is perhaps at the crucible of attention and evaluation of authenticity that this work stands as a relevant contribution to a balanced and culturally appropriate ethnomusicological engagement with non-Western cultural artistic forms. The understanding of "cultural purity"[9] results from categorizations developed and learned by a combination of academic and experiential practices. Taxonomies of genres and other cultural categories, while useful for analysis, comprehension, and dissemination of information, are unlikely to be optimal gauges of newly encountered or newly developed artistic forms. Evaluations of worth or authenticity in such cases, if tinged with limiting parameters, may be prone to suffer from prejudicial and inaccurate judgments.

8.2.2 Ethnodoxology: What Is Culturally Appropriate?

As a field developed mostly by Christian ethnomusicologists, ethnodoxology inherited some of the expectations that permeate the Western academic scene. Among them is the dichotomy of "indigenous traditional" versus "Western" music styles. Such perception may even be evident in the titles of works of ethnodoxologists, either because they were puzzled at some point in time, or, as in Morehouse's article "They're Playing *Our* Song!" because they predict that the audience may be attempting to categorize potential mixtures of musical genres, particularly those of indigenous cultures on the basis of this dichotomy.

Roberta King's dissertation on the Senufo church presented a challenge to this binary paradigm as early as 1989. She proposed three categories of African music styles at that stage: "western styles, traditional styles and the musics that are *hybrids* of western and traditional styles."[10] Each of these broad categories include multiple genres that could be

---

8. Conklin, "Body Paint, Feathers, and VCRs," 726.
9. Nettl, *Study of Ethnomusicology*, 405.
10. King, "Pathways," 7. Emphasis added.

perceived as belonging entirely to them. She appropriately asked the following questions:

> Is it right to impose upon one group of people what is appropriate for a different group? Should, for example, traditional people be forced to use song styles that are more appropriate for westernizing people? Must the peoples in transition between the traditional and westernizing worlds be compelled to choose between purely western or purely traditional song styles? Are westernizing peoples only interested in western music? When is music (song) appropriate for people and what is its relationship to Christian communication?[11]

The implied responses suggest that it is not right to impose song styles appropriate for westernizing people to traditional people, nor that it is the duty of peoples in transition to choose one of the two sides of the dichotomy "traditional" versus "western." She hinted at the fact that Westernizing peoples may not be interested only in Western music and addressed the core question of her thesis about the appropriate character of the music for a particular people and its relationship to Christian communication. King skillfully handled these questions throughout her dissertation, and as this research should have disclosed, suggested implied responses which concur with the thesis of this book.

Nonetheless, the questions still reveal the presence of the dichotomy as guiding principle for the discussion. The categories of "traditional people" and "westernizing people" presume a cultural identity that remains constant throughout the lifetime of individuals and their communities. As suggested by Harold R. Isaacs[12] and cited by Josef Sprotte earlier in this volume, group identity is not restricted to early life but undergoes modifications by enculturation. I suggest that this is a continuous process and that peoples, close communities, as well as individuals undergo changes of taste or preference for a number of reasons. These reasons may or not be expressly articulated by those who cross from one "camp" to another, but are, nonetheless, worthy of respect. Such changes can be likewise verified in the cultural move towards contemporary musical worship in innumerable churches across the world. Within the mass of Christian believers who participate in contemporary music one can find those who have grown up with this recent setting as the default church model as well

11. King, "Pathways," 7.
12. Isaacs, "Basic Group Identity," 26.

as older believers who, although brought up with a tradition of Western hymns, have come to appreciate the new style and to adopt it as a new version of their identity.[13] I cannot deny my personal tendency to adopt King's categorization. It is part of the educational and cultural mindset of which I have been a part. However, this insight should sound an alarm to ethnodoxologists to be aware of such preconceived ideas, help them prevent further imposition of an unbending categorization on others, and deter its use as gauges of what might be deemed "culturally appropriate."

Another question posed by King addresses the "peoples in *transition* between the traditional and westernizing worlds."[14] Unsurprisingly, both outsiders and insiders are prone to identify a hybrid culture, along with all its hybrid artistic and musical expressions, as a "transition." The term "transition," defined in the online Oxford Lexico Dictionary as "the process or a period of changing from one state or condition to another,"[15] assumes the existence of a fixed (at least temporarily) of a particular "state or condition" from or to which the total culture or particular forms move. Musical genres are the "states" as the term is used in the Oxford definition. To view Xerente musical fusion genres as "transitional" appears to portray an inherent instability (indeed it may be *un*stable since music is malleable) and potentially temporary. In fact, neither possibility can be totally denied, but the future outcomes of Xerente musical development remain open. The stabilization of a musical style/genre to the point that society acknowledges it as a clear category of music results from multiple factors which, as a rule, cannot be predicted.

I propose, therefore, that the fluid character of musical development, although forms and genres may admittedly sustain periods of relative stability, calls on ethnodoxologists to consistently allow the local community to drive the labeling of categories, considering primarily their insider's perception, and remain undisturbed by categorizations

13. This observation is the result of my personal experience with churches and individuals as well as a variety of literary resources. For instance: 1. Elmer Towns, *Putting an End to Worship Wars* (Amazon Digital Services, 1996/2014). Kindle ed. Elmer Towns is the cofounder of Liberty University which originally maintained traditional fundamentalist ideals, including in the area of music. 2. Robert Bakss, *Worship Wars: What the Bible Says about Worship Music* (Port Orchard, WA: Ark House, 2015). Kindle ed. Pastor Robert Bakss is a personal acquaintance. Coming from a strict traditionalist Baptist background, he went through a period of deep re-thinking of the musical preferences he held and imposed on his church, and eventually adopted a contemporary model for his church in Australia which his son, Ben Bakss, now pastors.

14. King, "Pathways," 7. Emphasis added.

15. See Oxford Learner's Dictionary, "Transition."

Applications and Conclusion 189

devoid of a linear continuum moving from traditional to Western. The bidirectional continuum of stylistic possibilities ranging from the traditional to Western music, with the transitional possibilities in the middle of the two, although common in Western thought, does not provide the most comprehensive way to incorporate the potential for cultural, musical, or otherwise artistic expression:

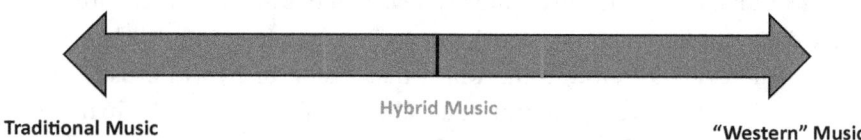

17—Linear continuum of music categories

An alternative, nonlinear view of style categorization could resemble a circle with multiple musical or artistic elements from which a people may draw, regardless of their (potentially recent) origin.

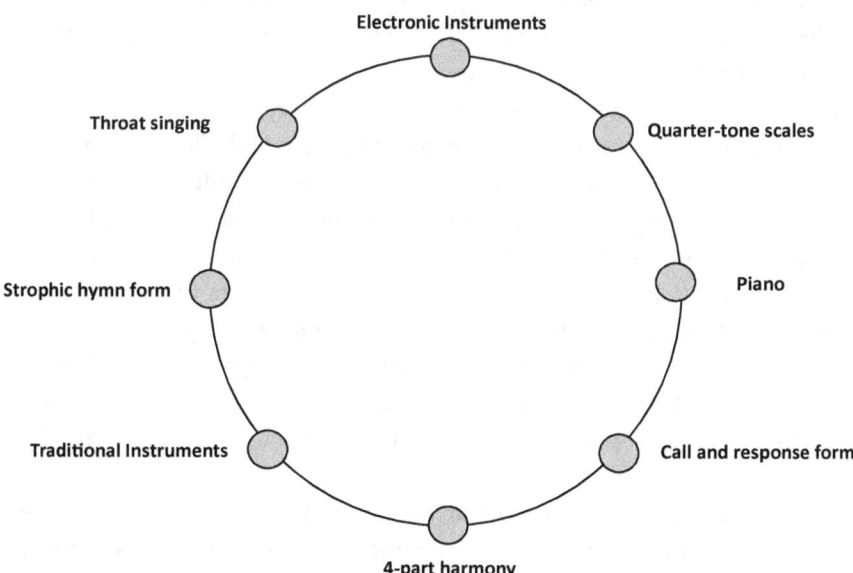

18—Palette representing potential musical style options

One of the issues with the linear categorization is its limited range and predetermined assignment of specific aspects to one or the other side. As this research has highlighted, the contemporary fusion compositions of the Xerente, which one could call "transitional" according to the linear paradigm, is rather a compilation of conscious and subconscious choices made by the composers and performers as to their music's elements. These elements were drawn from a circle of possibilities available to them and which had been part of their aural world for a considerable amount of time. For the Xerente, this music is perceived as "theirs," not a transitional form that will eventually have to move to one of the more stable ends (traditional or Western), nor an illegitimate or infertile hybrid.

The evidence around the world that fusion or hybrid artistic and musical forms have significant cultural value also brings this theme to the forefront. In November of 2018, for instance, *The Fuller Missiology Lectures* held its annual conference at Fuller Seminary with the theme "Global Arts and Witness in Multifaith Contexts,"[16] coordinated by Roberta King, bringing together speakers representing numerous political nations and multiple cultures that intersect and influence one another within those countries. Of the nine plenary speakers, no less than four addressed hybrid forms of artistic expression. In view of the proposal of ethnodoxology to study and help communities develop "their arts" for the kingdom of God as well as the relevance of what Western culture calls "fusion" or "hybrid" in countless cultural situations around the world, scholars are encouraging practitioners more and more to embrace a definition of "culturally appropriate" which *not only includes* but also *concentrates* on the reality at the present moment of intersection with a given community's life. The importance of encouraging and reminding the community of its cultural roots remains a central feature of ethnodoxology. However, as people who encourage creatives in each cultural instance, ethnodoxologists can engage with this creativity by advocating for ample freedom from restrictive genre perceptions. Local artists may choose to compose, draw, dance, or otherwise create outside of classic stylistic bounds utilizing their internal know-how to formulate culturally appropriate expressive arts.

An affirming implication of this study for ethnodoxology is the observable power of music to communicate Christian messages, human emotions, cultural identity, and inferred meanings, as well as its potential as an outlet for creativity and autonomy. The local agency of the Xerente has allowed Christian musicians to exercise their gifts through the musical

---

16. Fuller Studio, "FULLER Dialogues."

language which appears to connect most closely with their audience with which they are conversant. Meaning has been developed and allowed to progress through the manifold functions of the music styles at hand. Ethnodoxologists can be inspired to continue the work of advocacy of local worship arts by the integrated roles that these arts can attain in society.

8.2.3 Cultural Anthropology and "Transitional Forms"

Perhaps it was at the instigation of anthropological studies that ethnomusicology and even Western musicology began to celebrate the transgression of classically acknowledged forms and genres. Philip Tagg explains that the development of the Western understanding of "absolute music" became an institutionalized concept around the turn of the twentieth century and that it continued to influence the perception of music's meanings well into recent times.[17] Since its formal development in the nineteenth century, anthropology had demonstrated the presence of a plethora of "differences, diversity, and plurality"[18] among the nations of the world. It also provided evidence that similarities often derived from "cross fertilization" among societies which went through constant internal changes. According to Ruth Benedict, writing in the early 1940s, this complex picture of development contradicted "earlier students whose theories had been based on the assumption that each group of tribes had its own orderly evolution, hermetically sealed against outside influences."[19] Anthropology only came to terms with the concept of change as the "norm" in the 1950s.[20] But such perception takes time to be awarded an official seat in the halls of academic thought as well as in the general population. Along with ethnomusicologists, anthropologists can also succumb to the lure of excluding cultural expressions that appear to be viewed as "under development," transitional, hybrids, mixtures, or fusions. The present stage of musical life among the Xerente demonstrating signs of meaning, function, local competence, and agency indicates that these forms are not in a laboratory being examined for its potential benefits or negative outcomes. Xerente fusion genres are alive in the people's minds, being currently practiced as an integral part of their

---

17. Tagg, *Music's Meanings*, chapter 3.
18. Canclini, *Hybrid Cultures*, loc. 141.
19. Benedict, "Anthropology and Cultural Change," 244.
20. Nettl, *Study of Ethnomusicology*, 244.

Christian service. Therefore, it should be the object of inclusion and regard as demonstrative of Xerente culture in this fraction of time, whether it continues for years and decades to come, or whether it fades away and gives place to other musical practices.

Frederik Barth's approach to ethnicity brings to light another implication of the study of the Xerente Christian music movement for anthropology. Barth "wanted to part with anthropological notions of cultures as bounded entities, and ethnicity as primordialist bonds, replacing it with a focus on the interface between groups."[21] Hence, *Ethnic Groups and Boundaries*, edited by F. Barth, maintained its "focus on the interconnectedness of ethnic identities."[22] Ethnic "boundaries persist despite a flow of personnel across them."[23] The maintenance of ethnic distinctions, such as the Xerente perceive for themselves, does "not depend on an absence of mobility, contact and information."[24] An ethnic group must not necessarily be solely defined by the set of contemporary characteristics that the anthropologist uncovers during his or her encounter with the people. Barth explains that

> when one traces the history of an ethnic group through time, one is not simultaneously, in the same sense, tracing the history of "a culture": *the elements of the present culture of that ethnic group* have not sprung from the particular set that constituted the group's culture at a previous time, whereas the group has a continual organizational existence with *boundaries (criteria of membership)* that despite modifications have marked off a continuing unit.[25]

In fact, "most of the cultural matter that at any time is associated with a human population is not constrained by this boundary; *it can vary, be learnt, and change without any critical relation to the boundary maintenance of the ethnic group.*"[26] The relevant implication for anthropology of theories of ethnicity that allow for a porous cultural framework is that a population may continually maintain its ethnic boundaries, that is, hold to its distinctiveness as a "nation" while at the same time allow the integration of dissimilar elements from other societies. Along its history, the

---

21. Boston University Anthropology, "Emeritus Professors: Frederik Barth," para. 4.
22. Boston University Anthropology, "Emeritus Professors: Frederik Barth," para. 5.
23. Barth, *Ethnic Groups and Boundaries*, 9.
24. Barth, *Ethnic Groups and Boundaries*, 10.
25. Barth, *Ethnic Groups and Boundaries*, 38. Emphases added.
26. Barth, *Ethnic Groups and Boundaries*, 38. Emphasis added.

"cultural matter" which was associated with a given community can be added to and take on new forms.

The evidence of the present-day context of musical practice in the Xerente church supports Barth's theory despite the fact that his publication is half a century old. Despite the growing connection of the Xerente with the national Brazilian society, the Xerente have continually affirmed and sustained their ethnic identity, not only or primarily verbally or by keeping earlier cultural practices alive, but by varying them, learning new ones, and allowing themselves to be changed in accordance with the experiences of their lifetimes. Presumably, experienced contemporary anthropologists are prepared to accept the contemporary practices of Xerente or other indigenous groups as genuine. On the other hand, superficial attempts at evaluating the authenticity of current Xerente society and its musical and artistic expressions by means of static models may come short of correctly identifying the situation.

8.2.4 Historical and Sociological Implications

Historical records and recent reviews[27] of the process of assimilation, inculturation, and conquest discussed in this work have unfolded a complex journey of interactions among the various peoples that lived in South America, including those who came to colonize, conquer, or explore, as well as those who were brought as slaves against their will. The resulting Brazilian national ethos, Brazil's multiple regional cultures, as well as the indigenous ethnic groups spread throughout the country, did not develop according to a simple pattern of subjugation, i.e., "Portuguese conquerors" versus "Indians and African slaves." Population movements, cultural interactions and exchanges, along with linguistic adoption or rejection, were frequently caused or affected by those who were of the subjugated class. Musical, artistic, and social aspects intermingled and gave rise to new expressive forms which took root in some particular branch of the population. These forms continued to develop, at times becoming sedimented as a stable category but seldom ceasing its transformation.

History, in spite of its "fixed" dates and historians' formulaic descriptions of a particular era of the past, is seldom static. It is in constant flux, even when its actors are unaware of ongoing or upcoming changes.

---

27. For instance, see John Monteiro's and João Pacheco de Oliveira's research and publications cited in this book.

Recent Xerente history demonstrates the fluidity of a culture and the potential worldview and social changes in a given environment. Pr. Rinaldo and Pr. Guenther's six-decade-long work with the Xerente granted them an extended view of a wide range of possible modifications an ethnic group can undergo while maintaining group identity and a sense of ethnic patriotism. Although ethnographic research on Xerente culture is less than 100 years old, one can observe that social transformations in relation to clans, marriage, dress, religion, music, and many other aspects of the society have followed complex patterns of change involving individual and corporate, as well as internal and external powers. Furthermore, the fusion of musical elements from traditional and regional genres demonstrates the possibility that, even within an economically poor and clinically suffering society, new decisive voices can emerge calling for greater participation in the administration of their own future.

Certainly, historians and sociologists can confirm the likelihood of the above-mentioned developments in numerous periods of time in human history and all over the world. The Xerente musical example is not a rare situation to be studied from a historical or social point of view. Within the controversial history of interaction between original and immigrant peoples in Brazil during the last 500 years, the question of the participation of indigenous persons in the outcome of their destiny has indeed been viewed in contrasting ways. However, the recent history of Xerente social development, in contrast to the past, has been recorded more faithfully and much of it has been witnessed by those who are still alive and are able to retell. Thus, historians and sociologists, along with other researchers, can attain a strong sense of the fluid reality of a society by observing the developments in Xerente culture.

8.2.5 Implications for Contextualization in Missions

The history of Christianity demonstrates a variety of approaches to gospel preaching, disciple-making, as well as a host of actions perceived to be recommendations or commands in the Scriptures. The New Testament informs us that, after Christ's resurrection, the disciples received direct instructions to make disciples of all nations, reaching out to the whole world, both geographically and demographically, by proclaiming the Christian message and teaching believers the tenets of their faith along with their applications in real life.[28] These initial followers of Jesus became engaged in the mission of God of making disciples but concentrated on reaching primarily Jews, although the message was intended for all peoples. An unavoidable encounter with new customs and worldviews ensued in the following years and continues until today in the countless cross-cultural missionary activities around the world.

Missiologist Andrew Walls addresses the multiple tension points that developed precisely during those initial encounters of the gospel with new cultures. Convinced that some form of adaptation (Walls deplores the term "contextualization") took place early in the history of the Christian church, he develops a history of missions along the lines of these moments of transition from one culture to another. He explains:

> It is in the moments of transition, the process of diffusion across cultural boundaries, the points at which cultural specificities change, that the distinctive nature of the Christian faith becomes manifest in its developing dialogue with culture. *The process is clearly visible within the New Testament itself.* The Synoptic Gospels, rooted as they are in the soil of Palestine, set forth the Good News of Jesus in terms of the themes he himself preached, the Kingdom of God and the work of the Son of Man. But *how rarely the letters of Paul, addressed to the Hellenistic world of West Asia and Southern Europe, employ the term Kingdom of God; and they never once speak of the Son of Man.* Such Palestinian titles had little immediacy in the world of the new Christians; they required footnotes. In order to explain in the Greek world who Christ is and what he did and does, *a new conceptual vocabulary had to be constructed.* Elements of vocabulary *already existing in that world* had to be commandeered and turned towards Christ. And once that happened, and Hellenistic people began to see Christ *in their own terms*, a host of questions arose that Palestinian Jews, even those who had had a Hellenistic education and were at home in the language, felt no need to raise.[29]

Walls distinguishes the nature of the Christian faith from the multiple ways through which its message could be communicated. The language of the apostle Matthew, reporting the message, stories, as well as the vocabulary which Christ used to speak to his compatriots appears to have been too foreign for the Hellenistic world to have simply been literally translated and put forth as the message. Walls identifies the scarceness

---

28. Matt 28:18–20; Mark 16:15; Luke 24:46–49; Acts 1:8
29. Walls, "American Dimension," locs. 190–97. Emphases added.

(although not the complete avoidance) of the use of Hebrew terminology in the transmission of the gospel to other cultures. A "new conceptual vocabulary" was constructed from the elements of communication already present in the local culture, i.e., "in their own terms," in order to appropriately convey the message. This process, according to Walls, has been ongoing all around the world as Christianity has penetrated, in one form or another, new cultural milieus with distinct worldviews and diverse problems.

The ample use of the term "contextualization," however, is considerably recent. F. Ross Kinsler, in the 1978 article "Mission and Context: The Current Debate about Contextualization,"[30] links the introduction of the word with its current meaning to Shoki Coe, general director of the Theological Education Fund, and to Aharon Sapsezina, one of its associate directors, in 1972.[31] The Lausanne Congress of 1974 also dealt with this subject in one of its seminar groups.[32] Furthermore, the entire January 1978 edition of the *Evangelical Missions Quarterly* was dedicated to various possible applications of contextualization and the issues that surrounded them.[33] Although practical contextualization had already been intentionally introduced to missions practices earlier in the century, it was now becoming an integral part of the evangelical missiological discussion.

Within the context of adapting the message (without damaging the actual content) to the language of another culture, music and the arts stand out as coparticipants in need of similar adaptation in order to enable a settling of the Christian worldview in the hearts and minds of a given community. Although an issue often ignored by earlier missionaries of the modern missionary movement, the importance of using understandable musical and artistic communication in "foreign contexts" was brought to light by a few missiologists. In his 1925 book *Whither Bound in Missions*, Daniel Fleming, who had "caught his first enthusiasm for the Christian enterprise overseas" in the home of Rev. James C. R. Ewing in India, entreated the church at large and, more specifically, missionaries and missiologists to heed the movement towards adaptation and indigenization in missions' approaches:

---

30. Kinsler, "Mission and Context," 23–29. Kinsler was a Presbyterian missionary in Guatemala involved in theological education by extension.

31. Kinsler, "Mission and Context," 24.

32. Kinsler, "Mission and Context," 23.

33. Kinsler, "Mission and Context."

> We have slowly come to realize that the people of India can *play on their own home instruments chords of religious music that touch and move their own hearts.* They love their melodies. We now see that we have come with our foreign instruments; and, though the music has been that of the great Master, our inability to appreciate their instruments and our rough handling of them has left much to be desired. *Certain it is that in most fields we have not waited for the outer forms of religious expression to arise as the natural growth of the religious consciousness of the indigenous group.* We have gone into lands which have known only individual worship, and have *introduced congregational worship after a western pattern* with synods and presbyteries and conferences, with paid pastors, with deacons and elders, with standing committees and the like systems *wholly unlike what the native religious consciousness would have created if left to itself.*
>
> In the past fifteen years, however, *the devolution of initiative and powers and responsibilities from the foreign missions to the young Churches has received an immense amount of attention,* and many missions have taken radical steps in the way of transfer of authority and leadership. *For the most part it is a consciously accepted principle of missionary work that Churches should be developed among different peoples according to their genius and culture rather than presented readymade by westerners.*[34]

A more comprehensive and worldwide response of the missionary community to Fleming's call would only be seen later in the twentieth century. Nonetheless, his enthusiasm for the adaptive nature of Christian worship almost a century ago sounds just as refreshing in the present as it did then. Fleming had observed the power of connection that the "home instruments" possessed to move the hearts in India. Like contemporary ethnodoxologists, he expected musical worship to spring up from their own consciousness and to be communicated in their musical languages. He acknowledged the potential weakness of introducing foreign styles of worship as normative which missionaries had witnessed along the course of the modern missionary movement. Yet, he remained hopeful that the attention given during the previous fifteen years to the importance of "devolving" (transferring or entrusting) the "initiative and powers and responsibilities" to the "young [local] churches" was indicative that "the prevailing thought movements of [their] age"[35] represented a natural

---

34. Fleming, *Whither Bound in Missions*, 163–64. Emphases added.
35. Fleming, *Whither Bound in Missions*, viii.

and enduring change "in attitude and method."[36] It took approximately five decades for some of the ideas of contextualization to be graced with widespread approval within the missiological community, and they still face pockets of resistance among those who may find greater "safety" in the maintenance of patterns of worship and gospel communication rooted in widespread ecclesial practices of previous centuries.

What Fleming described as a change in attitude and method did not take root in Brazilian indigenous missions until later in the twentieth century. Among the Xerente, the introduction of Western church practices followed the earlier models of missionary work around which Brazilian missions' agencies had been organized since the beginning of the twentieth century. For better or for worse,[37] Western hymns were indeed introduced. Later came the *corinhos* and praise and worship styles, along with the technological capabilities to connect with regional popular genres through trips outside Xerente territory, as well as through radio, television, internet, and cellular phone media. Thus, the musical world of the Xerente expanded to include new Christian genres along with local folk or popular ones.

Accessibility to external resources and musical genres may in fact have effected change within the aural experience of the Xerente, as well as the development of new tastes, more than the missionaries did. In fact, technology has "altered the spatial and temporal boundaries of human interaction,"[38] ever since the telegraph was invented. The list of actors involved in the process of widening the range of musical interest among the Xerente, therefore, is not limited to missionaries with their Western hymns, but needs to include the participants of social and political programs that enabled the population to own and utilize modern means of communication, as well as the Xerente themselves who made the choice to use the devices.

---

36. Fleming, *Whither Bound in Missions*, viii.

37. The object of the discussion and analysis in this book is not to provide negative criticism of earlier cross-cultural practices (excluding, of course, any violent or coercive manipulation of indigenous peoples). It has been stated, and it is my personal conviction, that the introduction of Western hymnody into the Xerente church plants was not motivated by a conscious notion of indifference to local choices, nor by malicious prejudice, but simply by the pragmatic reason of the ready availability of a prepared hymnody, combined with deeply seated ideals of excellence in classic inculturation to which I, they, and many other cross-cultural workers (including missionaries) held until relatively recent times.

38. Carey, *Communication as Culture*, 204.

The historical development of Xerente Christian fusion genres carries important implications for future contextualization processes in mission endeavors. The perspectives attained through the study of the ethnodoxological situation in the Xerente church highlight the fact that missiology cannot rely on a "mathematical" process of methodology, or a "universal formula" that expects identical results every time an equation is solved. Rather, they suggest that a balanced approach should be developed that includes principles supported by the Christian Scriptures as well as ideas and best practices gained through observable examples of cross-cultural interaction. The musical and artistic development of each nation, society, tribe, or community varies from others in countless ways and requires individualized attention if one wishes to attain a clear picture of what is "culturally appropriate" in that particular context. Regardless of past (not necessarily negative) introductions of external artistic and musical forms and consequent blends which may have resulted from the interaction of cultural features, the demonstration of Christian love and support can be enacted by welcoming local agency and by encouraging the development of internal musical competence.

The response of each culture (acceptance, rejection, adaptation, etc.) to external influences may also differ according to potential internal predispositions. Likewise, within each people group, not every community member responds to them in the same manner. On the basis of research of multiple instances of musical choices in Asian Christian communities along their development, as well as examples from among indigenous groups in Brazil with which I have been acquainted, three distinct, but not mutually exclusive, predispositions were identified. They can significantly affect the outcome of the introduction of external music in a given society, as well as play central roles in new or continued culturally appropriate missionary efforts:

1. Some communities *may not have a high regard for their own (traditional) artistic features* and their interest for their own original arts may diminish when they encounter a(n) (apparently) more sophisticated culture.

2. A *dichotomy distinguishing sacred and profane aspects* imbedded into the culture may naturally lead to an expectation of a different musical or artistic form to be used for worship or other communication with a transcendent world. The theories of religion published by Emile Durkheim early in the twentieth century even claimed

that this dichotomy was a cultural universal.[39] This perception can indeed be observed among countless peoples, but it has not been proven to be truly universal.

3. *External musical and artistic forms may have become integrated into these cultures* in earlier decades and, in some cases, centuries. The elements which were integrated, presuming they did not eliminate older local forms, may have become "innate" and "natural," and internally perceived as authentically theirs. Thus, the community's musical and artistic world may have continued or developed a mindset of eclecticism in which the incorporation and multiplication of genres is viewed as a positive characteristic.[40]

In light of the above predispositions, it would be unlikely that the Baptist mission's efforts among the Xerente encountered a people that held their culture in low esteem. To this day, community members testify of the importance and emotional connection they sense with traditional music. From a strictly musical analysis, the traditional religious song genres do not differ significantly from communal songs of entertainment and of festivities. Apart from the lyrics and the functional role they played, the musical styles do not display clear distinctions between religious and secular ones. Hence, it is probable that this was not a predisposition that required them (from the perspective of their traditional worldview) to have a distinct musical form for the worship of God. It is possible that the earlier interactions with Catholicism and the use of standardized religious forms for Christian worship may have affected their early acceptance of evangelical hymns, but that they were viewed as additions to their ever-growing eclectic aural world rather than replacements or unavoidable new forms in order to be "Christian."

Continuing with an attitude of acceptance and incorporation, the Xerente likewise integrated regional music genres into their repertoire and developed interests and preferences that led to the contemporary musical fusion. Swee Hong Lim describes Christianity as a culture shaped through from multiple "sociocultural forces, and as it grows its roots in

---

39. Durkheim, *Elementary Forms of Religious Life*, 37. This is a republication of the original published by Allen & Unwin in 1915.

40. The predispositions and the research on Asian artistic worship forms mentioned in this section are further discussed in my article: Portugal, "Asian Worship Arts," 34–39. To request access, email elsen.portugal@bhcarroll.edu. For more on social acceptance of musical innovations, see Schrag and Neeley, "All the World Will Worship," 124–26.

the culture, its outlook and expression will change."⁴¹ At the intersection of missions' efforts with communities which have already adopted and incorporated Western elements, it is unrealistic and counterproductive to insist that they restrict their musical and artistic expressions to that which is believed to be historically or "authentically" traditional. Even before the growth of the ethnodoxology movement, John Butler commented that the confluence of diverse artistic forms, as in the case of India, could serve as "starting-points, the growth-stimuli, for whole new types of art."⁴² Christian art in India had received a "pervasive influence from the West,"⁴³ and had "had its bad side, destructive and divisive, but ha[d] also had its good side, as a constructive, seminal influence."⁴⁴ In fact, the musical and artistic elements actively participating in the life of such communities, "blended" as they may be, are likely to continue as the accepted norm, as demonstrated among the Xerente.

As heirs of the forces of globalization, both isolated indigenous and urban centers cannot entirely escape the contemporary and future cultural modifications and ensuing creations that will characterize their societies in years to come. The ethnodramatologist Julisa Rowe, a missionary working in Kenya with Arts in Christian Testimony, confirms this reality:

> As globalization continues in many countries, it is also important to look at developing theater styles that *fuse contemporary realities with traditional, indigenous forms*. Christian artists can blend the two worlds into an artistic heart language for today's urban audiences. Christian workers who truly desire to communicate Christ in a way that reaches to the heart of each culture, effecting change for the Kingdom of God, should seek dramas that are indigenous to each country, *whether historically indigenous or indigenous through fusion of contemporary culture and traditional cultural elements*. In such indigenous drama, ideas and actions are communicated in a powerful language that is truly understood by the people.⁴⁵

---

41. Lim, "Forming Christians through Musicking," 7.
42. Butler, *Christian Art in India*, 5.
43. Butler, *Christian Art in India*, 6.
44. Butler, *Christian Art in India*, 6.
45. Rowe, "Community Engagement through Ethnodramatology," 54. Emphases added.

The importance of local agency and the acceptance of what is internally deemed to be culturally appropriate for any given society has a prominent place in missiology in the twenty-first century. Jo-Ann Richards Goffe, a Jamaican ethnodoxologist[46] who has been engaged in cultural worship in Africa and the Caribbean since 2002 wholeheartedly embraces the advocacy of the use of local art forms for Christian worship and communication. Responding to occasional pressure from a non-Caribbean colleague insisting that Jamaicans *should not use* "foreign songs," she once said: "It was foreign missionaries who told us that our language and our music were not appropriate for worship. It is not right that foreign missionaries should now insist that we *must* use our own language and music in worship!" She came to believe that "people need to evolve on their own terms. *However*, we must *never* leave our own voices and sounds behind as we grow in discovering ourselves, being influenced by the "foreign" sounds. Often, there is a rejection of self that accompanies that, and we have to honestly search ourselves to ensure that this is not what we are doing. We don't have to reject our own in order to appreciate and enjoy the 'other.'"[47] Her statement reveals the importance of each people's autonomy or agency in evaluating and administering the direction of their own culture. It may imply a certain resentment of earlier practices, but also a self-consciousness that her personal (and national Jamaican) identity now incorporates elements that, while apparently borrowed from other cultures, *are* in fact *authentically* part of who she is. At the same time, she encourages a continual connection to an understanding of an earlier Jamaican cultural identity, calling for self-examination to "discover themselves," or else, a call for an authenticity that does not reject one's "own" to "appreciate and enjoy the 'other.'"

Daniel Fleming and John Butler, as scholars of the development of Christian art in Asia, suggested that each situation could call for either the rejection or acceptance of local forms. Through their writings they attempted to impress on the readers the importance of trust in the divine guidance, not only for the missionaries, but primarily for the local population. The implication of their suggestions affirms the need for a solid discipleship that leads to maturity among the new Christians, and a diminished dependence on outside leadership. Christian faith and love are testified in missions' efforts that hold to the relevance of obedience

---

46. Goffe, "Kom Mek Wi Worship 2." Also see Jo-Ann Faith Richards Goffe's personal website at http://www.joannfaithrichards.com/bio/.

47. Jo-Ann Faith Richards Goffe, in personal conversation on August 7–8, 2019.

to the divine mandate of proclaiming the gospel and discipling the nations. They are accompanied by the assurance in the associated promise of Jesus's presence with his emissaries on their journeys[48] and of the Holy Spirit as guide. Likewise, they imply that a demonstration of love towards the people whom missionaries serve includes the validation of their creative spirit in culture—maintaining discernment as to sinful practices—and of their voices as newly incorporated partners in ministry.

8.2.6 Spiritual Considerations

The Christian faith as described in the Scriptures calls for a personal commitment to the person of Christ, his teachings, and to key foundational elements they contain. As a personal faith it implies the need for individual authenticity from a psychological and sociological perspective. This study did not attempt to evaluate this type of authenticity, genuineness, or sincerity in the individuals. The responses of interviewees and the report of the missionaries who spend continuous time with them do not suggest that insincerity is common among Xerente Christians, and this text was written on the premise that they do possess a genuine Christian faith. Nevertheless, an authentic musical expression as discussed in this book does relate to a personal and genuine spiritual life in that it may allow for an uninhibited vehicle for confessing one's faith.

Xerente Christian fusion music compositions have become significant agents in the spiritual life of Xerente individuals and churches. These preferred genres have gained considerable space in church services, have provided opportunity for lyricists and musicians to participate in them, and have allowed the exercise of their gifts according to the New Testament Scriptures: "What then, brothers? When you come together, each one has a hymn, a lesson, a revelation, a tongue, or an interpretation. Let all things be done for building up (1 Cor 14:26 ESV). Furthermore, considering that the thematic content of the majority of songs are evangelistic or at least directed towards others in the church, they have become vehicles for the proclamation of the gospel to the Xerente in response to Mark 16:15 (ESV): "Go into all the world and proclaim the gospel to the whole creation," as well as modes of exhortation to faithfulness and growth for fellow believers.

48. Matt 28:20.

Early in the development of the Xerente church, the missionaries noted the key role of music in the total context of church services. Although church attendance may not have been contingent on the use of music even in those days, an impression remained in the mind of Pr. Rinaldo that music may have encouraged participation since then. The progressive integration of Xerente believers in the production and performance of musical genres with which they had grown accustomed could also have been essential to their spiritual maturity. Leadership training meetings, such as the one in Cabeceira Verde in June of 2019, integrate both musicians and leaders involved in preaching ministry. In contrast to the specializing characteristics of Western culture, musicians and preachers (especially those who can also sing or play an instrument) collaborate in a seamless fashion. This collegial development of leaders is a positive spiritual advance of which Xerente fusion genres could be considered to be an integral part.

The impact that Xerente Christian music has had on individuals, although more carefully analyzed in this research from cognitive and emotional (signpost of meaning), functional, and practical (signposts of competence and local agency) points of view as indicative of local authenticity, is not limited to these aspects. In fact, if the signposts utilized for this study do indeed demonstrate authenticity, they attest to genuine genres of musical expression *precisely because* their cognitive and emotional value (meaning) *is in line with the spiritual life of the believers*, seeing that they affirm their sincere faith in Christ, whom they worship "in spirit and truth" (John 4:23 ESV). Among the key functions performed by the fusion genres, those that promote spiritual growth, affirmation, and gospel proclamation are central in the minds of performers and other church members. Likewise, the prospects for becoming contributors to the spiritual practices in church meetings have been greatly expanded through the increased competence and agency of Xerente musicians.

The genres' spiritual significance is likely to continue and become intensified through indigenous projects being developed at this time. The example of relevance of authentic, culturally appropriate genres—so deemed because of their internal meanings, functions, and made possible through attained competence and local administration—extend far beyond the Xerente case. While spiritual growth in the Christian faith does not depend primarily on musical and artistic techniques to occur in a community, genuine expressions of faith can demonstrate the authentic nature of a community's faith, its depth of theological understanding, and its level of maturity. Christian churches need the encouragement, therefore, to advocate the use of sincere, heartfelt, musical and artistic expressions of faith that resound the sincere character of individual and corporate spirituality. The literature addressing the interaction between the arts and spirituality discuss three common roles of artistic forms: expression, unifier, and mediation (or as a catalyst).[49] Music, as in the Xerente context, can play a role in spirituality as an expression of faith, as a medium of promoting and maintaining unity, and as a catalyst or mediation to lead others to faith or a spiritual experience. Seldom, however, will these roles be completely isolated from one another. A more likely scenario is that of a symbiotic relationship between artistic form and spirituality, as suggested by the Christian poetess Luci Shaw:

> Does art impact our spirituality? Does spirituality affect our art? Yes. And yes. *The two seem symbiotic, each feeding on and in turn nourishing the other.* They work in tandem; it is hard to imagine an artist who is totally unspiritual in the sense of being out of touch with both created and unseen worlds. And it is hard to image a person full of the Spirit who is not in some way creative, innovative, world-disturbing.[50]

Her questions and conclusions warn against a complete isolation between a living art form and a living spirituality. Shaw's response applies to culturally appropriate (traditional, foreign, or fusion—whatever the context calls for) genres of music. These genres can *express* faith, while at the same time *nourishing* both others' and one's faith and its practice (spirituality). The relationship, therefore, is not a closed circuit, but rather a symbiotic relationship *"full of inexplicable transitions and showings, mysterious both in their origin and mechanism."*[51]

---

49. This condensed functional synopsis is based on multiple readings. My paper, "Artistic Works," addresses the roles of the arts in spirituality in greater depth. The following are important samples of the literature discussing the potential roles of the arts in spirituality: Rookmaaker, *Art Needs No Justification*; Hentschel, "Sensuous Music Aesthetics," 1–2; Sayers, *Mind of the Maker*; Stapert, *New Song for an Old World*; Shaw, "Art and Christian Spirituality," 114.

50. Shaw, "Art and Christian Spirituality," 114. Emphases added.

51. Portugal, "Artistic Works," 18.

8.3 SUMMARY

8.3.1 Historical Re-Evaluation of Musical and Cultural Development

If there are any universal principles that hold true in any society around the world, although it may not be possible to prove them true in every case, they could be thus stated: a) that societies are complex structures that resist totally binding categorizations, making it practically impossible to homogenize their perceptions, preferences, and beliefs in ways that no individual is excluded; b) that cultures are always changing in some form or another, potentially in every facet of their lives, attaining relative stability of form for certain aspects during an indefinite period of time, while regarding other aspects as malleable as a rule. In short, cultures are not homogeneous and are prone to continual change.

The indigenous Brazilian context holds true to the two principles above in that its complexity resists a universally binding description, and that it has changed and continues to change in a great number of facets of the societies that compose it. The Xerente people belong to this national context and is composed of individuals who may disagree with the general indications of authenticity of its musical fusion genres. Likewise, this society has been modified, not only by external but also internal choices, and displays characteristics today that it did not possess even in living memory.

The acknowledgment of the resulting blending of cultures and the multiple processes of ethnogenesis which occurred in the South American continent through European conquest and other forces as today's reality, does not imply a justification for the violence that was done to conquered nations and the methods of enslavement which were applied to Africans and Brazilian Indians. Indeed, South American indigenous populations suffered irreparable damage at the hands of their pretentious masters, but as highlighted by the most recent scholarship of Brazilian anthropologists and historians,[52] they also played a part in the future of their societies when they chose to submit, flee, or in some way adapt to the new social situations. The Xerente culture, which was facing a real danger of extinction at the beginning of the 1960s, has increased tenfold, attained land rights, and reimagined itself with a set of old and new features that

---

52. The "recent scholarship" to which this sentence refers encompasses works published by anthropologists and historians since the so-called "parting of the waters" marked by the scholarship of the late John Monteiro.

compose the society of today. The Xerente identity today encompasses elements that historically were not a part of it. It now includes the possibility and expectation of general literacy, public education, new building structures, media technology, transportation, and even new musical sounds. Within the framework of the total society, a Christian Xerente identity has also developed encompassing new daily and weekly rituals such as prayer, Bible reading, and church attendance. In conjunction, the new components of Xerente communities with which its members have become not only acquainted, but to which they have become accustomed, have presented new opportunities for creativity and development which they may not have thought possible before the recent decades. The new Christian musical genre(s) exemplify the potential for change within a given society that is willing to develop new "tastes" and seek out new possibilities beyond the framework of historical cultural features.

In this study, the potential malleable character of cultures has been applied to the development of categories of musical genre. Reflecting one of the cautiously universal principles stated at the beginning of this section, musical and artistic genres undergo modifications on a regular basis, either due to external influences (consciously or unconsciously adopted) or by some internal creativity that challenges a previously accepted set of norms. They often attain a relative stability of form or of criteria for inclusion within the consciousness of the cultures to which they belong for some time. These relatively stable plateaus in musical development represent the genres which have been primarily considered in this book. As the history of music demonstrates, not only in Brazil but around the world, genre boundaries are porous and receive external influences leading to permanent modifications (and the subsequent reaching of a new musical genre plateau), or else they may be internally modified. The insistence upon the restrictions of a particular genre, as well as the possibility of external influences on a culturally acknowledged one, can often give rise to potentially undue criticisms of newly developed forms and to evaluations that question the validity or the authenticity of the ensuing musical style. This book has maintained that an evaluation of authenticity of such genre(s) should grant a pre-eminent place to the internal voice of the community responsible for the modifications or fusion of elements if indeed a realistic and truthful assessment is to be made. As demonstrative of potential authenticity, therefore, I have considered corporate and individual meaning and function of the fusion genre to be signposts of their authentic character, together with the musical competence and local agency as practical markers of genuine integration of this musical practice into the present-day character of Xerente society.

8.3.2 Authenticity Re-Defined

The cultural authenticity of artistic forms as modeled in this study has drawn meaning from various applications of the term, such as individual psychological authenticity, authenticity related to genuineness for tourism, of material or immaterial cultural heritage, or of performing arts. These applications can both affect and interact with the way authenticity is perceived by those who make use of the term. In this book, the signposts used to indicate the potential authentic character of the Christian musical fusion genres of the Xerente suggest the following definition of authenticity:

> Authenticity of musical and other artistic expressions for a given culture can be defined by the internally acknowledged qualities of meaning and function inherent in the practice, connected with the competence of its qualified practitioners and the administration or agency of its stakeholders.

Stated in this manner, artistic cultural authenticity becomes less dependent on the old or exotic characteristics that have been associated with a given culture and more indicative of its present-day value to the local "owners" of the expression.

This concept is distinct from an evaluation of its "goodness" from an artistic or aesthetic point of view. A qualitative assessment of artistic practices can differ vastly depending on the worldview and presuppositions of the persons involved in the review. In *Creating Local Arts Together*, Brian Schrag offers a helpful clarification of this idea, a standard for "how good a work is and how it could be improved":[53]

> A created work is good insofar as its features work together to effect the purposes demanded by the context of its performance and experience. These purposes could include the work's theological correctness, accuracy of information communicated, ability to communicate, ability to touch people through its aesthetic quality, ability to motivate to action, etc.[54]

---

53. Schrag, *Creating Local Arts Together*, 245.
54. Schrag, *Creating Local Arts Together*, 245.

Schrag's definition is in line with the Bible commentator Matthew Henry's (1662–1714) interpretation of the Creator's assessment of creation as "very good" in Gen 1:31. Henry suggested, among several options, that creation is good because "it answers the end of its creation, and is fit for the purpose for which it was designed."[55] Although the "goodness" of a humanly created artistic practice does not present an equal parallel to divine creation, the insight Matthew Henry's comment brings to this discussion relates to *the definition* of what is good. As he suggests, good is that which "answers" or corresponds to the "end" of its creation, and "is fit" or appropriately suited "for the purpose for which it was designed." It is unlikely that all humanity could view every creature on land or in the sea as aesthetically pleasant to behold, or that every one of them is applicable to one's individual conception of suitability. The commentator appears to recognize the unlikelihood of such meaning to the declaration of a "very good" creation and appears to have identified a more precise sense for the term in the concept of "function" and "suitability." Within these parameters, evaluations of quality—or "goodness"—concerning an artistic genre, even if it transgresses traditional or extra-cultural boundaries of categorization or seems aesthetically unpleasant to others, could truthfully label as "good" those musical practices that fulfill their purposes and are well suited to the needs they address.

8.3.3 Worship and Missional Reviews

I chose to address the case of the Xerente because it is as a meaningful representative of the changing character of Christian music both in indigenous and non-indigenous contexts. Not only does it reveal significant considerations for the various fields that contributed to the discussion, but it also alerts the missiological community as well as local churches to the importance of a number of paradigm shifts in cross-cultural communication to which Christians are being called in the twenty-first century. In line with Walls's observation that the Christian message has consistently been adapted in its communicative form throughout church history since the apostles, the tradition that contends that Christian expressive forms need to be immutable when transported into other cultures cannot be well supported as "best practice" from a biblical or historical point of view. On this basis, a paradigm shift may be necessary

---

55. Henry, *Commentary of the Whole Bible*, "Genesis I."

in the missiological approach on the part of some. Furthermore, if led by human intuitions of value, authenticity, or permissiveness, Christians tend to infringe on biblical principles that caution against passing judgment on one another's conscience. For areas where a definitive moral ruling has not been given (even in cases of potential inadequacy due to an association with sinful practices, such as the "meat offered to idols"), the apostle Paul provides guidelines in Romans chapters 14 and 15 that indicate the importance of not judging another Christian's conscience in statements such as these: "Receive one that is weak in the faith, not for disputes over opinions" (Rom 14:1); "Who are you to judge another's servant? To his own master he stands or falls" (Rom 14:4); "One indeed judges one day above another; but another judges every day *the same*. Let each be fully assured in his own mind" (Rom 14:5); "But why do you judge your brother? Or why do you despise your brother? For we shall all stand before the judgment seat of Christ" (Rom 14:10); and "So then each of us shall give account concerning himself to God" (Rom 14:12).[56] Hence, the meaningful and functional character of a musical expression, although perceived by certain Christians as inappropriate or falsely motivated in the lives of their brothers and sisters, calls for an attitude of humility and equality as servants of the same God. This stance may involve, in many cases, another paradigm shift to an attitude of confidence and support towards those whose conscience sense no condemnation in practices not verbally or universally forbidden in Scripture.

In response to the observations discussed in this study, two vital paradigm shifts are necessary to construe a holistic missional character for Christian musical expression. The usual framing of music into the category of "worship," which, in turn, is further defined as moments of individual spiritual encounter with God, has limited the potential of music for the life of the church. Worship, as a broad category of thoughts and actions performed both to God and toward others, encompasses much more than musical moments of individual devotion or corporate singing within the framework of church services. Therefore, the potential practical applications of music clearly include "worship" in the sense of communication of God's message to others, such as the strongly evangelistic Xerente songs, as well as songs of testimony and edification directed towards fellow Christians. Culturally appropriate Christian music manifestations can serve as influential media to reach out to the surrounding

---

56. All Scripture citations in this paragraph are from the Logos Bible.

community as well as perform functions of individual and corporate worship to God. Thus, music practitioners and other church leaders could benefit the Christian church worldwide if they would distinguish between music and worship, realizing that these two are not the same thing. A concerted study of the Scriptures can lead to a more profound comprehension of the range of purposes which music and other artistic modalities can fulfill. Just as music's function involves much more than a way to express worship to God, so one's concept of worship will also benefit from a biblical study of the meanings and practices of worship which are part and parcel of the Christian faith.

8.4 CONCLUSION

The complexity of societies and the historical evidence of potential and real course changes that exist never seem to allow researchers to reach the end of all questions. This investigation into the character and authenticity of Xerente Christian fusion genres was no different in this aspect. When entering a research environment to explore a seemingly interminable number of resources, a scholar uncovers the existence of an exponential number of other avenues on which he or she will not be able to travel during that particular journey. Considerations on the life of precolonial indigenous peoples, the multiple responses and ethnogenetic processes that occurred since then, the musical developments among the Xerente before the 1960s, the potential internal presence of dichotomies in musical categories, questions about the origin of their musical system, the full effect of the availability of Western instruments and the media in Xerente musical perception, results of earlier syncretism in their worldview, influences and outcomes resulting from earlier migrations and individual moves to and from urban centers, and many more questions deserve to be given their proper attention, but were much broader than the scope of this research. Therefore, these other lines of inquiry had to be postponed for another opportunity, or else left for others to follow them.

This book has focused on the locally developed fusion of genres which Xerente musicians produce, noting how they have provided spiritual meaning and emotional support, and how they have come to fulfill crucial functions in the life of the Xerente evangelical churches. The porous nature of cultural and, in this case, musical forms support the view that musical genres are socially constructed plateaus along a seemingly endless trajectory of change. Musicians develop new genres, wittingly or unwittingly, through the transgression of earlier criteria. The Xerente fusion genres incorporate features from the culture's linguistic and musical tradition, as well as newly incorporated elements from regional styles. The blended character, however, is an appealing mode of communication in contemporary Xerente life and is now viewed internally as an integrated part of society.

Furthermore, the processes of meaning development and modification that occurred among the Xerente in relation to popular regional genres demonstrated that these newly composed Christian songs function *symbolically* (in the Peircean sense) as identity markers for various aspects of the Xerente Christian life and practice. My evaluation of the genuine or authentic character of these compositions was based on signposts of meaning, function, musical competence, and local agency. They provided evidence that these markers are capable of indicating, and do confirm, an internally acknowledged authenticity in these genres. As such, the resulting fused genres can stand as prime examples of contemporary, culturally-appropriate musical expressions for Christian worship. They provide active channels of spiritual engagement among Christians, as devotional exercises, and as proclamatory tools for all members of Xerente communities.

I am greatly indebted to the Xerente Christians and their missionaries for allowing me to examine this musical development among them. Their experience could encourage the re-evaluation of missiological perceptions of local cultural expressions among various people groups around the world.

The conclusions which I reached and shared here concerning the key topics of this book are written in hope that professionals and laymen in the various fields that contributed to the discussion further expand their horizons of creative possibilities beyond the boundaries of temporal criteria and culturally-determined dichotomies. Moreover, in view of the evident capacity of musical and artistic forms to serve as genuine expressions of faith, as unifiers, as identity markers, as well as catalysts of change, these conclusions also convey my express desire that the Christian missiological thrust of the twenty-first century may go beyond giving an approving consent to an increase in musical and artistic communication, but that these may become integrated into virtually all efforts of transmission of the gospel message and into the practices of discipleship.

Appendix A

Characteristics of Xerente Music

Rinaldo de Mattos
Miracema do Tocantins, 1996
(Revision for the internet: November 2003)
(English translation by E. Portugal, December 2018)

(Translator's note: The following observations deal specifically with traditional Xerente music)

INTRODUCTION:

Xerente music has not yet been properly studied. The following notes are only preliminary observations which call for deeper studies.

1. **Musical pitch inventory:**

    a. Preference is given to major intervals. The most frequent scale degrees are the 1st, 3rd, 5th, and 6th, as well as the repeat tonic;

    b. The 2nd scale degree was not found except as the 9th scale degree;

    c. Two scale degrees arrived at by minor intervals have not yet been found within the same music: those leading to the 4th and from the 7th degree to the tonic. When one is present, the other one is not.

2. **Rhythm:**

    a. The rhythm is always binary with the strong beat of the measure (e.g., 2/4) being stressed.

    b. In certain songs/pieces the strong beat is marked by the strong stomping of the right foot on the ground, while the left foot is only dragged, marking the weak beat;

    c. In other songs/pieces, such as those for the *naming of girls*, the strong beat is strongly marked by hitting club used by the *association singers* on the ground.

3. **Timbre:**

    The timbre is always mostly high-pitched rather than low-pitched. When the Xerente sings songs in Portuguese, for instance, they always pick a pitch higher than usual. In general they prefer singers with higher voice qualities.

4. **Choreography:**

    (Traditional) Xerente music is invariably accompanied by choreography (movement). One does not sing without moving. The Xerente also do not sing while sitting except for lament songs.

5. **How music is used:**

    a. Xerente music is exclusively ritualistic. It is only sung (performed) during ceremonies and rituals;

    b. The Xerente people does not "hum" songs. No one sings while working, fishing, or hunting. One sings only during ceremonies, as mentioned above, or when there is a "puxador" (pronounced "poo-shah-ʹdoe," a person who starts singing a song) who leads the singing.

6. **The gatekeepers of the songs:**

    Xerente music is not the people's property. They belong to certain specific social groups. They are:

    a. The shamans (*pajés*) who have a repertoire of appropriate (proper) songs, both for their *pajelânça* (the shaman's religious activities) and for the plaza songs (*cantigas "de pátio"*) which are usually sung at night;

b. The *associations or societies* (there are 4 male associations) that are responsible for "singing" the names of the girls during the naming ceremony as well as for leading the song in the event when the boys are secluded to the bushes before they receive their names. Each of the four associations have their proper repertoire. There is also the women's association, but it serves other functions.

7. **The "*puxadores*" of the song (leaders or initiators):**

In order for a common person in the Xerente society to sing, it is necessary that the music be "initiated" by a specialist who represents one of the gatekeepers of that particular music.

8. **The form of the musical verse:**

   a. Xerente songs are always short and have only one stanza. They display a system of verses divided into two musical phrases. The first phrase serves as a question, and the second one, with the music and lyrics somewhat modified, as the answer;

   b. In order for the people to follow the song, the *song initiator* (*"puxador"*) sometimes sings the first phrase once being followed by the people who join him in the repetition; another possibility is that the *"puxador"* sings the complete first phrase and the people join in for the second phrase.

   c. When performing a song, the first phrase is normally sung twice. The second phrase is also normally sung twice, and all continue repeating the whole verse many times until the song starter ends the song. We have not yet detected any sign to indicate that the music has come to an end and that it is time to stop singing.

   d. An exception to the short verses is the Wakedi song. This song is performed both by the women's association and by the men. It contains several stanzas. A curious fact is that Wakedi is the only Xerente name that may be given to both sexes.

9. **Lyrics and to whom they are addressed:**

   a. In the analysis of Xerente music the most difficult aspect is determining to whom the song is directed. Invariably there will be a second-person singular pronoun included, such as "tôka"

(Pt.: você; En.: you—singular), to whom the song is directed. Most of the time the lyrics are directed to mythological entities, that is, either to the spirits that inhabit the rivers and the bushes (in the case of the shamans), or to certain animals (in the case of folklore music, or "warræ nõkrêze"/plaza songs);

b. The only two songs directed towards human beings, as far as I know, are the Wakedi, which the men sing to the women, or the women sing to the men;

c. Once (and only once) I heard a group of shamans singing a song during an intense flooding season in which the second-person pronoun was the honorific at" (Pt.: o senhor; En.: you, sir), a pronoun which they use either when referring to "Bdâ" (the sun) as the cultural hero, or to "Waptokwa Zawre," the term used for God.

10. **Musical authorship:**

Within the Xerente worldview music has no human composer. The authorship of the songs which they sing is not attributed to any one person. They were all "left" by Bdâ, the cultural hero, just as the other aspects of their culture.

11. **Exemple of Xerente song—BRUPAHI: (see attached sheet music transcription)**

a. Text:

Brupahi,	Brupahi, Brupahi,
Bâtô prê	Bâtô prê
Bâtô prê æsãmræ kõ bâ	Bâtô prê æsãmræ kõ bâ
Bâtô præ sãmræ.	Bâtô præ sãmræ
	Brupahi.

b. When it is sung: The song Brupahi is sung during the girls naming ceremony, particularly when the same name is given to both of them at the same time. The second-person pronoun "bâ" is directed to the birds or the *brupahi*. It is a migratory bird (a type of large swallow) that, according to mythology, stood for boys and girls that had gone to sing alone in the bushes and that had transformed themselves into that bird while there. It is very difficult to translate, but, in essence it says that the singer is being seen by the brupahi bird, and is still singing with longing for the young children who had disappeared in the bushes (the jungle).

Appendix B

Xerente Musical Instruments

By Rinaldo de Mattos
INSTRUMENTOS MUSICAIS XERENTE[1]

Até onde vão os nossos conhecimentos, os principais instrumentos musicais usados pelos Xerente eram:

Kupawã: Espécie de corneta ou tubo feito apenas de uma taboca de (bambu) de cerca 35 a 45 cm de cumprimento com 4 a 5 cm de diâmetro. A taboca tem apenas função sonora do tubo sendo tocado pelos *sipsa* em dias de rituais nos horários de meia noite, 4 horas da madrugada, meio dia e cinco horas da tarde. O som do kupawã parece ser mais surdo e menos vibrante do que o do Kupawãhrâpo.

Kupawãhârpo: Usualmente confeccionado pela junção de dois produtos da natureza de grande potencial sonoro: uma cabaça oblonga, (medindo 30 a 40 cm de cumprimento, e cerca de 15 cm de diâmetro na parte mais larga do seu bojo) e uma taboca (bambu) (de 25 a 35 cm de cumprimento com 3 a 4 cm de diâmetro).

    A taboca exerce a função sonora do tubo que conduz o ar até a cabaça, que por sua vez exerce a função de caixa de ressonância (ou

---

1. Appendix B contains the original full text from which the information about traditional Xerente instruments was drawn. It is included in the original language here to register as a citable official source, rather than an unpublished document.

elemento potencializador). Tradicionalmente o bambu escolhido para o instrumento é formado por um único gomo, mas quando há mais de um, estes são furados permitindo a passagem de ar pelo tubo que tem uma extremidade completamente aberta. Esta extremidade é inserida na parte mais fina da cabaça, onde se encaixa com pouca folga, sendo definitivamente fixada com cera de abelha. Um furo lateral, feito na extremidade oposta do bambu serve de bocal, enquanto a parte mais bojuda da cabaça também é aberta para permitir a saída alti-sonora do ar soprado. Na aparência o instrumento pareceria com uma corneta soprada transversalmente, mas o som produzido pelo sopro do kupawãhrâpó, é grave, rouco e vibrante, e assemelha-se em seu timbre ao de um instrumento de sopro de madeira trincado, talvez um oboé com palheta vibratória.

Sua ornamentação final era completa com penas, e engenhosos trançados de talo de taboca bicolores, alternando o bege-areia com o preto. Seu uso tradicional era o de anunciar a chegada de um grupo Xerente em visita amistosa.

Sdupuzâ: Confeccionada ainda hoje com dois gomos de taboca diferentes ou no cumprimento ou no diâmetro, que variam respectivamente entre 15 a 20 cm, e de 1 a 1 ½ cm. Ambos os gomos de taboca são abertos em suas extremidades, e unidos por uma linha de tucum, recebem como ornamento final um trançado de talas de taboca cortado, que ainda ultrapassam a cobertura trançado em torno de 6 a 8 cm como se fossem franjas de uma saia comprida.

Mas era em tempo de guerra com outras tribos o Sdupuzâ revelava seu real valor e utilidade, proporcionando comunicação contínua entre os guerreiros sem serem percebidos pois seus sinais eram confundidos com pássaros cantantes

Zâ: Espécie de chocalho confeccionado com três elementos: a cabaça, a haste de madeira, e com fragmentos de casca de caracóis e pedras. Para confeccioná-lo uma cabaça redonda com aproximadamente 15 cm de circunferência em sua parte mais larga, é perfurada em seu eixo vertical. Esse eixo transpassado por uma haste ligeiramente cônica confeccionada de pau-brasil que possui 1 ½ cm de espessura em sua base, por onde é manuseada, e aproximadamente 8mm na extremidade superior que ultrapassa a cabaça em 4 a 6 cm. Para dar a sonoridade de chocalho são inseridos na cabaça fragmentos de casca de caracol ( ) e pedras brancas ( ) que produzem o som desejado.

Tal instrumento é de uso exclusivo dos Sekwa (pajés) que além de empregá-las em suas sessões de pajelança, as utiliza também nos warri nõkrêze, cânticos de terreiro, onde os pajés funcionam com Mestre de Cerimônia.

Kupkrnãihirê: Espécie de pife ou flauta confeccionada apenas com um gomo de taboca no qual são feitos sete furos: O maior, na extremidade tampada, serve como bocal para o instrumento, os outros seis são agrupados em três de cada lado o que possibilita o manuseio da mesma com as duas mãos. Duas dessas flautas eram tocadas apenas e ocasiões consideradas festivas não tradicionais, geralmente de noite, sendo provavelmente inserido na cultura Akwẽ pelo contato com os brancos, festividades tais como a festa do Divino. Segundo relatos sabe-se que uma das flautas, com tonalidade mais grave fazia o baixo e outra, com tonalidade mais aguda entoava a melodia da música.

Wanẽkumkrê: Tamborete confeccionado apenas pelo acoplamento de um couro de sucurijú a um tronco de madeira oco. O tronco variava muito pois era geralmente confeccionado com o tronco oco encontrado *in natura*. Algum acabamento era dado no tronco, que recebia em uma de suas extremidades, talvez a mais grossa, a pele de sucurijú esticada era amarrada com cordão de tucum, ainda não seca, para que a mesma, secando já no tronco, obtivesse a tonalidade desejada. O tamborete era tocado ou com uma vareta (wanẽkumkrêtkaze), ou com as próprias mãos. Sua utilização acompanhava as flautas usadas nos festejos de origem não-indígena. Ambos instrumentos eram considerados profanos, não sendo manuseados pelos sekwa.

Wapsãwanẽ: Corneta pequena e fina confeccionada apenas de um gomo de taboca de cerca 15 a 25 cm de cumprimento com 3 a 3 cm de diâmetro, possuindo um bocal, na extremidade tampada oposta a extremidade completamente furada. Seu som característico imitava o latido do cachorro, sendo tocada apenas pelos *sipsa* em ocasiões de alerta onde algum perigo ameaçava a comunidade, mas também era tocada cotidianamente pela manhã para anunciar a alvorada.

Kukrãinmõrturê: Pequena cabaça de apenas 8 cm de altura e 5 cm em sua parte mais larga, que era cerrada na parte superior por onde ficava pendurada à árvore, fazendo o bocal, recebendo também um furo lateral, que permitia apenas a produção de dois sons, um mais agudo e outro mais grave, quando se apertava o furo e quando se soltava respectivamente. Além de ser tocado pelos *sipsa* em sua estadia no *warã*, era também utilizada pelos visitantes para anunciar sua aproximação à aldeia.

Appendix C

Xerente Music Recordings, Transcriptions, and Lyrics

Transcriptions of Xerente Christian songs[1] analyzed in the dissertation and in this book

---

1. Some of the transcriptions displayed in this appendix do not contain the complete composition.

Ĩpkẽ wadkâ wa waza Jesus dawa

Lázaro Rowakro

Appendix C

Waptokwa Zawre Dawarze
Melodia tradicional, letra cristã

Comunidade Xerente
Cabeceira Verde

This is a traditional Xerente melody to which musicians in Cabeceira Verde gave a Christian text. The recording was made with about 15 people singing together, basically in unison, except for the addition of an alto line for the first half of the phrase at times. The accompaniment was simply the zâ or maracá.
The score above is 'metered' as 2/4 since most traditional Xerente music is in duple meter. This often does not apply to the length of time between phrases. This group seemed to have consistently (based on the puxador) changed the last note of the chord into 3 beats - thus the change of meter.

Kâ psêktabdi

João Simrãmĩ

Waptokwa Zawre damã danõkrêze

Marcelino

Dazakru sĩm warewdêhu

Ronaldo

Aisi hawim hã nã

Pasiku

Appendix C

1. Sample transcriptions of other Xerente Christian fusion songs recorded during the Cabeceira Verde Workshop in 2017

Isimẽm nori – Tiago 2:14

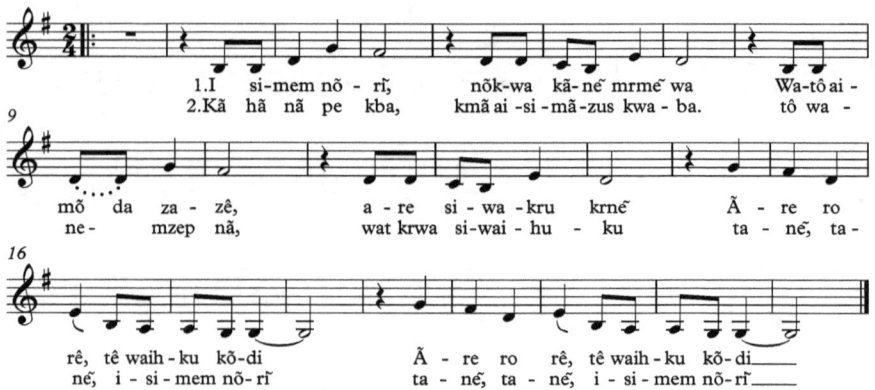

Dazaparwĕze

This song was recorded by a group of singers. The first time it was sung through, part B was only sung by the women who attempted to create some alto harmony. The only instrumental accompaniment is the zã.

Comunidade Xerente
Cabeceira Verde - July 2017

A
No- mõ - mõk - wa nrŏ - wa   hã   No- mõ - mõk - wa nrŏ - wa   hã

B
Tô hê-wa nsĭ wam   hã za hã   kri   wa   Tô hê-wa nsĭ wam   hã za hã   kri

A
wa   Ta- nĕ__ nmĕ__ wi wê kbu - re   Ta- nĕ__ nmĕ__ wi wê kbu - re

C
Wak - mad - kâk - wa   za - tôai - mõ   dat wa - ni - mrŏ

Wak - mad - kâk - wa   za - tôai - mõ   dat wa - ni - mrŏ

Acolhimento (Reception)

Onde é a casa de vocês?
Nas casas que são do Céu
Então venham todos
O Senhor vai nos levar para Ele.

Where are your homes?
In the Heavenly homes.
So, come all
The Lord will take us to Himself.

Wi wê aimõrĩ

Wató ĩsenã hã bdâdi

Comunidade Xerente
Transcribed by Elsen Portugal

This song is an adaptation of a traditional Xerente melody created musicians who met at Cabeceira Verde in July 2017. It is sung in unison primarily by the whole group, accompanied by the zâ only. Some people attempt to sing a parallel (3rds) line in some segments. The translation is:

Eu sou o caminho verdadeiro (I am the true way)
1. Eu sou pra vocês, o caminho pra vocês (I am for you, the way for you)
 Eu sou pra vocês, o caminho pra vocês
 Quem for meu seguidor, eu não o deixarei (Whoever is my follower, I will never leave him)
 Quem for meu seguidor, eu não o deixarei

2. Eu agora sigo a Jesus (Now I follow Jesus)
 Eu agora sigo a Jesus
 Agora eu vou ficar cantando pra Ele junto com as pessoas (Now I will continue singing for Him with the people)
 Agora eu vou ficar cantando pra Ele junto com as pessoas

Appendix C

2. Sample transcriptions of "traditional" Xerente songs

Arê Arê

Aimãsisi tô wahãrê

Traditional Xerente Song

Are Danõkrê Hã

Traditional Xerente Song

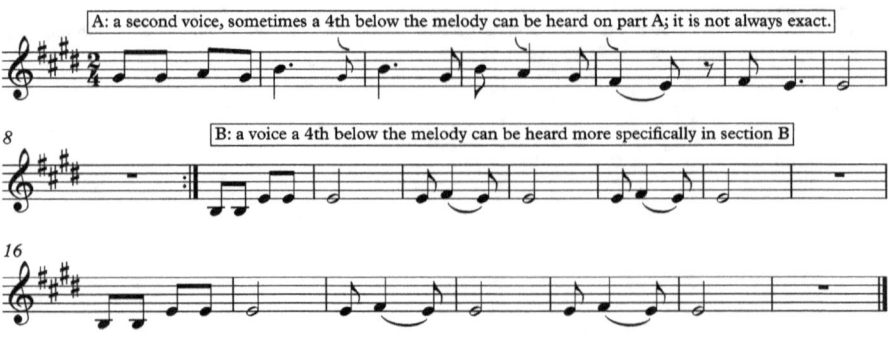

3. Lyrics of 25 songs recorded in Cabeceira Verde in 2017 with brief title or content explanations

1. Nmõmõp wanrõwa—Dazaparwẽze—Receiving—(written by the Xerente Church)

1. Nmõmõp wanrõwa hã?
Nmõmõp wanrõwa hã?
Tô hêwa nsĩ wam hã za hã, kri wa
Tô hêwa nsĩ wam hã za hã, kri wa

2. Tanẽ nmẽ wi wê kbure
Tanẽ nmẽ wi wê kbure
Wakmãdkâkwa zatô aimõ dat wanĩmrõ
Wakmãdkâkwa zatô aimõ dat wanĩmrõ

2. Wa tô ĩsenã hã bdâdi (written by the Xerente Church)

Wa tô aimõ ĩsenã hã bdâdi aimã kba hã
Wa tô aimõ ĩsenã hã bdâdi aimã kba hã
Nõkwa tĩkmãsasõ nẽ hã za hã ĩt rmẽ kõdi
Nõkwa tĩkmãsasõ nẽ hã za hã ĩt rmẽ kõdi

Wa watô tokto Jesus dakmãsasõ
Wa watô tokto Jesus dakmãsasõ
Tokto wa za damã krĩnõkrê akwẽ nõrai mẽ
Tokto wa za damã krĩnõkrê akwẽ nõrai mẽ

3. Waptokwa Zawre dawarze (aisawi nã re)—Prayer—(written by the Xerente Church)

1. Waptokwa Zawre watô amõ awarnĩ
Waptokwa Zawre watô amõ awarnĩ
Tô aimõ Jesus danĩsizep nã
Tô aimõ Jesus danĩsizep nã

2. Tô btâ bâ wê aimõ at wa waihâkâ
Tô btâ bâ wê aimõ at wa waihâkâ
Tô aimõ ĩsenã, wat azawi da
Tô aimõ ĩsenã, wat azawi da

4. Wi wê aimõrĩ—Invitation—(tôkai sô tet tahrânĩ)—(written by the Xerente Church)

1. Tôkai sô tet tahrânĩ Jesus hã,
Tôkai sô tet tahrânĩ Jesus hã,
kaisô, kaisô, kaisô tet tahrânĩ
kaisô, kaisô, kaisô tet tahrânĩ

2. wi tô wê datmẽ aimõrĩ azanã
wi tô wê datmẽ aimõrĩ azanã
wi wê, wi wê, wi wê datmẽ aimõrĩ
wi wê, wi wê, wi wê datmẽ aimõrĩ

5. Ĩsimẽm nori—James 2:14 (mrẽtôrê)—Teaching

1. Ĩsimẽm nõrĩ, nõkwa kãnẽ mrmẽ wa,
Watô aimõ dazazê, are siwakru krnẽ
Ãre ro rê, tê waihku kõdi
Ãre ro rê, tê waihku kõdi

2. kãhã nã pe kba, kmã aisimãzus kwaba
tô wanẽmzep nã, wat krwasiwaihuku
tanẽ, tanẽ, ĩsimẽm nõrĩ
tanẽ, tanẽ, ĩsimẽm nõrĩ

6. **Hêwa nsĩm hã tô Waptokwai ktabi (João Sĩmrãmĩ)—Our True Father Is the One from Heaven**

Note: in the audio recording this song is mislabled as "Kâ psêktabdi."

The lyrics speaks of various attributes of God and Jesus: "the first," "the older brother", "our friend," and so forth.

Hêwa nsĩm hã tô Waptokwai ktabi	kãnẽ mãt wasku psênĩ
tahã mãt wakrãiwatbronĩ	tahã tô romkuiwẽ ktabi
tahã tô ĩsnãkrta ktabi	kãtô wakmãdkâkwai ktabi
kãtô dure ĩsistu ktabi	
kãnẽ mãt wam wasku psênĩ	Are nmãzi za mnĩ dat krẽwai wa
wat dazazêzem hawi	akwẽ nõrĩ za tô krssakrẽ
	tazi za tê datom zêĩdi
Are Jesus tô wazdekba ktabi	Are Jesus dat wa waihku psêdi
kãtô dure wapãi ktabi	nõkwa tê dazazê nẽ hã
kãtô wasiwaikẽ ktabi	

7. **Kâ psêktabdi (João Sĩmrãmĩ)—Excellent Water**

Note: this song is mislabled under the title: "Hêwa nsĩm hã tô Waptokwai ktabi"

God's good water saves; so let us go to Him!

Kâ psêktabdi Waptokwa datê hã tahã zatô wapkẽhi
Kâ psêktabdi Waptokwa datê hã tahã zatô wapkẽhi
Tanẽ nmẽ arê kba tô kbure tô tammõ wawahtu kwaba
Tô tahã tô ĩpsê tmẽ
Tanẽ nmẽ arê kba tô kbure tô tammõ wawahtu kwaba
Tô tahã tô ĩpsê tmẽ

Nõkwap sa tô tahã? Nõkwap sa tô tahã?
Tahã tô Jesus hã kãtô dure Waptokwa
Nõkwap sa tô tahã? Nõkwap sa tô tahã?
Tahã tô Jesus hã kãtô dure Waptokwa

8. **Waptokwa daknã [wa] nõkwa mãr kõdi (João Sĩmrãmĩ)— Without God No One Has Anything**

Note: this song is registered under the title "Waptokwa daknã [wa] nõkwa mãr kõdi."

Essence of the text: *If someone does not have God, he does not have any thing. So, let us go to Him. He has built a good house for us in Heaven. There it is very good. God loves all of us and you, too.*

1. Waptokwa daknā wa nõkwa mār kõdi
tanẽ nmẽ arê kba tô kbure datmẽ
hêwa nsĩ māt krim pê wazô sabunĩ
tô tazi za rowẽ zawre ktabi

2. Waptokwa tô kbure dat wazawidi
tanẽ nmẽ tôka dure ĩsiwaikẽ

wi azanā datmẽ aipkẽ sĩkdâ nā
tanẽ wa zatô aipkẽhrinĩ

3. Waptokwa zatô mnĩ dakra wdakurnĩ
are tkai wa za hā dapra kõdi
tô aināka wa za tanmĩzazârnĩ
tô tazi za dasittê kburõinĩ

9. Ĩpkẽ wadkâ wa waza Jesus dawa—(Lázaro Rowakro)—When I Am Sad, I Will Pray to Jesus

The lyrics alternate "when I am sad" with "when I am crying," "worried," "weak," sick, etc, followed by the chorus each time.

CHORUS:
Ĩpkẽ wadkâ wa waza Jesus dawa zatô ĩm waihkânĩ
Ĩwwai wa waza Jesus dawa zatô ĩm waihkânĩ
Ĩpkẽ zako wa waza Jesus dawa zatô ĩm waihkânĩ
Ĩpakuwa wa waza Jesus dawa zatô ĩm waihkânĩ
Ĩhâze wa waza Jesus dawa zatô ĩm waihkânĩ
Ĩpahi wa waza Jesus dawa zatô ĩm waihkânĩ

Tô tanẽ dure tôka tô ĩsenā Jesus dawari
Zatô Jesus tôka aiwaihkâ nĩ are zatô dure tôka aipkẽtoinĩ

Tanẽ nmẽ mātô Jesus kriĩ pê wazô sabunĩ
hêwa nsĩ wa mātô wanõwa kriĩ pê mātô wazô hrinĩ

Tanẽ nmẽ dure tôka dazakru Jesus dam sawidi
Tô dure tônmẽm hā akwẽ tô ĩsenā mātô dasimā smĩstunĩ

10. Ĩsimẽm nõrĩ (Lázaro Rowakro)—My Brothers (and Sisters)

My brothers, I am happy when we meet here. God has chosen us to Himself; so let us go to Him, etc.

Ĩsimẽm nõrĩ ĩtoiti wa tônmẽ wasiwaikrãm wa
Ĩsimẽm nõrĩ ĩtoiti wa tônmẽ wasissu wapkẽ toi wa

Tô tanẽ mãtô Jesus dasimã wanmĩstunĩ
Tanẽ nmẽ arê ĩsenã damẽ wawahtu kwaba

Ĩsimẽm nõrĩ ĩtoiti wa tônmẽ wasiwaikrãm wa
Ĩsimẽm nõrĩ ĩtoiti wa tônmẽ wasissu wapkẽ toi wa

Tôka dure waimẽ aipkẽtoi wa aisimẽ hã aikrtamrê hã kâri
Are kanẽ kmã aimrẽmẽ tôka dure Jesus taisawidi

Ĩsimẽm nõrĩ ĩtoiti wa tônmẽ wasiwaikrãm wa
Ĩsimẽm nõrĩ ĩtoiti wa tônmẽ wasissu wapkẽ toi wa

Tô tanẽ mãtô wahêmba Abraão, Isaque kãtô Jacó
mãtô dasimã smĩstunĩ are mãtô dure dasimẽ dat simrõ

Ĩsimẽm nõrĩ ĩtoiti wa tônmẽ wasiwaikrãm wa
Ĩsimẽm nõrĩ ĩtoiti wa tônmẽ wasissu wapkẽ toi wa

Tô tanẽ mãtô Jesus wanõr mã ropistunĩ
Nmãzi za mnĩ dat krẽwai wa zatô wanõrĩ dasimẽ dat wanĩmrõ

11. Waptokwa mãtô wam ropistunĩ (Lázaro Rowakro)—God Has Promised Us

God has promised us that one day He will give us very good things. Therefore we are happy. Jesus has called us and chosen us. Let us, then, work for Him!

Waptokwa Zawre mãtô wam ropistunĩ
Waptokwa Zawre mãtô kmã krãinĩstunĩ
Smĩsi btâ nã mãtô wamã tamrmēnĩ
Za hã wanõr mã rowẽ zawre dat sõmnã

Tanẽ nmẽ wanõrĩ wapkẽ toiti
Jesus mãtô wanõrĩ wazaihrãnĩ
Kãtô dure mãtô wanmĩstunĩ
Damã wanõrĩ za hã wanĩpi da
Tanẽ nmẽ mãtô wanĭpttênĩ
Wanõr mã mãtô rowaskunĩ
Tanẽ nmẽ wanõrĩ wapkẽ toiti
Jesus mãtô wanõr mã tasihêĭkrenĩ

Smĩsi btâ nã watô wapkẽ wadkânĩ
Are Jesus mãtô wapkẽtoinĩ
Smĩsi btâ nã watô wapakuwanĩ
Are Jesus mãtô wawaihkânĩ
Tanẽ nmẽ mãtô wanĭm akwẽ
damã wanĭpi re mãtô kmãdkâ psênĩ

Wakra kãtô dure wamrõ
wanĭm akwẽ mãtô kmãdkâ psênĩ
Tanẽ nmẽ wanõrĩ wapkẽ toiti
Jesus mãtô dasimã wazaihrãnĩ

Tôka dure tõnmẽ aipkẽ wadkâ wa
Zatô Jesus tôka aipkẽtoinĩ
Aipakuwa wa zatô aisipttênĩ
Jesus kbure akwẽ tmã sawidi

Waptokwa Zawre mãtô wam ropistunĩ
Waptokwa Zawre mãtô kmã krãinĩstunĩ
Smĩsi btâ nã mãtô wamã tamrmēnĩ
Za hã wanõr mã rowẽ zawre dat sõmnã

Tanẽ nmẽ wanõrĩ wapkẽ toiti
Jesus mãtô dasimã wanmĩstunĩ
Tanẽ nmẽ waza wanĭpinĩ
Are waza dure damã waanõkrênĩ

Tanẽ nmẽ mãtô wakmãdkâ psênĩ
Wanĭm akwẽ mãtô kmãdkâ psênĩ
Wakra kãtô dure wamrõ
wanĭm akwẽ mãtô kmãdkâ psênĩ

Tôka dure tõnmẽ aipkẽ wadkâ wa
Zatô Jesus tôka aipkẽtoinĩ
Aipakuwa wa zatô aiwaihkânĩ
Dure Jesus akwẽ tmã sawidi

12. Wê aimõrĩ Jesus datmẽ (Lázaro Rowakro)—Come to Jesus

Wê aimõrĩ Jesus datmẽ zatô Jesus tôka aisaparnĩ

Wê aimõrĩ Jesus datmẽ zatô Jesus tôka aipkẽhrinĩ

Tô ĩsenã wi datmẽ aimõrĩ zatô Jesus romkunẽ aim kutõrnĩ

Tô ĩsenã wi datmẽ aimõr wa zatô aisapronĩ dasimẽ hêwa nsĩ ku

13. Waptokwa Zawre damã danõkrêze (Marcelino Kasuwamrĩ)—Hymn to God
We have the Holy Spirit; Thus we serve God

Waptokwa Dahêmba wakmã mãrd mnõdi
Tanẽ nmẽ mãtô dat wanõrĩ
Danĩpĭ damã wat krdakmãdkâ mnõ da

Tàkãhã dazakru mãtô sã mnĩ
Tanẽ nmẽ Waptokwa dapkẽ toiti

Wasisu zahã krwanmrõ mnõ nmẽ
Tanẽ nmẽ wa tokto ĭpkẽ toiti
Waptokwa damẽ krinẽ mnõ wa

14. Wazô dahrâ wa waza ĩmõrĩ (Valmir Hkâwẽ)—When He Calls Me I Will Go

Translation of the traditional hymn "When the Roll is Called Up Yonder."

1. Nmãzi Waptokwa Zawre danĩm hrâze mnĩ dat hrâ wa
Nmãzi rowẽ zawre snã awẽ wa
Tazi tô kbure akwẽ tkai wa dazô tsikrãikõtõ Nmãzi mnĩ wazô dahrâ wa waza ĩmõrĩ

Nmãzi mnĩ wazô dahrâ wa
Nmãzi mnĩ wazô dahrâ wa
Nmãzi mnĩ wazô dahrâ wa
Nmãzi mnĩ wazô dahrâ wa, waza ĩmõrĩ

2. Ta btâ nã dazazeĩkwa tô kbure za krãiktõnĩ Hêwa nsĩ ku dasimẽ dat simrõi da
Ta btâ nã dazazeĩkwa za pkẽ to zawre ktabdi Nmãzi mnĩ wazô dahrâ wa waza ĩmõrĩ

3. Ĩpkẽ toi snã wazatô krdazô ĩnmĩpari
Wazatô tônmẽ damrmẽze ĩt krwasku
Nmãzi zatô Waptokwa ĩstõm hã bdâ za vam hrinĩ
Nmãzi mnĩ wazô dahrâ wa, waza ĩmõrĩ.

15. Rowẽ si (Valmir Hkâwẽ)—Only Good Things

Translation of an unidentified Western hymn.

1. Tônmẽ hã wanĩm romkmãdâ tkai wam hã Wazatô nmãzi rmẽnĩ

Arê kba Jesus datmẽ,
Zatô aimõ wapkẽ hrinĩ
Tô ta dawtẽsi za nõkwa pkẽ hrinĩ
Are rowẽ tmã sõmrnĩ

2. Tônmẽ mhã wanĩm rokmãdkâ kunẽ mnõ Wazatô aimõ wat rẽmẽ

Waptokwa Zawre dakmã hêwa nsĩ wa
Tazi rowẽ tmã zawredi
Waptokwa Zawre datmẽ hêwa nsĩ ku
Zatô aimõ dat wanĩmrõ

3. Dazazeĩkwa za tô siwaikrãmĩ
Nmãzi za hêwa nsĩ wa
Tô tazi za hã nõkwa hâze kõdi
Tazi rowẽ zawredi

16. Azabba krĩmõr zêĩdi (Valmir Hkâwẽ)—I Want to Walk By Your Side

Translation of Just a Closer Walk with Thee

1. Jesus daknã ĩnĩptê kõdi
Jesus dat ĩnĩptê kõ wa
Romkunẽ at ĩm kutõrĩ
Azabba aimõ krĩmõr da

Azabba krĩmõr zêĩdi
Tô ĩsenã ĩt azawi da
tô btâ bâ aimõ ĩt awar da
twa kãnẽ, ĩkmãdkâkwa, tô kãnẽ

2. Tkai wam hã romkmãdkâ nã
Nõkwa ĩkmã sapka kõdi
Are Jesus mãtô ĩnmĩstunĩ
Jesus tô ĩkmãdkâkwai ktabi

3. tâkãhã tka nmãzi ĩt rmẽ wa
nmãzi ĩnĩ tkai krowi sbre wa

za ĩhêbba Jesus saprõnnĩ
watô aimõ tô ĩsenã dazazê

17. Hêwa nsĩ ku hã bdâdi—(Valmir Hkâwẽ)—The Way of the Cross

Translation of the traditional hymn "The Way of the Cross Leads Home."

1. Wakmãdkâkwa mãtô bdâdi wam hrinĩ
Aimõwi hã mãr kõdi
nmãnãsi za hã aimõ ĩzbre kõdi
tô tahã bdâdi ĩt rmẽ wa

Hêwa nsĩ ku wazatô ĩmõrĩ
Hêwa nsĩ ku wazatô ĩmõrĩ
Wakmãdkâkwa damẽ wazatô ĩmõrĩ
Hêwa nsĩ ku wazatô ĩmõrĩ

2. Tô ĩsenã waza tâkãhã bdâdi
aimõ ĩsimã kmãdâkâ
hêwa nsĩm hã ro wat waikẽ zepuku
Wakmãdkâkwa dat sõmrĩ hã

3. Romkmãdkâ kunẽ watô rmẽ pêsê
aipâ za hã ĩt krêwai kõdi
Jesus damẽ si waza krĩmõrĩ
Hêwa nsĩ ku damẽ ĩmõe da

18. Ĩnẽmrzep nã ĩpkẽ toiti—(Valmir Hkâwẽ)—I Thank God for My Life

Song Translation

1. Ĩnẽmrzep nã ĩpkẽ toiti
Ĩnõwam hã romkmãdkâ mnõ
kãtô kbure ro ĩt rmẽ mnõ nã
Romkmãdkâ pê dat krĩm sõmr mnõ nã
ĩpkẽ to, ĩpkẽ wadkâ
Romkunẽ aimõ dat krĩmrmẽ psê mnõ
tô ĩsenã damã ĩpkẽ toiti

2. Hêwa kmã dure ĩpkẽ toiti
Hêwa(ka?) nwa simtã mnõ
bdâdi pê tô rom nĩrnã nẽ
Romkunẽ tô aimõ krãnkwa (krãikwa?) nẽ
Romkmãdkâ (tu?) aimõ ĩt kwanĩ mnõ

Aimõ Jesus dat hri psêkwa
wasi mnõ rkopre mnõze
ĩnĩwari dat kmã wakrãm mnõ
ĩnmĩpari tetõ krsrowaptâkâ

3. Jesus damã ĩpkẽ toiti
ĩnõkwakrê mãt tadkânĩ
Rowẽ zawre mãt ĩm hrinĩ
tetõ dure dat krĩwaihâkâ
ĩsiwaikẽ nã dure ĩpkẽ toiti
ĩwwaire tkrĩ pkẽ toi mnõ
Ro ĩm kunẽ wa dat krĩ kusbi mnõ
btâ bâ ĩpkẽ toi snã wa krĩnẽ

19. Nmãzi za mnĩ Waptokwa—(Valmir Hkâwẽ)—One Day Christ Will Return

Hymn Translation

1. Nmãzi za mnĩ Waptokwa
Dakra dure dakurnĩ
Tazi za tô kbure akwẽ
tkai wa dazô tsikrãikõtõ

Tô da toi snã zamnĩ tamõr nĩ
dazazẽikwa aimõ dat simrõ mnõ da
Ainãka wa za tanmrãnĩ
Tammõ za datmẽ wahudu

2. Are kbure akwẽ kõdi
tô dat smistu nõrai wtẽsi
za tamõ datmẽ wahudu

hewa nsĩ ku zahã dat simrõi mnõ da

3. Kanẽ mãt Waptokwa Zawre
akwẽ mã ropistunĩ
datmẽ kwasikwanĩ mnõ wa
zatô aimõ dasimẽ dat wanimrõ

4. Tô isenã mã ropistu nĩ
dazô wanmĩpar kwaba
nmãzi za bdâ wawaptkã wi
zatô aimõ kbure dat rowaihuku

20. Aisĩm hawim hã nã (Pasiku)

Go in the ways of God to hear well His plans . . .

Waptokwa Zawre danĩm bdâdi nã
wi tô wê aimõr wẽ nã
aisĩm romãdkâ wẽ zawre
wat wapar wẽ pibumã

Tanẽ nmẽ
aisĩm romãdkâ wẽ zawre
wat kmãdkâ wẽ pibumã

Tanẽ nmẽ
wi tô wê aimõr wẽ nã
aisĩm romãdkâ wẽ zawre
wat wapar wẽ pibumã

Dazakru mba hã akwẽ nõrĩ
Tet aisô danmĩpar wẽ
aisĩm hawim hã nã wê
aismĩ wẽ nã

Tanẽ nmẽ

wi tô wê aimõr wẽ nã
aisĩm romãdkâ wẽ zawre
wat wapar wẽ pibumã

Wapkẽhrikwa mãtô mnĩ
aisaprõnnĩ
wi tô wê aimõr wẽ nã
aisĩm romãdkâ wẽ zawre
wat wapar wẽ pibumã

Waptokwa Zawre zatô aipâ
aimõ saprõnnĩ
tô nmãinnĩ aimõrze mba
aipâ aisiwẽttê nã

Tanẽ nmẽ
wi tô wê aimõr wẽ nã
aisĩm romãdkâ wẽ zawre
wat wapar wẽ pibumã

21. Dazakru sĩm warewdêhu wa aire romzakrã—Ronaldo—In the Village of Warewdêhu There Used to Be Darkness

In the Village of Warewdêhu people used to walk in darkness, but now Jesus came for us and so everyone walks in the light. His light will never end.

Dazakru sĩm warewdêhu wa aire romzakrã wa kwanmrõ mnõze tô tazim si
Are tokto mãtô Jesus kãnẽ waimã ĩmãntamĩnĩ
tâkâhã hawi zatô mẽ romkuiwẽ wa kbure krdanõmrõ

Are tô tahã romkuiwẽ za sikutõr kõdi (2x)

Ambâ nõrĩ, pikõĩ nõrĩ, aikte nõrai zemã
wasi bdâdi hirê watô smĩstu psênĩ
tanẽ nmẽ wapkite snã wasisa ktab snã
damẽ si tô ĩsenã snã wakmã kba

22. Kãnẽ Waptokwa damrmẽze—Mateus Sirnãwẽ—This Is the Word of God

This is a hymn composed by Mateus when his one-year-old son died. He had said he would have a service of thanksgiving whether his son recovered or died. The song says that God has already told him that it would happen this way. God loves His children, my children and my wife. God, who makes the plans, He took one of my children to Himself. He had told me that on that day.

Kãnẽ mãtô Waptokwa wamã tamrmẽnĩ, tamrmẽnĩ:
Ĩkra nõrĩ wa ĩt aisawidikwa taisawidikwa
Tôka, kãtô aimrõ kãtô aikra nõrĩ
Watô aismĩstukwa, watô aiwazrêkwa ĩsimã

Tanẽ nmẽ wat smĩsi btâ nã romkmãdâ aim hri kwa
smĩsi aikra watô ĩsimẽ saprõ, ĩsimẽ
watô ro aim waskukwa, watô aimã kba imrẽmẽ tô tahã btâ nã

Watô ĩmrẽmẽ aimã kba, ĩmrẽmẽ
Ro za ĩkrãiwatbro kba mnõ nã watô ro aimã waskukwa

Ĩkra nõrĩ wa ĩt aiwaihkudikwa ĩprai nẽm kba nã
tô btâ bâ watô aimẽ kba krĩnẽ krainẽm kbaze mba
watô aiwãitêkwa, watô aikuparkwa, watô aipkẽnmrõkwa

Tanẽ nmẽ, bâtô ro kmã kahõs psêkwa
Kãnẽ watô aimã kba ĩmrẽmẽ
Wi tô aisõkrê kwaba, wi tô krainẽm kwaba, ĩpra
watô ro aim waskukwa
watô aimã kba ĩmrẽmẽ tô tahã btâ nã

23. Waptokwa Dakra dam sawidi (Mateus Sirnãwẽ)—God loves His Children

Waptokwa dakra damsawidi
Waptokwa dakra damsawidi
Dakra mã mãtô ropistunĩ
"Dasimẽ zatô dat wanimrõ".

Waptokwa tô waptokwai ktabi
Tanẽnmẽ mãtô wanmĩstunĩ
Tanẽnmẽ mãtô wapkẽhrinĩ
Tanẽnmẽ wanõrĩ wapkẽ toiti

Tanẽ nmẽ arê kba damẽ
Dazabba damẽ krwanmrõ mnõ da
Tanẽ nmẽ arê kba damẽ
Dazabba damẽ krwanmrõ mnõ da

Waptokwa danmĩzawi sawre nmẽ
Mãtô dawaikwam hawi wawazrênĩ
Danmĩzawi mãt kbure mã wasku psênĩ
Dammrmẽze mãt kbure mã rmẽnĩ

24. Waptokwa damẽ krĩmõr da (Augusto Damsõkẽ)—God Has Called Me to Walk with Him

Waptokwa damẽ krĩmõr da mãtô ĩzaihrânĩ,
dasimã mãtô ĩwazrênĩ romkunẽ hawi

dasimã mãtô ĩnmĩstunĩ
damrmẽze ĩt krwasku mnõ da.

Tôka dure ĩsiwaikẽ, zatô aisaihrânĩ,
danõwa aisiwasku da, zatô btâ aihrinĩ.

Mãtô ĩzaihrânĩ, dasimã,

Zãtô ĩsaihrânĩ, dasimã,
danõwa aisiwasku pibumã
Waptokwa dazazê nã

25. Tokto ĩpkẽ toiti (Mateus Sirnãwẽ)—Now I Am Happy

Waptokwa wazatô dakmãdâkâ
Waptokwa wazatô dakmãdâkâ

Tanẽ nmẽ wa tokto ĩpkẽ toiti
Tanẽ nmẽ wa tokto ĩpkẽ toiti

Romkunẽ mãtô ĩm kutõrnĩ
Romkunẽ mãtô ĩm kutõrnĩ

Appendix D

Musical Symbol and Meaning
Abbreviated Article

MUSICAL SYMBOL AND MEANING: A SEMIOTIC APPROACH TO A DIVERSE CHRISTIAN MUSICAL PERCEPTION
Elsen Portugal

October 26, 2018

INTRODUCTION

Although the vastness of the field of semiotics and the unusual application of its principles to areas of Christian music may seem controversial, the time invested, however, is likely to be rewarded with a greater comprehension of the process of meaning creation, and a more graceful understanding for the views of others. This paper challenges the presumed universality of music's meanings and the potential resulting unfairness to other musical systems through the examination of the process of meaning development on the basis of Peircean categories. Along the centuries an absolutist view of the meaning of music has led to the imposition of foreign styles in cross-cultural interactions around the world. Understanding the potential for limitless connotations for each genre, style, or musical element is central to a positive and culturally appropriate development of Christian musical practices at national, communal, and denominational levels.

WHAT IS A "SIGN?"

Daniel Chandler defines semiotics as "the study not only of what we refer to as 'signs' in everyday speech, but of anything which 'stands for' something else."[1] The use of signs can be found in various instances in Scripture and their meanings are often variable. In the area of music, the range of perceptions conveyed through musical patterns is verifiably immense. "Meaning is not 'transmitted' to us—*we actively [interpret texts and the world] according to a complex interplay of [frames of reference]*."[2]

SEMIOTICS: FOUNDATION AND DEVELOPMENT

The study of *semiotics* owes its modern development to the work of Swiss linguist Ferdinand de Saussure[3] and of the American philosopher Charles Sanders Peirce.[4] Music(al) semiotics follows similar principles and incorporates ideas from the fields of ethnomusicology, psychology, and the social sciences.[5] Semiotician Thomas Turino explains: "Music has a great multiplicity of potentially meaningful parameters sounding simultaneously, and its status as a potential collective activity helps explain its particular power to create affect and group identities."[6] Along with ethnomusicologists, music semioticians contest the idea that "music is a universal language." "Music is no more a universal 'language' than (verbal) language itself. Being a universal phenomenon does not mean that the same sounds, musical or verbal, have the same meaning in all cultures."[7] Leonard Meyer, in 1956, identified "universalism" or "the belief that the responses obtained by [musical] experiment or otherwise are universal, natural, and necessary," as an error.[8] Although some semioticians admit to the existence of "bioacoustic" universals in music,[9]

---

1. Chandler, *Semiotics for Beginners*, introduction.
2. Chandler, *Semiotics for Beginners*, introduction. Emphasis added.
3. See Joseph, "Ferdinand de Saussure."
4. See Atkin, "Peirce's Theory of Signs."
5. See Tagg, *Music's Meanings*.
6. Turino, "Signs of Imagination," 249.
7. See Tagg, *Music's Meanings*.
8. Meyer, *Emotion and Meaning in Music*, 5.
9. See Tagg, *Music's Meanings*.

musics do not carry clearly equal meanings as demonstrated in Balkwill and Thompson's study.[10]

PEIRCEAN SEMIOTIC CONCEPTS

American philosopher Charles Peirce's semiotic concepts have played vital roles in the research of numerous musical semioticians and authors around the world, such as Eero Tarasti, Umberto Eco, Thomas Turino, Oscar Salgar, José Luis Martinez, Philip Tagg, and Jean-Jacques Nattiez. His concepts involve a series of trichotomies used for the analysis of *semiosis*, the process of creating and understanding meaning. Two of his most important trichotomies can be highly valuable for this study. The first and central triad of elements identified by Peirce involves the *sign* (also termed *representamen* in his notes), the *object*, and the *interpretant*.[11] The *sign* is the form that carries the meaning, whether it is material or not. The *object* is that to which the sign refers, and the *interpretant* is the "sense made of the sign,"[12] which this paper often terms 'perception'. This triad of elements systematizes the stations through which a message is carried by musical mediation. If a composer *intends* to communicate an emotion or a mood (the "object") to a given audience, he chooses a musical language, potentially with multiple layers of signification, to create a piece of music (the "sign"). This music may be transcribed for individual performance and/or recorded for general audiences to access. Upon performing or hearing this piece, "every individual 'negotiates' musical meaning in a different manner"[13] presumably assisted by naturally-embedded perception skills together with multiple layers of culturally-induced cues. The second trichotomy labels types of signs as the *icon*, the *index*, and the *symbol*. *Icons* are "signs bearing physical resemblance to what they stand for."[14] Although this is more easily perceived in the visual realm, certain musical sounds can also bear a resemblance to known aural cues in life. *Indices* are "signs connected [to the object] either by causality, or by spatial, temporal or cultural proximity, to what they stand for."[15] "This sign

---

10. See Balkwill and Thompson, "Cross-Cultural Investigation."
11. Tagg, *Music's Meanings*, 60.
12. Chandler, *Semiotics for Beginners*, "Signs."
13. Salgar, "Musical Semiotics," 4.
14. Tagg, *Music's Meanings*, 161.
15. Tagg, *Music's Meanings*, 162.

type ... is particularly important in music semiotics to the extent that all musical sign types can be considered as at least partially indexical."[16] A musical *index* is any type of sonic reference which is partly iconic (or "sounds like" something one could naturally hear in common life) but also denotes a larger concept than what is heard. The *symbol* is also called *arbitrary sign*. "A *sign* can be called *arbitrary* when its semiosis exhibits no discernible elements of structural similarity (*icons*), or of proximity or causality (*indices*), between sign and object/interpretant."[17] As a general rule, the association between an object and sign functioning as a *symbol (arbitrary sign)* arises by "convention" and not due to any clear resemblance to the object.

COMMUNICATION, MEANING, AND EMOTION

Texts on musical semiotics tend to intertwine the ideas of music's *meaning* and its power to evoke *emotions*. The relationship between the affective (*emotional*) response to the musical stimuli and the creation of meaning is complex and even the most knowledgeable scholars have not yet completely understood it from a psychological perspective. Several models attempt to explain human response. One twenty-first-century medical/psychological study by two Swedish psychologists, Patrik Juslin and Daniel Västfjäall, identifies six distinct brain mechanisms involved in emotional response to music:

1. Brain stem reflex—a response reflecting a perception of urgency.
2. Evaluative conditioning—prompted by earlier pairing of the musical stimulus to either positive or negative experiences.
3. Emotional contagion—whereby the listener perceives emotional content and "mimics" it leading to personal emotion.
4. Visual imagery—when the listener creates mental pictures which interact with the musical stimulus.
5. Episodic memory—when the music evokes a memory from the listener's life due to association with an earlier event.

---

16. Tagg, *Music's Meanings*, 162.
17. Tagg, *Music's Meanings*, 163. Emphasis added.

6. Musical expectancy—when a musical feature violates, delays, or confirms how the listener expects the music to continue.[18]

Juslin and Västfjäall's mechanisms, 2–5 in particular, display a certain relationship to Peircean sign types, and therefore, to the creation of meaning. According to the authors, the brain responds according to "evaluative conditioning" (2) by the "pairing of musical stimulus with positive or negative experiences of the past." Thus, music serves as a *symbol* (or *arbitrary sign*), since the sonic material evokes the memory of the emotion of the previous event because the event and the music occurred in synchrony. "Emotional contagion" (3) is believed to take place when the listener "perceives the emotional expression of the music," and by "mimicking" it he or she internalizes and adopts the emotion. For emotion to occur, the subject would need familiarity with the stylistic tools, or emotive features of the song or piece. For this to take place, a certain level of inculturation would be necessary. The implication is that such musical stimulus would be an *index* sign type, which would, in turn lead listeners to first "feel" the emotion it indicates, and then potentially deduce meaning. The mechanism of "visual imagery" (4) is particularly relevant for musical therapy. The images entertained by the listener may result from a Guided Imagery and Music (GIM) approach, as conceived by musical therapist Helen Lindquist Bonny, or be fully spontaneous. Music, in such cases, could be *iconic*, *indexical*, and *symbolic*—at least partially—through the same instantiation. "Episodic memory" (5) best undergirds the use of music as a *symbol*. Juslin and Västfjäall explain that "episodic memory is one of the induction mechanisms that have *commonly been regarded as less 'musically relevant' by music theorists*, but recent evidence suggests that *it could be one of the most frequent and subjectively important sources of emotion in music*."[19]

THE PEIRCEAN *SYMBOL* AND THE MEANINGS OF CHRISTIAN MUSIC

Musicians, music listeners, and Christian worshipers develop attachments to different genres, styles, or pieces along the course of their lives. Intracultural perspectives can indeed lead common practices to

---

18. See Juslin and Västfjäall, "Emotional Responses to Music."

19. See Juslin and Västfjäall, "Emotional Responses to Music"; Sloboda and O'Neill, "Emotions in Everyday Listening."

crystallize to such extent, that *symbols* are transformed into *icons* and *indices*. The *symbolic* features of a musical genre, style, or piece can become so ingrained in the conscience of a people group, a community, or a society, that it *becomes iconic or indexical* for that culture, or else, it begins to "sound like" a specific emotion, event, identity, idea, etc. These culturally bound *icons* and *indices* lend themselves to becoming distinctive social markers and motivators.

Evidence gathered through surveys clearly indicates that the meaning of a piece of music is not identical to all individuals within a given culture. The musical *sign* reaches the *interpretant* stage of semiosis guided by multiple personal cues, thus allowing multiple (accurate or not) meaning perceptions to exist. Philip Tagg gives as example an experiment with 607 listeners for whom he played the song *The Dream of Olwen* by Charles Williams. Although the most common responses were "love" and "romance," many conceived of "waving corn," "rolling hills," "flowing hair," and even "shampoo" and "Austria." Thomas Turino presents a valuable example of how differently people can perceive a musical stimulus. When playing a recording of Jimi Hendrix's "The Star-Spangled Banner" at Woodstock for university students who were "not yet born in the late sixties," he notes that they displayed various reactions. One particular older gentleman, who had lost his son to drugs, found Hendrix's performance very disturbing. For that man, Hendrix's routine was *indexical* and even *iconic* for being on drugs. Hendrix's performance does indeed make use of *iconic* sounds (ex.: bombs—a likely criticism of the Vietnam War), as well as *indexical* interludes (ex.: "taps" indicating the death of soldiers). The total performance could be viewed as *symbolic* of the drug scene, since drugs are not seen on the video, the sounds produced by the guitar are not typically produced by the action of taking drugs, and the band sings no lyrics about drugs. As informed people, listeners perceive an *indexical* association of this performance with drugs and the cultural revolution of the sixties. But without initial acquaintance with the culture (i.e., knowing the United States, recognizing the national anthem as a symbol of this country, knowing how the anthem is traditionally sung, understanding the events of the era—the war, the cultural revolution, etc. and possibly many other factors) a foreign individual from an isolated people group would not hear Hendrix's performance and deduce any meaning resembling the above-mentioned indexical perception among Americans. By means of a simple questionnaire requesting individual answers to eight Christian music samples, this author confirmed the same trend towards a perception of *symbolic* meaning among the participants of a questionnaire in two churches in one city.

INTENDED MEANING AND INTERFERENCE

Sound may be produced intentionally or not. As the examples offered have demonstrated, much of this "meaning" arises from a series of cultural and personal factors along the course of *semiosis*. Disruption of intended meaning, according to Philip Tagg, can be attributed to what he terms *codal interference*, one of two aspects of breakdown of communication. Another plausible explanation to the great number of music *interpretants* is given in the semiotician/linguist Umberto Eco's concept of "Open Work." In a 2015 article of the literary journal *The Context*, Dr. Prayer Elmo Raj described Eco's thesis that artists (writers, painters, musicians, etc.) often create works that are open for multiple meanings.[20]

CONCLUSION

This paper has reviewed concepts developed by multiple key semioticians of the Western world, focusing on two of Charles Peirce's trichotomies. The study of the process of semiosis demonstrates the importance of the listener as the effectual "interpreter" of the message, intentionally or not intentionally delivered. Some musical material develops *iconic* and *indexical* values due to an *initial symbolic function*, that is, the musical material was *first of all* associated with (an) event(s), and concurrent emotions and meanings—a distinct function of the Peircean *symbol*, before it could become a cultural *icon* or *index*. While the focus of application for semiotics in this study has its benefit for "navigating" through a variety of Christian music perceptions, it has incorporated concepts from secular semioticians involved with various communicative practices, as well as intentionally cited examples from Christian and secular musics. Utilizing semiotic guidelines, the findings of this paper affirm the fluidity of meaning found in classical, popular, and church music styles and do not justify the attribution of value and meaning labels on musics that may not be one's personal preference.

---

20. Elmo Raj, "Text and Meaning."

Appendix E

Xerente Mission Records

1. HOW THE VIGILS CAME TO BE IN XERENTE VILLAGES

Rinaldo de Mattos
Translated and adapted by Elsen Portugal

Certain regions of the State of Tocantins inherited fragments of the traditional Catholic feasts of the northeast, with few religious expressions but rather with much dancing and alcoholic drinks that last the entire night. As a result of the drunkenness state of participants, the behavior in these feasts is loose and, as a rule, leads to a lot of fighting and contentiousness. It is not rare for physical aggression leading to bodily harm and even death to take place.

Xerente believers have already identified these feasts as something bad, and the faithful believer, within the Xerente understanding, does not attend these feasts.

A certain day many years ago a young Christian man from the church in the village of Porteira (Nrõzawi) by the name of Tiago Wakuke came to think this: "well, if unbelievers spend the whole night dancing and drinking 'for Satan' [in his terms], why can't we, believers, spend the whole night praying to God? . . ." Based on these thoughts he had the initiative of organizing a night of prayer in his village, exactly on the same date when one of these feasts was taking place not very far from there. Many took part in this first meeting.

In the neighboring village of Salto (Kripre), another Xerente believer, Valci Sinã, adhered to the idea and, together with Tiago, organized an all-night prayer meeting at the house of Paulinho Waĩkarnãse, one of the Christian believers. His house was on the margins of the Piabanha River (Ribeirão), a tributary of the Tocantins River. I also took part in this meeting. It was from this point on that these all-night prayer meetings began to be known as "vigils" ("Vigília").

These vigils grew and became traditional. Today, the majority of Xerente churches plan vigils to which all the other churches are invited. These meetings may bring together twenty churches or more along from the Xerente reservation area. Sometimes more than 300 people take part in them.

2. XERENTE VILLAGES WITH CHURCHES

Rinaldo de Mattos—August 2015
Translated by Elsen Portugal

(With additions from information provided by Lázaro Rowakro Xerente)
(Updated by Mário Luiz Gomes Moura—September 2018)

Churches with Baptist Affiliation:

Well-established:

1. **Village: Porteira Nrõzawi**—Leaders: Pr. Pedro Waĩkainẽ, Tiago Wakukepre and other leaders

2. **Village: Salto Kripre**—Leaders: Pr. Silvino Sirnãwẽ and Betânia Kuzadi

3. **City: Tocantínia Krikahâ**—Leaders: Pr. Sinval Waĩkazate and Bolivar Sinãrĩ

4. **Village: Cabeceira Verde Mrãiwahi**—Leaders: João Brito Simrãmi, Tiago Mrãkrãwekõ and Carlinho Waikarnãse

5. **Village: Novo Horizonte Warewdêhu**—Leaders: Pedro Mmĩrkopte and Leonardo Kuzêiro

6. **Village: Jenipapo Mrãzawrerê**—Leaders: Nelson Wdêrêhu and Suelene Kuzadi

Church in the process of organization (being established):

1. **Village Nova Jerusalém** (?)—Leader: Lázaro Rowakro
2. **Village Sdarãrê**—Leaders: Nelson Sipahimẽkwa and Alonso Smiwaibu
3. **Village Riozinho Kakumhu**—Leaders: Marcelino Kasuwamrĩ and Osmar Kurbepte
4. **Village Brejinho Tkiburê**—Leaders: Lucas Wakukepre and Eduardo Kumserã
5. **Village Funil Sakrêpra**—Leader: José Silva Sromne
6. **Village Canaã**—Leader: José Valter Sõnhã—used to belong to the Congregação Cristã do Brasil (Christian Congregation of Brazil) denomination
7. **Village Recanto da Água Fria Kâwahâ Zase**—Leaders: Alfredo Snãromti and Adalton Pizumẽkwa
8. **Village Brejo Comprido Wrakurerê**—Leaders: Juraci Saparzane and Valmir Hkâwe
9. **Village Santo Antônio Mrãite**—Leaders: Edmilson Kumkawe and Deuzimar Mmirkopte
10. **Village Nova do João Mandi**—Leaders: Nelson Praze and Otávio Wdêkruwe
11. **Village Campo Grande Pakre**—Leaders: Maurício Kbazaksêkõ and Valdomiro Simnãwe with his children

Villages /Farms/Residences with small population in which a leader lives and where some sporadic meetings take place in view of establishing a church

1. **Village Karêhu**—Leaders: Couple Valteir Tpêkru and Patrícia Brudi
2. **Village Fortaleza Mrãinĩsdu**—Leaders: Couple Manoel Sawrekmõzê and Eunice Brupahi
3. **Village Suprawahâ**—Leaders: Edvaldo Kmõmse and Valnice Kuzadi
4. **Village Morrão**—Leaders: Cacique Altino and Samuel

5. **Farm Sítio Novo (?)**—Leader: Valter Dbazanõ (non-Indian married with an indigenous woman)
6. **Village Aldeinha Kâwahâ**—Leaders: Gilson Dbatêkrdu and Vitorino Mãrawe
7. **Village Monte Belo Srãpre**—Leader: Mateus Sirnãwẽ
8. **Village Rio Preto (?)**—Leader: Bento Wakukepre
9. **Village Nova -Próximo a aldeia Suirêhu**—Leader: Sandoval Krãrãte
10. **Residence Sucupira (?)**—Leaders: Couple Jonair Ainãksêkõ and Wanda Brudi
11. **Residence Angelim (?)**—Leader: Basílio Dbazanõ (new believer)
12. **Village Serra Verde (?)**—Leader: Whoshington Prawã
13. **Village Zé Brito Spohurê**—Leaders: Ricardo Sawrepte and Gilvan (?)
14. **Village Akehu**—Leader: Paulinho Kmõrê
15. **Village Brejo Comprido Kãwrakurêrê Nisdu**—Leaders: Juraci Saparzane and Valmir Hkâwe
16. **Village Brupre**—Leaders: Milton Srênõkrã and Valperino
17. **Village Buriti Kuiwdêhu**—Leader: Edmilson Simawe
18. **Village Traíras Brupkarê**—Leader: Jeová
19. **Village Cachoeira**—Leader: Kmorê
20. **Village Bêtãnia**—Leader: Edvan Wdêkruwe

CHURCH ASSOCIATED WITH THE *CONGREGAÇÃO CRISTÃ DO BRASIL* DENOMINATION:

1. **Village Paraíso Kakrãiwdê**—Leader: Genivaldo Romkre

CHURCH ASSOCIATED WITH THE *FOUR-SQUARE GOSPEL* DENOMINATION:

1. **City of Tocantínia (Krikahâ)**—Leader: Adilson Warõ

CHURCHES ASSOCIATED WITH THE *ASSEMBLY OF GOD* DENOMINATION:

1. **Village Brejo Verde Mrãirê**—Leaders: José Kumrĭzdazê and Adailton Hêssukamekwa—Ministry of Monte Sião—Rio de Janeiro—RJ
2. **Village Cabeceira da Água Fria Kâwahâ Nĩsdu**—Leaders: Nilson Wazase and Nilda Sibakadi—Ministry of Ágape—Palmas

There are a total of twenty-two active local churches with local leaders, as well as eighteen nuclei (villages, farms, residences) where the name of the Lord is proclaimed. The estimated Xerente population is presently of 4,000 people. Approximately 1,000 people have converted to the gospel. There are three ordained pastors.

Observation: The question marks in parentheses indicate that our source did not remember the precise name of the location or of the person at the moment, neither in Xerente, nor in Portuguese.

Bibliography

Almeida, Maria Regina Celestino de. "John Manuel Monteiro (1956–2013): um legado inestimável para a Historiografia." *Revista Brasileira de História* 33 (2012) 399–403. https://www.researchgate.net/publication/260768510_John_Manuel_Monteiro_1956-2013_um_legado_inestimavel_para_a_Historiografia/stats.

Almeida, Rita Heloísa de. *O Diretório dos Índios: Um Projeto de "Civilização" no Brasil do Século XVIII*. Brasília, Braz.: Editora UnB, 1997.

Anais do XVI Encontro Regional de História da Anpuh-Rio: Saberes e Práticas Científicas. "O Evangelho Não Destrói Culturas." *Encontro*, 2014. http://www.encontro2014.rj.anpuh.org/resources/anais/28/1400426618_ARQUIVO_encontro2014_anpuh_pgrigorio_oevangelhonaodestroiculturas.pdf.

Anchieta, José de. *Cartas, Informações, Fragmentos Históricos e Sermões do Padre José de Anchieta: (1554–1594)*. Rio de Janeiro: Ed. Civilização Brasileira, 1933.

Andrade, Oswald de. "Erro de Português." *Faraco & Moura. Língua e Literatura* 3 (1995) 146–47.

"Anthropologists! Anthropologists!" *Anthropologizing* (blog), June 20, 2011. https://anthropologizing.com/2011/06/20/anthropologists-anthropologists/.

Ashton, Mark, et al. *Worship by the Book*. Edited by D. A. Carson. Grand Rapids, MI: Zondervan, 2002.

Associação Linguística Evangélica Missionária. "História." https://web.archive.org/web/20190101061833/http://wycliffe.org.br/alem/historico.php.

Atkin, Albert. "Peirce's Theory of Signs." In *Stanford Encyclopedia of Philosophy*, Stanford University, 2006. https://plato.stanford.edu/entries/peirce-semiotics/.

Avery, Tom. "Music of the Heart: The Power of Indigenous Worship in Reaching Unreached Peoples with the Gospel." *Mission Frontiers Magazine*, July-August 1996. http://www.missionfrontiers.org/issue/article/music-of-the-heart.

Bailey, David M. "Cultivating and Contextualizing Arts in Worship for Minority Groups." In *Worship and Mission for the Global Church*, edited by James R. Krabill, locs. 7169–214. Pasadena, CA: William Carey Library, 2013. Kindle ed.

———. "Three Obstacles to Overcome." In *Worship and Mission for the Global Church*, edited by James R. Krabill et al., locs. 10869–918. Pasadena, CA: William Carey Library, 2013. Kindle ed.

Bailey, John M., ed. *Pursuing the Mission of God in Church Planting*. Alpharetta, GA: North American Mission Board, 2006.

Bakss, Robert. *Worship Wars: What the Bible Says about Worship Music.* Port Orchard, WA: Ark House, 2015. Kindle ed.

Balkwill, Laura-Lee, and William Forde Thompson. "A Cross-Cultural Investigation of the Perception of Emotion in Music: Psychophysical and Cultural Cues." *Music Perception: An Interdisciplinary Journal* 17 (1999) 43–64. https://pdfs.semanticscholar.org/fd2f/e5df348eb9d055ddee8586cf31a13ad0df7b.pdf.

Balonek, Michael T. "You Can Use That in the Church? Musical Contextualization and the Sinhala Church." Master's thesis, Bethel University, 2009.

Barth, Fredrik. *Ethnic Groups and Boundaries: The Social Organization of Culture Difference.* Long Grove, IL: Waveland, 1998. Kindle ed.

Bateman, Herbert W. *Authentic Worship: Hearing Scripture's Voice, Applying Its Truths.* Grand Rapids, MI: Kregel Academic & Professional, 2002.

Begbie, Jeremy S., and Steven R. Guthrie, eds. *Resonant Witness: Conversations between Music and Theology.* Grand Rapids, MI: Eerdmans, 2011. Kindle ed.

Behague, Gerard. "Brazil." In *The New Grove Dictionary of Music and Musicians*, edited by Stanley Sadie and J. Tyrrell, 3:221–44. London: Macmillan, 2001.

Benedict, Ruth. "Anthropology and Cultural Change." *The American Scholar* 11 (1942) 243–48. http://www.jstor.org/stable/41203587.

Bergamaschi, Maria Aparecida, and Juliana Schneider Medeiros. "História, memória e tradição na educação escolar indígena: o caso de uma escola Kaingang." *Revista Brasileira de História* 30 (2010) 55–75. https://dx.doi.org/10.1590/S0102-01882010000200004.

Bertolini, Carolina. "Performance Musical e Reconhecimento: a etnomusicologia da relação entre os povos Sateré-Mawé e Tikuna através do estudo do grupo musical Kuiá, da Aldeia Inhãa-bé." Master's thesis, Manaus: Universidade Federal do Amazonas, 2016. https://tede.ufam.edu.br/bitstream/tede/5745/5/Disserta%c3%a7%c3%a3o%20-%20Carolina%20Bertolini.pdf.

Best, Harold. *Unceasing Worship: Biblical Perspectives on Worship and the Arts.* Downers Grove, IL: InterVarsity, 2003.

Biblioteca Brasiliana Culta José Mindlin. "Sousa, Gabriel Soares de." https://digital.bbm.usp.br/handle/bbm/4795.

Blache, Martha. 1988. "Folclor y cultura popular." Revista de Investigaciones Folclóricas 3 (December). University of Buenos Aires, Instituto de Ciencias Antropológicas.

Black Image Band. "History." https://web.archive.org/web/20191029235551/http://blackimage.com.au/history/.

Blacking, John. *Music, Culture, and Experience.* Edited by Reginald Byron. Chicago: Chicago University Press, 1995.

Boehme, Ron. *The Fourth Wave: Taking Your Place in the New Era of Missions.* Seattle, WA: YWAM, 2011.

Bondanella, Peter. *Umberto Eco and the Open Text: Semiotics, Fiction, Popular Culture.* Cambridge: University of Cambridge Press, 1997. Kindle ed.

Borchert, Gerard L. *Worship in the New Testament: Divine Mystery and Human Response.* St. Louis: Chalice, 2008.

Borges, Gerson. *Ser Evangélico Sem Deixar de Ser Brasileiro.* Viçosa, Braz.: Editora Ultimato, 2016.

Boston University Anthropology. "Emeritus Professors: Frederik Barth." https://web.archive.org/web/20181216062229/http://www.bu.edu/anthrop/people/emeritus/f-barth/.

Brand, Hilary, and Adrienne Chaplin. *Art and Soul: Signposts for Christians in the Arts.* Downers Grove, IL: InterVarsity, 2001.
Brueggemann, Walter. *Worship in Ancient Israel: An Essential Guide.* Nashville, TN: Abingdon, 2005.
Bruner, E. M. "Abraham Lincoln as Authentic Reproduction: A Critique of Postmodernism." *American Anthropologist* 96 (1994) 397–415.
Buker, Raymond B. "Missionary Encounter with Culture." *Evangelical Missions Quarterly* 1 (1964) 9–18.
Butler, John F. *Christian Art in India.* Madras, Ind.: The Christian Literature Society, 1986.
Camêu, Helsa. "Música Indígena." *Revista Brasileira de Folclore* 2 (Sept/Oct 1962) 23–38.
Carey, James W. *Communication as Culture: Essays on Media and Society.* New York: Routledge, 1988.
Carone, Edgard. "Tratado Descritivo do Brasil em 1587." *Revista de Administração de Empresas* 11 (1971) 97–98. https://www.scielo.br/j/rae/a/N39T7Fh7SSBfc5Pzx589jNh/?lang=pt.
Carson, D. A. *Christ and Culture Revisited.* Grand Rapids, MI: Eerdmans, 2008.
Chandler, Daniel. *Semiotics for Beginners.* http://visual-memory.co.uk/daniel/Documents/S4B/.
———. *Semiotics: The Basics.* London: Routledge Taylor & Francis, 2017. Kindle ed.
Chenoweth, Vida. *Melodic Perception and Analysis.* Ukarumpa, Papua New Guinea: Summer Institute of Linguistics, 1972.
———. "Spare Them Western Music." In *Worship and Mission for the Global Church,* edited by James R. Krabill, locs. 119–23. Pasadena, CA: William Carey Library, 2013. Kindle ed.
Collinge, Ian. "Moving from Monocultural to Multicultural Worship." In *Worship and Mission for the Global Church,* edited by James R. Krabill, locs. 10980–1065. Pasadena, CA: William Carey Library, 2013. Kindle ed.
Collins, Paul M. *Context, Culture, and Worship: The Quest for Indian-ness.* Kashmere Gate, Delhi: Indian Society for Promoting Christian Knowledge, 2006.
Conferência Nacional dos Bispos do Brasil. "Festas do Divino Espírito Santo Celebram a Religiosidade Popular Brasileira." http://www.cnbb.org.br/festas-do-divino-espirito-santo-celebram-a-religiosidade-popular-brasileira/.
Conklin, Beth A. "Body Paint, Feathers, and VCRs: Aesthetics and Authenticity in Amazonian Activism." *American Ethnologist* 24 (1997) 711–37. https://www.jstor.org/stable/646806.
Corbitt, J. Nathan. *The Sound of the Harvest: Music's Mission in Church and Culture.* Grand Rapids, MI: Baker, 1998.
Costen, Melva W. *African American Christian Worship.* 2nd ed. Nashville, TN: Abingdon, 2007.
Crouch, Andy. *Culture Making: Recovering our Creative Calling.* Downers Grove, IL: InterVarsity, 2008.
Crowley, Roger. *Conquerors: How Portugal Forged the First Global Empire.* New York: Random House, 2015.
DeNeui, Paul H., ed. *Communicating Christ through Story and Song.* Pasadena, CA: William Carey Library, 2008.
Dicionário Online de Portugues (Dicio). "Sucuriju." https://www.dicio.com.br/sucuriju/.

———. "Taboca." https://www.dicio.com.br/taboca/.
Dickinson, Edward. *Music in the History of the Western Church*. New York: Scarce Scholarly Books, 1969.
Dowley, Tim. *Christian Music: A Global History*. Minneapolis: Fortress, 2011.
Dreyer, Elizabeth A. *Passionate Spirituality: Hildegard of Bingen and Hadewijch of Brabant*. New York: Paulist, 2005.
Durkheim, Emile. *The Elementary Forms of Religious Life*. 1915. Reprint, Mineola Park, NY: Dover, 2008.
Dushkina, Natalia. "Historic Reconstruction: Prospects for Heritage Preservation or Metamorphoses of Theory?" In *Conserving the Authentic: Essays in Honour of Jukka Jokilehto*, edited by Nicholas Stanley-Price and Joseph King, 83–94. Rome: ICCROM International Centre for the Study of the Preservation and Restoration of Cultural Property, 2009. https://www.iccrom.org/sites/default/files/publications/2019-11/iccrom_ics10_jukkafestchrift_en.pdf.
Dye, T. Wayne. *Bible Translation Strategy: An Analysis of Its Spiritual Impact*. 1980. Reprint, Dallas: Wycliffe Bible Translators, 1985.
Echoes of a Friend. "Rebirth Brass Band - Why Your Feet Hurt." YouTube, June 11, 2014. https://www.youtube.com/watch?v=M4ojemNyy9Y.
Eco, Umberto. *A Theory of Semiotics*. Bloomington, IN: Indiana University Press, 1976.
Elmo Raj, P. P. "Text and Meaning in Umberto Eco's The Open Work." *The Context* 2 (2015) 326–31.
Enriquez, León. "A Peircean Model for Music and Sound-Based Art: A Pragmatist Approach to Experiences in the Artistic Use of Sound." Paper presented at the Electroacoustic Music Studies Network Conference "Meaning and Meaningfulness in Electroacoustic Music," Stockholm, June 2012. http://www.ems-network.org/IMG/pdf_EMS12_enriquez.pdf.
Fabbri, Franco. "A Theory of Musical Genres." In *Popular Music Perspectives*, edited by D. Horn and P. Tagg, 52–81. Göteborg, Swed.: International Association for the Study of Popular Music, 1981. https://www.tagg.org/xpdfs/ffabbri81a.pdf.
Farhadian, Charles E., ed. *Christian Worship Worldwide: Expanding Horizons, Deepening Practices*. Grand Rapids, MI: Eerdmans, 2007.
Feld, Steven. *Sound and Sentiment: Birds, Weeping, Poetics, and Song in Kaluli Expression*. Durham, NC: Duke University Press, 2012.
Fernandes, Felipe Munhoz Martins. "Do Parixara ao Forró, do Forró ao 'Parixara': uma Trajetória Musical." Master's thesis, São Carlos, SP, 2015.
Fleming, Daniel Johnson. *Contacts with Non-Christian Cultures*. New York: Doran, 1923.
———. *Each with His Own Brush*. New York: Friendship, 1938.
———. *Heritage of Beauty*. New York: Friendship, 1937.
———. *Whither Bound in Missions*. New York: The International Committee of Young Men's Christian Associations, 1925.
Fortunato, Frank, ed., with Paul Neeley and Carol Brinneman. *All the World Is Singing: Glorifying God through the Worship Music of the Nations*. Tyrone, GA: Authentic, 2006.
Fuller Studio. "FULLER Dialogues: Global Arts and Witness." https://fullerstudio.fuller.edu/fuller-dialogues-global-arts-and-witness/.
Fundação Biblioteca Nacional. "A Carta de Pero Vaz de Caminha." http://objdigital.bn.br/Acervo_Digital/Livros_eletronicos/carta.pdf.

Global Ethnodoxology Network. "Arts for a Better Future." https://www.worldofworship.org/artsforabetterfuture/.
———. "Core Values." https://www.worldofworship.org/core-values/.
———. "Ethnodoxology." https://www.worldofworship.org/what-is-ethnodoxology/.
———. "Ethnodoxology Values." Unpublished, 2019. On file.
Goffe, Jo-Ann Richards. "Kom Mek Wi Worship 2—di Revilieshan." *YouTube*, May 17, 2017. https://www.youtube.com/watch?v=V8GDM609QHs&feature=youtu.be.
Goldsborough, Bob. "Videa Chenoweth, Ethnomusicologist and First Marimbist to Play Carnegie Hall, Dies at 90." *Chicago Tribune*, January 11, 2019. https://www.chicagotribune.com/news/obituaries/ct-met-vida-chenoweth-obituary-20190111-story.html.
Gonzaga, Luiz. *Baião*. https://image.slidesharecdn.com/luiz-gonzaga-baiao-150105165152-conversion-gate02/95/luiz-gonzagabaiao-1-638.jpg?cb=1420476798.
Good, Allison Good. "Jazz Messengers." *Tablet*, August 2, 2011. https://www.tabletmag.com/sections/arts-letters/articles/jazz-messengers.
Graciana, Carmelita. "Pastor Guenther Carlos Krieger e o Evangelho." *Cristocentrado* (blog), July 22, 2012. http://cristocentrado.blogspot.com/2012/07/pr-guenther-carlos-krieger-e-o-povo.html.
Gross, Richard H. "Stained Glass as a Vehicle for Spiritual Growth." In *Stained Glass*, 113–20. Raytown, MO: Stained Glass Association of America, 2015.
Grupo Povos e Línguas (Group Peoples and Languages). "História da Missão entre os Povos Indígenas do Brasil" ("History of Mission among Indigenous Peoples of Brazil"). https://web.archive.org/web/20171113214444/https://portal.povoselinguas.com.br/artigos/historia-das-missoes/historia-da-missao-entre-os-povos-indigenas-do-brasil/.
Gupta, Akhil, and Ferguson, James. "Beyond 'Culture': Space, Identity and the Politics of Difference." *Cultural Anthropology* 7 (1992) 6–23.
Hale, Chris. "Reclaiming the Bhajan." *Mission Frontiers* 23 (2001) 16–17.
Hall, Dave. "The Centrality of Worship." *Mission Frontiers* 23 (2001) 28–29. https://www.missionfrontiers.org/issue/article/the-centrality-of-worship.
Handler, Richard, and Jocelyn Linnekin. "Tradition, Genuine or Spurious." *The Journal of American Folklore* 97 (1984) 273–90. https://doi.org/10.2307/540610.
Harris, Robin P. "Dealing Effectively with Opponents on the Field." In *Worship and Mission for the Global Church*, edited by James R. Krabill, locs. 9309–453. Pasadena, CA: William Carey Library, 2013. Kindle ed.
———. "The Great Misconception: Why Music Is Not a Universal Language." In *Worship and Mission for the Global Church*, edited by James R. Krabill, locs. 3066–74. Pasadena, CA: William Carey Library, 2013. Kindle ed.
———. *Storytelling in Siberia: The Olonkho Epic in a Changing World*. Urbana, IL: University of Illinois Press, 2017. Kindle ed.
Harris, Trudier. "Genre." *The Journal of American Folklore* 108 (1995) 509–27. https://doi.org/10.2307/541658.
Hastings, Adrian. *African Christianity*. New York: Seabury, 1976.
Henry, Matthew. *Commentary on the Whole Bible*. Vol. 1, *Genesis to Deuteronomy*. Christian Classics Ethereal Library. https://www.ccel.org/ccel/henry/mhc1.Gen.ii.html.

Hentschel, Frank. "The Sensuous Music Aesthetics of the Middle Ages: The Cases of Augustine, Jacques de Liège and Guido of Arezzo." *Plainsong and Medieval Music* 20 (2011) 1–29. doi:10.1017/S0961137110000173.

Hesselgrave, David J. *Today's Choices for Tomorrow's Mission: An Evangelical Perspective on Trends and Issues in Missions*. Grand Rapids, MI: Academic Books, 1988.

Hiebert, Paul J. *Anthropological Reflections on Missiological Issues*. Grand Rapids, MI: Baker, 1994.

———. *Mission et Culture*. St-Legier: Editions Emmaüs, 2002.

Hill, Jonathan D., ed. *History, Power, and Identity: Ethnogenesis in the Americas, 1492–1992*. Iowa City: University of Iowa Press, 1996.

História do Brasil. "Brasil Pré-Colonial—Características, História, Resumo." https://www.historiadobrasil.net/brasil_colonial/pre_colonial.htm.

Hodges, Catherine. "Ethnomusicology in Mission: What It Isn't, What It Is, and Why It Matters Anyway." *Ethnomusicology News* 5 (1996) 4–6. https://www.historia.uff.br/stricto/teses/Dissert-2007_MACHADO_Marina_Monteiro-S.pdf.

Hodgson, Renata. "Perceptions of Authenticity: Aboriginal Cultural Tourism in the Northern Territory." PhD diss., University of Western Sydney, 2007.

Hunt, Ernest H. *Spirit and Music*. Bristol, UK: St. Stephen's Printing Works, 1922.

Hunt, T. W. *Music and Missions: Discipling through Music*. Eugene, OR: Wipf & Stock, 1987.

Huron, David. "Models of Emotion." *Music 829D: Music and Emotion*. The Ohio State University. https://web.archive.org/web/20100703020750/https://musiccog.ohio-state.edu/Music829D/Notes/Models.html.

———. *Sweet Anticipation: Music and the Psychology of Expectation*. Cambridge, MA: MIT Press, 2006.

Hustad, Donald P. *Jubilate! Church Music in the Evangelical Tradition*. Carol Stream, IL: Hope Publishing, 1980.

Idowu, E. Bolaji. *Towards an Indigenous Church*. London: Oxford University Press, 1965.

Ingalls, Monique M. *Singing the Congregation*. Oxford: Oxford University Press, 2019. Kindle ed.

Indígenas do Brasil. "The Indigenous Peoples of Brazil." https://brasil.antropos.org.uk/.

Instituto Antropos. "Brazilian Indigenous Ethnic Groups." http://instituto.antropos.com.br/v3/index.php?option=com_content&view=article&id=562&catid=19&Itemid=58.

———. "Terena." https://web.archive.org/web/20210120035613/https://instituto.antropos.com.br/site/terena/.

International Council on Monuments and Sites. "The Nara Document on Authenticity (1994)." https://www.icomos.org/en/charters-and-texts/179-articles-en-francais/ressources/charters-and-standards/386-the-nara-document-on-authenticity-1994.

Irvine, Martin. "Structural Linguistics, Semiotics, and Communication Theory: Basic Outlines and Assumptions." https://web.archive.org/web/20180329200951/http://faculty.georgetown.edu/irvinem/theory/Semiotics_and_Communication.html.

Isaacs, Harold R. "Basic Group Identity: The Idols of the Tribe." *Ethnicity* 1 (1974) 15–41. New York: Harper & Row, 1974.

Jackson, Bruce. *Fieldwork*. Urbana, IL: University of Chicago Press, 1987.

Jamison, Todd (pseud.). "House Churches in Central Asia: An Evaluation." *The Evangelical Missions Quarterly* 43 (2007) 188–96.

Johnson, Stephen. "What Is a . . . Tone Poem?" *Classical Music* (blog), June 10, 2016. http://www.classical-music.com/article/what-tone-poem.
Jordan, Ivan, and Frank Tucker. "Using Indigenous Art to Communicate the Christian Message." *The Evangelical Missions Quarterly* 38 (2002) 302–9.
Joseph, John E. "Ferdinand de Saussure." *Linguistics* (2017). https://doi.org/10.1093/acrefore/9780199384655.013.385.
Juslin, Patrik N., and Daniel Västfjäall. "Emotional Responses to Music: The Need to Consider Underlying Mechanisms." *Behavioral and Brain Sciences* 31 (2008) 559–621. https://web.archive.org/web/20180219000856/http://nemcog.smusic.nyu.edu/docs/JuslinBBSTargetArticle.pdf.
Kidd, Jenny. "Performing the Knowing Archive: Heritage Performance and Authenticity." *International Journal of Heritage Studies* 17 (2011) 22–35.
Kim, Joy Hyunsook. "Diaspora Musicians and Creative Collaboration in a Multicultural Community: A Case Study in Ethnodoxology." Master's thesis, Graduate Institute of Applied Linguistics, 2018.
King, Roberta. "Ethnomusicology." In *The Evangelical Dictionary of World Missions*, edited by Scott Moreau, 327. Grand Rapids, MI: Baker, 2000.
———. *Pathways in Christian Music Communication: The Case of the Senufo of Côte d'Ivoire*. PhD diss., Fuller Theological Seminary, 1989.
———. "Singing the Lord's Song in a Global World: The Dynamics of Doing Critical Contextualization through Music." *Evangelical Missions Quarterly* 42 (2006) 68–74.
———. "Telling God's Story through Song." *Evangelical Missions Quarterly* 38 (2002) 295–98.
———. *A Time to Sing: A Manual for the African Church*. Nairobi, Ken.: Evangel, 1999.
Kinsler, F. Ross. "Mission and Context: The Current Debate about Contextualization." *Evangelical Missions Quarterly* 14 (1978) 23–29.
Kivy, Peter. *Introduction to a Philosophy of Music*. Oxford: Oxford University Press, 2002.
Krabill, James R., et al., eds. *Worship and Mission for the Global Church*. Pasadena, CA: William Carey Library, 2013. Kindle ed.
Kraft, Charles H. *Anthropology for Christian Witness*. Maryknoll, NY: Orbis, 2011. Kindle ed.
———. *Christianity in Culture: A Study in Dynamic Biblical Theologizing in Cross-Cultural Perspective*. 2nd ed. Maryknoll, NY: Orbis, 2005. Kindle ed.
———. "The Incarnation, Cross-Cultural Communication, and Communication Theory." *The Evangelical Missions Quarterly* 9 (1973) 277–84.
Kuss, Malena. *Music in Latin America and the Caribbean: An Encyclopedic History*. Vol. 1, *Performing Beliefs: Indigenous Peoples of South America, Central America, and Mexico*. Austin, TX: University of Texas Press, 2004.
Lee, Vernon. *Music and Its Lovers: An Empirical Study of Emotional and Imaginative Responses to Music*. London: Allen & Unwin, 1932. Kindle ed.
Leite, Yonne, and Bruna Franchetto. "500 anos de línguas indígenas no Brasil." In *Quinhentos Anos de História Lingüística do Brasil*, edited by Suzana A. M. Cardoso et al., 15–62. Salvador: Secretaria da Cultura e Turismo do Estado da Bahia, 2006.
Lena, Jennifer C., and Richard A. Peterson. "Classification as Culture: Types and Trajectories of Music Genres." *American Sociological Review* 73 (2008) 697–718.

Léry, Jean de. *History of a Voyage to the Land of Brazil*. Los Angeles: University of California Press, 1992.
Levin, Theodore. *Where Rivers and Mountains Sing: Sound, Music, and Nomadism in Tuva and Beyond*. Bloomington, IN: Indiana University Press, 2010.
Lexico. "Transition." https://www.lexico.com/en/definition/transition.
Lidório, Ronaldo. *Comunicação e Cultura*. São Paulo: Editora Vida Nova, 2014.
———. *Indígenas do Brasil: Avaliando a Missão da Igreja*. Viçosa, Braz.: Editora Ultimato, 2005.
———. "Indigenous Peoples of Brazil." https://web.archive.org/web/20190126014603/https://brasil.antropos.org.uk/.
———. *Introdução à Antropologia Missionária*. São Paulo: Editora Vida Nova, 2011.
———. *Missões: O Desafio Continua*. Belo Horizonte, Braz.: Editora Betânia, 2003.
Lidório, Ronaldo, and Isaac Costa de Souza, eds. *A Questão Indígena—Uma Luta Desigual*. Viçosa, Braz.: Editora Ultimato, 2008.
Lidório, Ronaldo, and Rossana Lidório. *Comunicação, Interculturalidade e Ética*. N.p.: Simplissimo, 2016. Kindle ed.
Lima, Layanna Giordana Bernardo. "Os Akwẽ-Xerente no Tocantins, território indígena e as questões socioambientais." PhD diss., Universidade de São Paulo, 2017. https://www.teses.usp.br/teses/disponiveis/8/8136/tde-11042017-082645/pt-br.php.
Lim, Swee Hong. "Forming Christians through Musicking in China." *Religions* 8 (2017) 1–10. https://doi.org/10.3390/rel8040050.
Lim, Swee Hong, and Lester Ruth. *Lovin' on Jesus*. Nashville, TN: Abingdon, 2017.
Little, Christopher. "A New Agenda: De-Americanization." *Evangelical Missions Quarterly* 42 (2006) 496–505.
Loh, I-To. "Contextualization versus Globalization: A Glimpse of Sounds and Symbols in Asian Worship." *Colloquium* 2 (2005) n.p. http://ism.yale.edu/sites/default/files/files/Contextualization%20versus%20Globalization.pdf.
———. *Hymnal Companion to Sound the Bamboo: Asian Hymns in Their Cultural and Liturgical Contexts*. Chicago: GIA, 2011. Kindle ed.
———. *In Search for Asian Sounds and Symbols in Worship*. Singapore: Trinity Theological College, 2012.
———. "Ways of Contextualizing Church Music: Some Asian Examples." In *Worship and Mission for the Global Church*, edited by James R. Krabill, locs. 1443–618. Pasadena, CA: William Carey Library, 2013. Kindle ed.
Luciano, Gersem dos Santos. *O Índio Brasileiro: O Que Você Precisa Saber sobre os Povos Indígenas do Brasil de Hoje* (The Brazilian Indian: What You Need to Know about the Indigenous Peoples of Today's Brazil). N.p.: SECAD, 2006.
Machado, Marina Monteiro. "A Trajetória da Destruição: Índios e Terras no Império do Brasil." Master's thesis, Universidade Federal Fluminense, 2006.
Marsh, Clive, and Vaughan S. Roberts. *Personal Jesus*. Grand Rapids, MI: Baker Academic, 2012.
Martinez, José Luis. "A Semiotic Theory of Music: According to a Peircean Rationale." Paper presented at the Sixth International Conference on Music Signification, University of Helsinki, December 1–5, 1998. http://hugoribeiro.com.br/biblioteca-digital/Martinez-A_semiotic_theory_music.pdf.
Mascarenhas, Mário. *Método Rápido para Tocar Teclado*. Vol. 1. São Paulo, Braz.: Irmãos Vitale Editores, 1991.

Mattos, Rinaldo de. "Características da Música Xerente." Unpublished file, 1996. Revised in 2003.
———. "Entrevista sobre os Xerente e a Missão Batista." *Missões Nacionais,* 1999/2003. https://web.archive.org/web/20101030211408/www.missoesnacionais.org.br/upload/arquivos/entrevista-xerente-02-99.doc.
———. "Instrumentos Musicais Xerente" ("Xerente Musical Instruments"). Unpublished file based on Mattos's personal research in the years between 1960 and 1998.
———. "Messianismo Existencial Xerente" ("The Xerente Existential Messianism"). *Revista Antropos* 3.2 (2009) 27–38. https://web.archive.org/web/20190102143422/http://revista.antropos.com.br/downloads/dez2009/Artigo%204%20-%20O%20Messianismo%20Xerente%20-%20Rinaldo%20de%20Mattos.pdf.
Maybury-Lewis, David. *The Savage and the Innocent.* London: Evans, 1965.
McGowan, Chris, and Ricardo Pessanha. *The Brazilian Sound: Samba, Bossa Nova and the Popular Music of Brazil.* Playa del Rey, CA: Culture Planet, 2014. Kindle ed.
McGravan, Donald A. *The Bridges of God: A Study in the Strategy of Missions.* New York: Friendship, 1955.
Merriam, Alan P. *The Anthropology of Music.* Evanston, IL: Northwestern University Press, 1964.
Merriam-Webster Dictionary. "Affect." https://www.merriam-webster.com/dictionary/affect.
———. "Authentic." https://www.merriam-webster.com/dictionary/authentic.
———. "Genre." https://www.merriam-webster.com/dictionary/genre.
———. "Traditional." https://www.merriam-webster.com/dictionary/traditional.
Meyer, Leonard B. *Emotion and Meaning in Music.* Chicago: Chicago University Press, 1956. Kindle ed.
Meyers, Megan Marie. "Developing Disciples through Contextualized Worship in Mozambique: Grazing and Growing." PhD diss., Fuller Theological Seminary, 2015.
Missão Novas Tirbos do Brasil. "História da Missão." https://novastribosdobrasil.org.br/historia/.
Missões Nacionais. "Who We Are." https://missoesnacionais.org.br/quem-somos/.
Monteiro, John M. "Tupis, Tapuias e Historiadores: Estudos de História Indígena e do Indigenismo." PhD diss., State University of Campinas, 2001. http://biblioteca.funai.gov.br/media/pdf/TESES/MFN-12944.pdf.
Morehouse, Katherine H. "'They're Playing Our Song': Functions of Western Hymns and Indigenous Songs in the History of the Non-Western Church, with a Case Study of the Maninka People in Kankan, Guinea." *Global Forum on Arts and Christian Faith* 5 (2017) A18–47. http://www.artsandchristianfaith.org/index.php/journal/article/view/34/34.
Moreira, Gabriel Ferrão. "O Estilo Indígena de Villa Lobos (Parte I): Aspectos Melódicos e Harmônicos." *Per Musi* 27 (2013) n.p. https://www.scielo.br/j/pm/a/DT8GWXRZjyj6NBkpPvmKWjF/?lang=pt.
Moynahan, Michael E. "Liturgy, Art, and Spirituality." *Liturgical Ministry* 5 (1996) 108–20.
Murphy, John P. *Music in Brazil: Experiencing Music, Expressing Culture.* New York: Oxford University Press, 2006.

Musical Instrument Museums Online. "Revision of the Hornbostel-Sachs Classification of Musical Instruments by the MIMO Consortium." http://www.mimo-international.com/documents/Hornbostel%20Sachs.pdf.

Music Genres List. "What Is a Music Genre?" http://www.musicgenreslist.com/what-is-a-music-genre/.

Nacaomestica.org. "Diretório que se Deve Observar nas Povoações dos Índios do Pará, e Maranhão, enquanto Sua Majestade Não Mandar o Contrário." https://web.archive.org/web/20191212111635/https://www.nacaomestica.org/diretorio_dos_indios.htm.

Nattiez, Jean-Jacques. *Music and Discourse: Toward a Semiology of Music*. Princeton, NJ: Princeton University Press, 1990.

Neeley, Paul. "Why Indigenous Hymns Failed." *Ethnodoxology News* 2 (1993) n.p.

Negrão, Héber. "Música: Uma Flecha que Atravessa o Coração." *Paralelo 10*, n.d. https://ultimato.com.br/sites/paralelo10/2017/10/musica-uma-flecha-que-atravessa-o-coracao/.

Nettl, Bruno. *The Study of Ethnomusicology*. 3rd ed. Urbana, IL: University of Illinois Press, 2015.

Nezhad, Somayeh Fadaei, et al. "A Definition of Authenticity Concept in Conservation of Cultural Landscapes." *International Journal of Architectural Research* 9 (2015) 93–107. https://web.archive.org/web/20210226044446/http://orcp.hustoj.com/wp-content/uploads/2016/01/2015-A-definition-of-authenticity-concept-in-conservation-of-cultural-landscapes.pdf.

Nida, Eugene. *Customs and Cultures*. New York: Harper & Row, 1954.

Oliveira, João Pacheco, and Carlos Augusto da Costa Freire. *A Presença Indígena na Formação do Brasil*. Brasília, Braz.: Ministério da Educação, 2006.

OMF Thailand. "Isaan." https://web.archive.org/web/20150409213125/https://omf.org/thailand/isaan/.

Opstal, Sandra van. *The Mission of Worship*. Downers Grove, IL: InterVarsity, 2012.

Oshana, Marina. "Autonomy and the Question of Authenticity." *Social Theory and Practice* 33 (2007) 411–29.

Oswald, John. *A New Song Rising in Tibetan Hearts: Tibetan Christian Worship in the Early 21st Century*. Thailand: Central Asian Publishing, 2001.

The Oxford Dictionary of Philosophy. "Authenticity." https://www.oxfordreference.com/display/10.1093/acref/9780199541430.001.0001/acref-9780199541430-e-298?rskey=YtbCTk&result=299.

Oxford Learner's Dictionaries. "Fusion." https://www.oxfordlearnersdictionaries.com/us/definition/english/fusion?q=+fusion.

———. "Transition." https://www.oxfordlearnersdictionaries.com/us/definition/english/transition_1?q=transition.

Pacheco de Oliveira, João. *O Nascimento do Brasil e Outros Ensaios*. Rio de Janeiro: Contra-Capa, 2016.

Pacheco de Oliveira, João, and Carlos Augusto da Rocha Freire. *A Presença Indígena na Formação do Brasil*. Brasília, Braz.: Ministério da Educação, 2006.

Peterson, David. *Engaging with God: A Biblical Theology of Worship*. Downers Grove, IL: InterVarsity, 1992.

Pettan, Svanibor, and Jeff Todd Titon, eds. *The Oxford Handbook of Applied Ethnomusicology*. Oxford: Oxford University Press, 2015.

Pioneers. "Isaan Worship: A Pioneer in Isaan, Thailand." https://web.archive.org/web/20150909065433/https://www.pioneers.org/connect/connect-full-view/isaan-worship.

Piper, John. *Let the Nations Be Glad: The Supremacy of God in Missions*. Grand Rapids, MI: Baker, 2003.

Portugal, Elsen. "Artistic Works: Potential Roles in Christian Spirituality." Irving, TX: B. H. Carroll Theological Institute, 2018. Unpublished paper.

———. "Asian Worship Arts and Church Growth: Learning from the Past, Wisdom for the Future." Irving, TX: B. H. Carroll Theological Institute, 2017. Unpublished paper.

———. "Fusion Music Genres in Indigenous Brazilian Churches: An Evaluation of Authenticity in Xerente Christian Contexts." PhD diss., B. H. Carroll Theological Institute, 2019. https://www.tren.com/e-docs/search.cfm?p150-006.

———. "Introduction to Ethnodoxology: An Academic Warrant." Irving, TX: B.H. Carroll Theological Institute, 2016. Unpublished paper.

———. "Musical Choices in Early Baptist Missions among the Xerente." *Intégrité: A Faith and Learning Journal* 17 (2018) 82–92.

Povos e Línguas do Brasil. "Conheça os Nossos Parceiros." https://web.archive.org/web/20190105134551/https://portal.povoselinguas.com.br/organizacoes-parceiras/.

———. "História de Missão entre os Povos Indígenas do Brasil." https://web.archive.org/web/20171113214444/https://portal.povoselinguas.com.br/artigos/historia-das-missoes/historia-da-missao-entre-os-povos-indigenas-do-brasil/.

Povos Indígenas do Brasil. "Índios Isolados." https://web.archive.org/web/20160818123611/https://pib.socioambiental.org/pt/c/no-brasil-atual/quem-sao/Indios-isolados.

———. "List of Indigenous Peoples." https://pib.socioambiental.org/en/List_of_indigenous_peoples.

———. "Quadro Geral dos Povos." https://pib.socioambiental.org/pt/Quadro_Geral_dos_Povos.

———. "Xerente." https://pib.socioambiental.org/en/Povo:Xerente.

Priberam Portuguese Dictionary. "Sesmarias." https://dicionario.priberam.org/sesmarias.

Price, Leslie Blake. "Bluegrass Nation: A Historical and Cultural Analysis of America's Truest Music." Honors thesis, University of Tennessee, May 2011. https://trace.tennessee.edu/utk_chanhonoproj/1465/.

Ramseyer, Robert L. "Christian Mission and Cultural Anthropology." In *Exploring Church Growth*, edited by Wilbert R. Shenk, 108–16. Grand Rapids, MI: Eerdmans, 1983.

Roberts, Bob, Jr. *Glocalization: How Followers of Jesus Engage a Flat World*. Grand Rapids, MI: Zondervan, 2007.

Rookmaaker, Hans. *Art Needs No Justification*. Downers Grove, IL: InterVarsity, 1978.

Rouget, Gilbert. *Music and Trance*. Chicago: The University of Chicago Press, 1985.

Rowe, Julisa. "Community Engagement through Ethnodramatology." *Orality Journal: The Word Became Fresh* 5 (2016) 51–54.

Ryken, Leland. *Culture in Christian Perspective: A Door to Understanding & Enjoying the Arts*. Portland, OR: Multnomah, 1986.

Sacks, Oliver. "The Power of Music." *Brain* 129 (2006) 2528–32.

Salgar, Óscar Hernández. "Musical Semiotics as a Tool for the Social Study of Music." *The Society for Ethnomusicology: Ethnomusicology Translations* 2 (2016) 1–33. Translated by Brenda M. Romero. https://scholarworks.iu.edu/journals/index.php/emt/article/view/22335/28281.

Santaella, Lucia. "Sound and Music in the Domain of Rhematic Iconic Qualisigns." *Signata* [*Online*] 6 (2015) 91–106. http://signata.revues.org/1065.

Saurman, Todd W. "Singing for Survival in the Highlands of Cambodia: Tampuan Revitalization of Music as Cultural Reflexivity." In *Music and Minorities in Ethnomusicology: Challenges and Discourses from Three Continents*, edited by Ursula Hemetek, 95–103. Vienna, Aust.: Institut für Voksmusikforschung und Ethnomusikologie, 2012.

———. "Singing for Survival in the Highlands of Cambodia: Tampuan Revitalization of Music as Mediation and Cultural Reflexivity." PhD diss., Chiang Mai University, 2013.

Sayers, Dorothy. *The Mind of the Maker: The Expression of Faith through Creativity and Art*. 1941. Reprint, New York: Open Road Integrated Media, 2015. Kindle ed.

Schaeffer, Francis A. *Art and the Bible*. Downers Grove, IL: InterVarsity, 1973.

Schiavini, Fernando. "Indigenismo e Politica Indigenista." *Fernando Schiavini* (blog), n.d. https://web.archive.org/web/20190206042835/http://fernandoschiavini.com.br/indigenismo/

Schoen, Max. "The Experience of Beauty in Music." *The Musical Quarterly* 17 (1931) 93–109. http://www.jstor.org/stable/738642.

Schrag, Brian. *Creating Local Arts Together: A Manual to Help Communities Reach Their Kingdom Goals*. Edited by James R. Krabill. Pasadena, CA: William Carey Library, 2013.

———. *Make Arts for a Better Life: A Guide for Working with Communities*. Oxford: Oxford University Press, 2018.

Schrag, Brian, and Paul Neeley. *All the World Will Worship: Helps for Developing Indigenous Hymns*. 3rd ed. Duncanville, TX: EthnoDoxology, 2005.

Schrag, Néstor García. *Hybrid Cultures: Strategies for Entering and Leaving Modernity*. 1995. Reprint, Minneapolis: University of Minnesota Press, 2005.

Schroeder, Ivo. "Política e Parentesco nos Xerente." São Paulo: Universidade de São Paulo, 2006. Doctoral Dissertation in Anthropology.

———. "Os Xerente: Estrutura, História e Política." ("The Xerente: Structure, History, and Politics"). *Sociedade e Cultura* 1 (2010) 67–78.

Sharp, Daniel. "A Satellite Dish in the Shantytown Swamps: Musical Hybridity in the 'New Scene' of Recife, Pernambuco, Brazil." Master's thesis, University of Texas at Austin, 2001.

Shaw, Luci. "Art and Christian Spirituality: Companions in the Way." *Direction* 27 (1998) 109–22. http://www.directionjournal.org/27/2/art-and-christian-spirituality.html.

Siering, Friedrich Câmera. "Conquista e Dominação dos Povos Indígenas: Resistência no Sertão dos Maracás. (1650–1701)." Master's thesis, Universidade Federal da Bahia, 2008.

SIL International. "Arts and Ethnomusicology." https://www.sil.org/arts-ethnomusicology.

Skoglund, Herbert. "New Shape of Evangelical Churches in Japan." *The Evangelical Missions Quarterly* 9 (1973) 176–80.

Sloboda, John A., and Susan A. O'Neill, S. A. "Emotions in Everyday Listening to Music." In *Music and Emotion: Theory and Research*, edited by Patrik N. Juslin and John A. Sloboda, 415–29. Oxford: Oxford University Press, 2001.
SophyaAgain. "Brasil, Brasil—Samba to Bossa Nova (4 of 4)." *YouTube* Playlist, 2007. https://www.youtube.com/watch?v=ttACvoyuVbM&list=PLn752vupXEfEsx3CL nLRRBAT6oePD8ovN&index=6&t=0s.
Spradley, James P. *The Ethnographic Interview*. Long Grove, IL: Waveland, 1979. Kindle ed.
Sprotte, Josef Joachim. *The Hurons—Ethnogenesis and Identity through the Centuries: A Comprehensive Research Based on Theories of Ethnicity*. Berlin: Xen-Imago, 2014. Kindle ed.
Staden, Hans. *Duas viagens ao Brasil*. 1557. Belo Horizonte, Braz.: Itatiaia, 1974.
Stańczyk, Xawery. "Authenticity and Orientalism: Cultural Appropriations in the Polish Alternative Music Scene in the 1970s and 1980s." In *Eastern European Popular Music in a Transnational Context: Beyond the Borders*, edited by Ewa Mazierska and Zsolt Győri, 75–99. Palgrave European Film and Media Studies. Cham, Switz.: Palgrave Macmillan, 2019.
Stapert, Calvin. *A New Song for an Old World: Musical Thought in the Early Church*. Cambridge, UK: Eerdmans, 2007.
Stokes, Martin. "Music and the Global Order." *Annual Review of Anthropology* 33 (2004) 47–72. https://www.jstor.org/stable/25064845.
Tagg, Philip. *Music's Meanings*. New York: The Mass Media Music Scholars' Press, 2013.
Tan, Sooi Ling. "Transformative Worship in a Malaysian Context." In *Worship and Mission for the Global Church*, edited by James R. Krabill, locs. 4904–5117. Pasadena, CA: William Carey Library, 2013. Kindle ed.
Tarasti, Eero. *A Theory of Musical Semiotics*. Bloomington, IN: Indiana University Press, 1994.
Taylor, J. P. "Authenticity and Sincerity in Tourism." *Annals of Tourism Research* 28 (2001) 7–26.
Thomas, Eliza. "Ethnodoxology: What It Means and Why It's Essential for Church Planting." *International Mission Board* (blog), September 7, 2016. https://www.imb.org/2016/09/07/ethnodoxology-means-essential-church-plantin/.
Titon, Jeff Todd, ed. *Worlds of Music: An Introduction to the Music of the World's Peoples*. 5th ed. Belmont, CA: Schirmer Cengage Learning, 2009.
Towns, Elmer L. *Putting an End to Worship Wars*. 1996. Reprint, n.p.: Destiny Image, 2014. Kindle ed.
Traditional Instruments of the World. "Reco Reco." https://traditionalmusicalinstrumentsblog.wordpress.com/2018/09/21/reco-reco/.
Treier, Daniel J., et al., eds. *The Beauty of God: Theology and the Arts*. Downers Grove, IL: InterVarsity, 2007.
Turino, Thomas. "Signs of Imagination, Identity, and Experience: A Peircean Semiotic Theory for Music." *Ethnomusicology* 43 (1999) 221–55. https://www.researchgate.net/publication/279975234_Signs_of_Imagination_Identity_and_Experience_A_Peircian_Semiotic_Theory_for_Music.
University of Manitoba. "Moieties." https://web.archive.org/web/20190325205237/https://www.umanitoba.ca/faculties/arts/anthropology/tutor/descent/unilineal/moiety.html.

UOL Educação. "Invasão do Brasil—Não foi Cabral quem 'descobriu' o Brasil." https://educacao.uol.com.br/disciplinas/historia-brasil/invasao-do-brasil-nao-foi-cabral-quem-descobriu-o-brasil.htm?cmpid=copiaecola.

Varga, Somogy, and Charles Guignon. "Authenticity." In *The Stanford Encyclopedia of Philosophy* (Fall 2017 Edition), edited by Edward N. Zalta. https://plato.stanford.edu/archives/fall2017/entries/authenticity/.

Veith, Gene Edward, Jr. *State of the Arts: From Bezalel to Mapplethorpe*. Wheaton, IL: Crossway, 1991.

Vidal, Laurent. "La Présence Française dans le Brésil Colonial au XVIe Siècle." *Cahiers des Amériques latines* 34 (2017) 17–38. https://doi.org/10.4000/cal.6486.

Volgsten, Ulrik. "Music, Culture, Politics Communicating Identity, Authenticity and Quality in the 21st Century." *Nordisk Kulturpolitisk Tidsskrift* 17 (2014) 114–31. https://www.idunn.no/doi/10.18261/ISSN2000-8325-2014-01-07.

Walls, Andrew F. "The American Dimension in the History of the Missionary Movement." In *In Earthen Vessels: American Evangelicals and Foreign Mission, 1880–1980*, edited by Joel Carpenter and Wilber Shenk, 1–25. Grand Rapids, MI: Eerdmans, 1990.

———. *Missionary Movement in Christian History: Studies in the Transmission of Faith*. Maryknoll, NY: Orbis, 1996. Kindle ed.

Webber, Robert E. *The Complete Library of Christian Worship*. Nashville, TN: StarSong, 1993.

Wewering, Silvia Thêkla. *Povo Akwẽ Xerente: Vida, Cultura, Identidade*. Belo Horizonte, Braz.: Editora Rona, 2011.

White, James F. *Protestant Worship: Traditions in Transition*. Louisville, KY: Westminster/John Knox, 1989.

Wilson-Dickson, Andrew. *The Story of Christian Music: From Gregorian Chant to Black Gospel*. Minneapolis, MN: Augsburg Fortress, 1992.

Wolterstorff, Nicholas. *Art in Action: Toward a Christian Aesthetic*. Grand Rapids, MI: Eerdmans, 1980.

Yates, Wilson. "Reflections on Art and Spirituality." *ARTS* 3 (1991) 20–23.

———. "Spirituality and the Arts: A Personal Exploration of the Importance of Art in the Spiritual Journey." *ARTS* 24 (2012–13) 14–19.

www.ingramcontent.com/pod-product-compliance
Lightning Source LLC
Chambersburg PA
CBHW071242230426
43668CB00011B/1551